BELFAST
AND THE
IRISH LANGUAGE

Fionntán de Brún

EDITOR

FOUR COURTS PRESS

Set in 10.5 on 12.5 point Ehrhardt for
FOUR COURTS PRESS LTD
7 Malpas Street, Dublin 8, Ireland
e-mail: info@four-courts-press.ie
http://www.four-courts-press.ie
and in North America by
FOUR COURTS PRESS
c/o ISBS, 920 N.E. 58th Avenue, Suite 300, Portland, OR 97213.

SPECIAL ACKNOWLEDGMENT

This publication was grant aided by Foras na Gaeilge

Urraithe ag

Foras na Gaeilge

A catalogue record for this title
is available from the British Library.

ISBN (10 digit) 1–85182–938–5 hbk
ISBN (13 digit) 978–1–85182–938–5 hbk

ISBN (10 digit) 1–85182–939–3 pbk
ISBN (13 digit) 978–1–85182–939–2 pbk

Printed in England
by MPG Books, Bodmin, Cornwall.

Contents

Int én bec
ro léic feit
do rinn guip
glanbuidi:
fo-ceird faíd
ós Loch Laíg,
lon do chraíb
charnbuidi.

The little bird which has whistled
from the end of a bright-yellow bill:
it utters a note above Belfast Lough –
a blackbird from a yellow-heaped branch.

Anonymous (ninth century)

Introduction

FIONNTÁN DE BRÚN

The historical focus of these essays is largely the period from the late eighteenth century onwards, where the Irish language ceased to function as the everyday language of social interaction and exchange in the Belfast area but was instead vested with a new significance as part of the cultural inheritance of the Irish people, a thing to be consciously regarded and located within the discourse of culture and politics, a language that many felt bound to preserve and to revive. The question of whether or not the use of the Irish language was to be encouraged duly became part of the broader political question that separated Irish/Ulster unionism from Irish nationalism. The political engagement of the Irish language must inevitably form part of the scope of this book, yet the intention here is chiefly to consider the role of the language in the cultural and social history of Belfast, in particular the attempts to consciously preserve and extend the use of Irish in society as part of what is known as the 'revival'.[1]

Among the earliest manifestations of culture and society in the Belfast area was the naming of places – Falls, Shankill, Ardoyne, Malone. The first documented reference to the name Belfast occurs in AD 668 and the Lagan is mentioned in Ptolemy's famous map of *c*.AD 150. All of these Irish names yield important information about the history of these settlements, as do later place-names such as Skegoneill (*Sceitheog an Iarla* 'the earl's thorn bush'), which may refer to the murder of William de Burgo in 1333, itself a turning point in an era dominated by strife between the Anglo-Normans and native Irish, between the twelfth and sixteenth centuries. The establishment of the charter for Belfast in 1613 marks the beginning of a period where Belfast became indisputably in the control of the English and Scots under Arthur Chichester and where the native Irish were restricted to outlying areas. However, by 1757 there were 556 'Papists' within the city and small communities established outside the city ramparts at the Mill Gate and on the Shore Road. The growing influence of Irish speaking Catholics in Belfast at this period can explain the Irish name of the Christmas market of the time, Margymore (*an margadh mór* 'the big market'). Indeed, there is evidence that the Irish language at this time was not the exclusive preserve of the Catholic population; a source from the late eighteenth century mentions Irish being the language spoken by both Dissenters and Papists in Rademon, Co. Down.

---

1 A fairly recent study, O'Reilly (1999), specifically investigates the politics of the Irish language in Northern Ireland.

The decline of the Irish language in the nineteenth century, precipitated by the Famine, signalled a new phase for the language where that part of the population that had been mostly Irish speaking, the Catholics, turned instead to English. Hence, many of the Catholic poor who poured into industrial Belfast in the latter part of the century were ignorant of the Irish language or were at least actively ensuring that their children would not be saddled with a language that had come to be associated with poverty. The preservation of the Irish language was unlikely to have been a priority for those who had struggled to survive starvation, not to mention typhoid and cholera. Yet the city which received a growing number of poor native Irish speakers into its population throughout the nineteenth century was a city which had in the previous century been synonymous with radical ideas, whose Presbyterian middle class celebrated the Enlightenment and the French revolution and sought an Irish Republic in the 1798 Rebellion. This passion for ideas encouraged a flowering of interest in the Irish language and music and a commitment to halt its decline. Initiatives such as the Harpers' Festival of 1792, which proposed 'to revive and perpetuate the ancient music and poetry of Ireland', and the publication of an Irish language magazine, *Bolg an tSolair* (Miscellany), in 1795, harnessed the dynamism of Belfast's enlightened middle class to the cause of cultural revival.

Thus, whilst the appetite for rebellion had receded as Belfast's mercantile class devoted its attention to managing the industrial boom and population explosion of the nineteenth century, some of the intellectual values established by the previous generation prevailed. Where the Irish language was concerned, no one reflected that marvellous intellectual energy better than Robert MacAdam whose intervention in the affairs of the language as an antiquarian, a scholar and revivalist was critical to the fortunes of the language in Ulster. Indeed, MacAdam the industrialist/antiquarian seems to have embodied the very essence of the Irish language revival which has been a feature of the cultural life of Belfast for over two centuries. Cultural revival as an elixir against what John Montague has described as Belfast's 'iron bleakness',[2] seems to be quite literally the case with MacAdam. Iron was his stock-in-trade, and his Soho Foundry is likened to a vision of hell by Aodh Mac Domhnaill, the foremost of the Irish scribes whom MacAdam employed to collect and compile literature in the Irish language.

The effusion of interest in the Irish language that brought about the founding of the Ulster Gaelic Society in 1830 and the manifold scholarly projects commissioned by Robert MacAdam began to wane from the 1860s onwards. Where the mainly Presbyterian middle class of Belfast had previously embraced the Irish language, there are many signs in this period that

2 'Home again', *Collected poems* (1995), p. 8.

attitudes were becoming much less favourable. Yet the locus for the re-emergence of the Irish language in the early 1890s was a familiar one: the Belfast Natural History and Philosophical Society, in which MacAdam and like-minded Irish revivalists had held office, was the first venue for an Irish class conducted by P.S. Ó Sé, a Customs and Mail officer from Kerry. In 1895, this class formed the first Belfast branch of the Gaelic League, a seminal event to which the contemporary Irish language movement owes its existence. The membership of the inchoate Belfast Gaelic League included bishops and clergy of most denominations together with individuals with quite opposite political allegiances, notably R.R. Kane, the Orange Grand Master, and Cathal Ó Seanáin of the Irish Republican Brotherhood.

While it would be difficult to ascribe a common motivation to such a diverse group, there is no doubt that, for some of them, their interest in cultural revival was a reaction to, or at least an escape from, what the novelist Forrest Reid called the 'tyranny of commercial materialism' which weighed heavily on Belfast (Hay 2004: 123–4). This was certainly the view of perhaps the most important proponent of cultural revival in Belfast at the turn of the twentieth century, Francis Joseph Bigger. 'With increased growth and the introduction of large manufactories,' Bigger contended, 'there is no doubt that Belfast has fallen behind in culture and art.'[3] Salvation was to be achieved through the Gaelic revival and the promotion of art and literature, otherwise 'life becomes sordid and mean, the enrichment of a few is accomplished, and the degradation of the masses ensured'.

The recognition that industrialization had impoverished the masses and desensitized the middle class pointed to the inevitable engagement of the cultural revivalists with the political and economic issues of their time. Confirmation that the separation of culture and politics was no longer viable came as the Gaelic revival began to be located ever-increasingly in the discourse of national politics. This was a development which had a direct impact on the now numerous Belfast branches of the Gaelic League. The original group's transition from benign enthusiasts engaged in a largely intellectual pursuit to membership of a national cultural organization was indicative of the many changes which would overcome the Gaelic League itself from its first meeting of nine men in Dublin in July 1893. The main thrust of those changes was to move the League into a national political domain, by a number of stages, culminating in the adoption of an explicitly political constitution in 1915 at the loss of one of its founders, Douglas Hyde. Hyde conceived of the League as a popular cultural organization whose mission was to 'de-anglicize' Ireland while remaining strictly non-political and non-sectarian. Yet it was in the many responses to Hyde's own call for 'the necessity for de-

3 'Art and culture in old Belfast', *Uladh*, 1 (1904), 12.

anglicizing Ireland', that the virtual impossibility of maintaining a strictly non-political course was proven.

Among those who dismissed the notion of a non-political cultural movement was James Connolly who, writing in the Belfast periodical, *The Shan Van Vocht*, in 1897, addressed the phenomenon of the growing number of associations – literary, Irish language and commemoration committees – engaged in the preservation of 'national sentiments':

> If the National movement of our day is not merely to re-enact the old and sad tragedies of our past history, it must show itself capable of rising to the exigencies of the moment, it must demonstrate to the people of Ireland and the world at large that Irish nationality is not merely a morbid idealising of the past, but is also capable of formulating a distinct and definite answer to the problems of the present, and a political and economic creed capable of adjustment to the wants of the future. This concrete political and social ideal, I believe, will be best supplied by a frank acceptance, on the part of all earnest Nationalists, of the Republic as the goal of our endeavours. (8 January 1897: 7)

Indeed, Connolly's view of the political importance of the Irish language movement was shared not only by many of those who took up membership of the Gaelic League, but by one of its co-founders, Eoin Mac Néill who, in 1913, famously made a call in the organization's periodical, *An Claidheamh Soluis* (The Sword of Light), for the establishment of a body of volunteers,[4] and found support for this call from Pádraig Pearse.

In general terms, the political evolution of the Gaelic League was also witnessed in Belfast but the advent of partition in 1922 forced the northern Irish language movement into an acceptance of the limitations of pursuing a political agenda in a state which was avowedly hostile to their aims. This did not, of course, mean that proponents of the Irish language abandoned their political aspirations or, in the case of many, their adherence to Republican ideals or involvement in Republican activisim. Rather, the notion of challenging the Northern Ireland state to take responsibility for advancing the status of the Irish language was considered entirely futile. Ironically, the near total absence of a viable agenda of political activism for the Irish language to an extent provided the circumstances in the North for the type of non-political Gaelic League originally envisaged by Douglas Hyde. For more than forty years after partition the Irish language movement in Belfast cultivated a thriving social, recreational movement which aspired to an alternative Gaelic Ulster and which effected an unlikely alliance with the Gaeltacht society of west

4 'The North began', *An Claidheamh Soluis*, 1 November 1913.

Donegal. A further irony was that, while overwhelmingly nationalist and anti-partitionist in outlook, the northern Irish language movement was under-pinned by a robust sense of provincial loyalty to Ulster Irish which had its roots in an early split in the Belfast Gaelic League over Irish dialects which led to the founding, in 1911, of An Ardscoil Ultach (The Ulster High School). Rather than pursuing a political agenda, Belfast Irish speakers devoted them-selves instead to sedulously cultivating a model of Gaeldom which they found in the Donegal Gaeltacht. The Donegal writer Seosamh Mac Grianna describes how Belfast Irish speakers would treat his native Rann na Feirste (Rannafast) like a shrine:

> To give Belfast people their dues, it would do the Gaels of Rannafast no harm if they [Belfast people] were to keep coming to them until the world ended. For they were people who never sullied anything Gaelic that they came across ... I have to say that they were as respectful in Rannafast as a pious person is at a church altar ... They criticized neither person nor place and they did valiant work for the [Irish] language.[5]

There is a real sense in the four decades after partition of a hidden Ulster of Irish revivalism which enjoyed hardly any relations with statutory author-ities and which was entirely alienated from the culture of the state. One inci-dent described in the Ulster Irish language monthly *An tUltach* (The Ulsterman) is worth recounting. Included in a series of reports on Irish lan-guage events in Belfast in the 1950s is an account of the reporter visiting the artist John Luke as he worked on his famous City hall mural, depicting the history of Belfast, commissioned for the Festival of Britain in 1952.[6] Discussing Luke's work with him on top of thirty-foot high scaffolding, *An tUltach*'s reporter was astounded to be told that, while the imagery centred on Arthur Chichester reading the Belfast Charter in 1613, the artist's style was indebted to the artwork of the Irish monastic scribes. 'One wonders what the Corporation would have to say if they could read what I have written here,' concludes the reporter, indicating that the artist's avowal of Irish monas-tic influences would have got him into trouble with the city fathers.

Thus, the situation of the Irish language in Belfast and in Northern Ireland was the same as it was in the days of the pre-Treaty Gaelic League – ignored by the state but championed by a very active and effective self-help movement which engendered a powerful social dynamic. Nevertheless, while the need to deal with the reality of partition was accepted by forming an

---

5 'A thuilleadh scríbhneoireachta le Seosamh Mac Grianna in eagar ag Nollaig Mac Congáil, cuid 2' in *Feasta* (Iúil 2003), 21. (My translation.)   6 'Tuairisg na cathrach', *An tUltach*, 3 (1953), 9–11. See also John Hewitt (1978), 80–2.

Ulster organization within the Gaelic League, Irish speakers in the North kept a keen eye on developments in the rest of Ireland where the promotion of the Irish language was accepted as the responsibility of the state. Yet while the Dublin government remained ostensibly committed to the Irish language, it was painfully apparent to many people, including Irish speakers in the North, that this commitment had been only partially honoured. Among the most powerful voices to emerge in the 1950s and 1960s to challenge the state's record on the Irish language in the south was Máirtín Ó Cadhain, a native of Connemara, a Republican Socialist and an exceptionally talented writer of fiction and polemic. Ó Cadhain's radicalism was enthusiastically received by groups like Cumann Chluain Ard (the Clonard Club), a radical branch of the Belfast Gaelic League, who recognized that his practical, people-based approach to Irish language politics could be acted on immediately, with or without the state's approval.

In particular, Ó Cadhain's belief in the primacy of urban centres for the successful survival of the Irish language was shared by Belfast Irish speakers who eagerly responded to his challenge that not a single street outside of the Gaeltacht had been claimed by the Irish language.[7] Co-operative schemes were established with a view to financing the building of houses for Ireland's first urban Gaeltacht on the Shaw's Road in west Belfast. The houses were completed in 1969 and were soon complemented by the city's first Irish-medium school, Scoil Ghaeilge Bhéal Feirste (Belfast Irish Language School)[8] in 1971. The Shaw's Road community laboured stoically in the time-honoured tradition of self-help, carrying the burden of a non-funded voluntary school, with a vastly increased enrolment, until state grant-aid was eventually ceded in 1984.

In the years that followed the founding of the Shaw's Road Gaeltacht, Belfast had undergone changes that guaranteed the city a place in the headlines of the international news media. The political conflict in the six counties of Northern Ireland claimed over 3,000 lives with many thousands physically injured and traumatized. The corollary of the polarization of Catholic nationalist and Protestant unionist communities was the intense politicization of cultural expression and identity. The Irish language became fixed in many eyes as a badge of Catholic nationalist identity and, indeed, the aftermath of the 1981 hunger strike witnessed a resurgence of interest in Irish among republicans who were inspired by the use of the Irish language among republican prisoners in Long Kesh.

Yet, while the Irish language was bound up with the ubiquitous question of national identity, the determination of those who had championed the importance of the language for 'all classes and creeds', including Cumann Chluain Ard and the Shaw's Road families, ensured that the language did not

7 Ó Laighin (1990: 442).   8 Now Bunscoil Phobal Feirste (Belfast Community Primary School).

become entirely subsumed by the political agenda. The success of this aspiration can be measured by the existence today of a significant number of Protestants who have embraced Irish without eschewing their political allegiance to unionism. The work of the Ultach Trust since 1989 has focussed on promoting an inclusive image for the Irish language which transcends political and communal divisions. Certainly, one of the truths that emerges from these essays is that the political significance of the Irish language is not fixed through time but has occupied different spaces in the politico-cultural map at various times.

The commitment made by the British government in the 1998 Good Friday Agreement to 'take resolute action to promote the [Irish] language' (9) may well mark an improvement in the fortunes of the language movement. Self-help by sheer necessity has, to some extent, already been replaced by state-funding. Whether or not the new era of state-funded language projects will consolidate the efforts of formerly voluntary groups or sap their life-force is a matter for speculation. One intriguing new development, outlined in the final essay of this book, is the proposal for a Gaeltacht quarter in west Belfast which will depend for its success on the ability of its proponents to turn cultural capital into material wealth. Stranger things have happened.

The first essay in this book follows in the steps of John O'Donovan, the celebrated scholar and first professor of Celtic at Queen's University, whose study of Irish place-names has become part of national heritage, not to mention drama. Pat McKay traces the origin and meaning of numerous Belfast townlands, rivers and ancient territorial divisions giving form and substance to the fragmented narrative of the city's earliest antecedents. In 'The Irish language in Belfast until the eighteenth century', Aodán Mac Póilin discusses the recorded use of Irish in the Belfast area and in particular the bardic sources of the seventeenth-century *Leabhar Cloinne Aodha Buidhe* (The Book of Clandeboy). The two essays by Art Hughes which follow, investigate principally the life and work of Robert MacAdam, the apotheosis of the Irish language revival in nineteenth-century Belfast, and include a very comprehensive account of the societies and individuals, most notably the Irish scribes, who were engaged in the language revival of the time. The fortunes of a community of fish and fruit dealers from the Omeath Gaeltacht who settled in Belfast in the latter part of the nineteenth century are traced in the subsequent essay by Fionntán de Brún where the social history reposited in the census returns of the early twentieth century forms a central source of information.

Aodán Mac Póilin's study of the Belfast language revival from 1892 to 1960, illuminates the cultural history of a period that witnessed the most important political and constitutional changes of the modern era. The origins and growth of the Gaelic League and the accession of what Mac Póilin terms 'Catholic communalism' in the Irish language movement in the new Northern

Ireland is carefully elucidated in this piece. The role and impact of the Shaw's Road urban Gaeltacht is the subject of Gabrielle NigUidhir's essay in which she returns to her 1991[9] study of that community. The influence of this initiative on the Irish language in Belfast generally and the many practical and theoretical bilingual issues which it presents, particularly now that it spans three generations, are as diverse as they are intriguing.

The attitudes of Belfast Protestants towards the Irish language are surveyed by Gordon McCoy in an essay that draws on extensive interviews carried out by the author which gauge the experience Protestants have of the Irish language and the associations it holds for them. A fascinating by-product of this essay is the insight it affords into the attitudes of Catholics towards the Irish language as elicited through encounters with Protestant learners.

The last two essays of this volume represent a contemporary perspective from two participant observers, both working in their respective fields of Irish-medium education and Irish language economic development. Seán Mac Corraidh assesses the development of Irish-medium education from single school to an entire sector which requires a multiplicity of support structures and services to consolidate its rapid growth. The final essay, 'The Gaeltacht Quarter: promoting cultural promiscuity and wealth', as its post-modern title suggests, makes a highly original case for embracing hybridity and exploiting the material potential of cultural wealth. The discourse of enterprise and urban economic development is applied here to harness an inherited tradition of self-help to modern urban enterprise.

Even within the fairly well-defined parameters of these essays, there may well be areas of interest to which it has not been possible to give proper attention. In the case of literature in Irish written in or about Belfast, it was thought best to refer the reader to Aodán Mac Póilin's recent essay in *The Cities of Belfast* (2003).[10] Where the study of census figures is concerned, one trusts that the need for a large-scale statistical analysis of the data pertaining to the Irish language will, in the future, attract the attention of scholars in this area. Possible shortcomings notwithstanding, it is sincerely hoped that this volume will not only enhance our understanding of the outworking of the Irish language revival but will initiate equally a reconsideration of the place of cultural revival in the development of a nineteenth-century industrial city.[11]

9 Maguire (1991). 10 'Irish language writing in Belfast after 1900'. 11 See Hunt (2004) for an interesting exploration of cultural revival in British industrial cities of the nineteenth century.

Belfast place-names and the Irish language[1]

PATRICK McKAY

Belfast

While the beginnings of Belfast as a city can be traced mainly to the eighteenth and nineteenth centuries, its name, and indeed a substantial proportion of the place-names within it, date back to a much earlier period and have their origin in the Irish language. In fact, the first documented reference to Belfast is found as early as AD 668 when the Annals of Ulster record *Bellum Fertsi eter Ultu agus Cruitne*, that is, 'the war (or battle) of the *Fersat* between the Ulstermen and the Cruithin'.[2] *Fersat* is the Old Irish form of the Modern Irish word *fearsaid* 'sand-bank ford' and the ford referred to was across the mouth of the river Lagan at the spot where the town (and later city) of Belfast was to grow up.

In 1910 the identification of Belfast with the site of the aforementioned battle in AD 668 was challenged by Hogan,[3] who suggested that the *Fertas* in question was the former ford at the head of the Lower Bann where it flows out of Lough Neagh at Toomebridge in Co. Antrim which is referred to as *Fertas Tuamma*, that is, 'the sand-bank ford of Toome' in the early tenth-century *Tripartite Life of Saint Patrick*.[4] The identification of the true site of the *Fertas* hinges on the respective locations of the two population groups who are described as protagonists in the battle, i.e. the *Ulaid* (Mod. Ir. *Ulaidh*) and the *Cruitne* (Mod. Ir. *Cruithne*). The term *Ulaid* (literally 'Ulstermen') in its strict tribal sense always referred to the *Dál Fiatach* and it is clearly in this sense that it is used in the Annals of Ulster in 668. The *Dál Fiatach* were the original rulers of Ulster from Navan Fort outside Armagh city but in the course of the fifth century they were driven eastwards and made their headquarters in the Downpatrick area. During the following centuries they began to expand northwards into the north of the modern county of Down and south of county Antrim and this would naturally have brought them into con-

---

1 This essay is intended to complement excellent earlier work on the place-names of Belfast by the late J.B. Arthurs and the late Deirdre Flanagan (née Morton), published in the first series of the *Bulletin of the Ulster Place-Name Society* (1956–7) and also Deirdre Uí Fhlannagáin's 'Béal Feirste agus Áitainmneacha Laistigh', published in B.S. Mac Aodha (ed.), *Topothesia: essays in honour of T.S. Ó Máille* (Galway, 1982), pp 46–64, translated by A.J. Hughes and published as 'Deirdre Flanagan's "Belfast and the place-names therein" in translation', in *Ulster Folklife*, 38 (1992), 79–97. 2 *The Annals of Ulster*, ed. Seán Mac Airt and Gearóid MacNiocaill (Dublin, 1983), i, p. 138. 3 Edmund Hogan, *Onomasticon Goedelicum* (Dublin, 1910), p. 414b. 4 *Bethu Phátraic: the Tripartite Life of Patrick*, ed. Kathleen Mulchrone (Dublin, 1939), p. 100.

flict with the resident *Dál nAraide*, at this time commonly referred to by their ethnic title *Cruthin* (also, *Cruithne*). The ford over the mouth of the Lagan was obviously of considerable strategic importance and would have been on the natural path of northward expansion of the *Dál Fiatach*. While the *Cruthin* (Mod. Ir. *Cruithin*) were indeed settled around Toome as well as in the Belfast area in 668, Toome lies a long way to the north-west of Downpatrick and it is highly unlikely that we would find the *Dál Fiatach* engaged in warfare with the *Dál nAraide* so far away from their centre of power at such an early period. The case for accepting Belfast rather than Toome as the site of the 'battle of the ford' in 668 therefore seems beyond question. In the afore-mentioned entry in the Annals we are informed that the *Dál nAraide* king was defeated and slain in the battle and no doubt this opened the way for the *Dál Fiatach* to establish themselves in the Belfast area. This opinion is corrobo-rated by the evidence of three place-names which point to *Dál Fiatach* set-tlement, namely the Cave Hill, Glengormley and, possibly, Dunmurry (see p. 22 below).

The modern Irish name of Belfast is, of course, *Béal Feirste* meaning 'mouth of (or approach to) the sand-bank ford' and it is clear that the ele-ment *Béal* was added to *Fearsaid* at a later date. At this point it is worthwhile correcting a common misconception, namely that *Béal Feirste* means 'mouth of the Farset', the Farset being a little river which is now covered by High Street and which flows into the Lagan close to where the latter enters Belfast Lough. In fact, there are no examples in Irish place-names of the use of the element *béal* to refer to the foot of a river[5] and it is likely that the Farset, like Belfast itself, is named from the *fearsaid* or sand-bank ford which was an important crossing place on the Lagan, linking the modern counties of Antrim and Down.[6]

PLACE-NAMES IN THE CO. ANTRIM PORTION OF BELFAST

Shankill

Everyone is familiar with the name Shankill Road, but Shankill is also the name of the civil parish which comprises all of the county Antrim portion of the city (that is, the portion which lies west of the Lagan), with the excep-tion of a tiny portion in the south which is in the parish of Drumbeg. There is now no trace of the original parish church of Shankill but the site is marked by St Matthew's Church of Ireland church on the Upper Shankill Road, in the graveyard of which there is a *bullaun* stone or holy water font from the

5 J.B. Arthurs, 'Place names and dialects' in E. Evans (ed.), *Belfast in its regional setting* (1952), p. 193. 6 D. Uí Fhlannagáin, 'Béal Feirste agus Áitainmneacha Laistigh', p. 50.

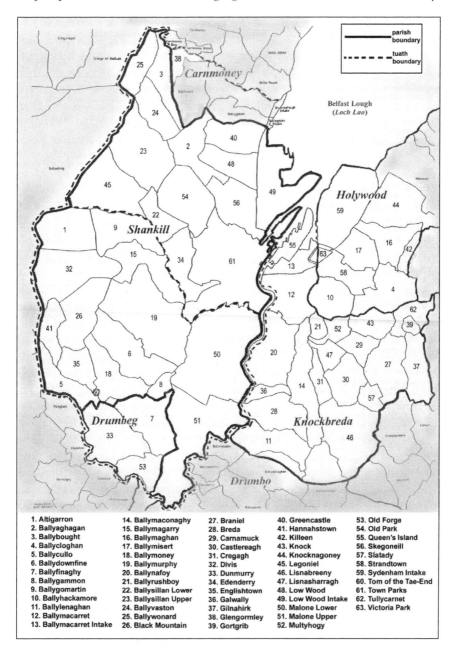

1. Altigarron	14. Ballymaconaghy	27. Braniel	40. Greencastle	53. Old Forge
2. Ballyaghagan	15. Ballymagarry	28. Breda	41. Hannahstown	54. Old Park
3. Ballybought	16. Ballymaghan	29. Carnamuck	42. Killeen	55. Queen's Island
4. Ballycloghan	17. Ballymisert	30. Castlereagh	43. Knock	56. Skegoneill
5. Ballycullo	18. Ballymoney	31. Cregagh	44. Knocknagoney	57. Slatady
6. Ballydownfine	19. Ballymurphy	32. Divis	45. Legoniel	58. Strandtown
7. Ballyfinaghy	20. Ballynafoy	33. Dunmurry	46. Lisnabreeny	59. Sydenham Intake
8. Ballygammon	21. Ballyrushboy	34. Edenderry	47. Lisnasharragh	60. Tom of the Tae-End
9. Ballygomartin	22. Ballysillan Lower	35. Englishtown	48. Low Wood	61. Town Parks
10. Ballyhackamore	23. Ballysillan Upper	36. Galwally	49. Low Wood Intake	62. Tullycarnet
11. Ballylenaghan	24. Ballyvaston	37. Gilnahirk	50. Malone Lower	63. Victoria Park
12. Ballymacarret	25. Ballywonard	38. Glengormley	51. Malone Upper	
13. Ballymacarret Intake	26. Black Mountain	39. Gortgrib	52. Multyhogy	

Townlands and civil parishes of Belfast and district

original church. The name of the church is first recorded in 1306 when it is referred to as *Ecclesia Alba*, 'white church'.[7] The name Shankill is not recorded in any Irish-language source but it clearly derives from Irish *Seanchill* 'old church' and this name appears to have replaced the earlier name at a later stage, some time after the construction of a 'new' church adjacent to the afore-mentioned ford across the mouth of the River Lagan. The name of this later church is recorded in 1306 as *capella de Vado* 'the chapel of the ford'[8] and its site is marked by St George's Church of Ireland church at the bottom of High Street. The civil parish of Shankill contains twenty-nine townlands.

The Falls and Malone

The Falls Road, which forms one of the main thoroughfares in the west of the city, is as well known as the Shankill. Like Shankill, the name Falls orig-inally had much wider significance, for it referred to one of the native Irish petty kingdoms of the area. The name of the territory appears as *Tuoghnefall* in seventeenth-century English documents and is likely to go back to Irish *Tuath na bhFál* 'petty kingdom or territory of the enclosures or fields'. In modern Irish the word *fál* usually means 'hedge, fence' but in place-names it often refers to the area enclosed by a hedge or fence and in the case of *Tuath na bhFál* this is its most likely meaning.

In early seventeenth-century English documentation, the name of the Falls is invariably linked with Malone and it is clear that by that time the two dis-tricts were regarded as forming a single territorial unit. However, Malone was originally a *tuath* or petty kingdom in its own right. Nowadays the original dis-trict of Malone is represented by the large townlands of Malone Lower and Malone Upper which between them stretch all the way from the bottom of the Ormeau Road to Sir Thomas and Lady Dixon Park near Dunmurry. However, Malone is not documented as a townland in the early seventeenth century and it is clear that it was so designated at a later date – probably in the eighteenth century. The name Malone is not recorded in the Irish language and there is an element of uncertainty as to its derivation. The first element is clearly Ir. *Maigh* 'plain' and it is interesting that the district is referred to as 'the plains of Malone' in eighteenth-century documents. According to *Gasaitéar na hÉire-ann* the original Irish name of the townland of Malone Upper is *Maigh Lón Uachtair*.[9] In 1957 Deirdre Morton (later Deirdre Flanagan) suggested that the element *lón* in *Maigh Lón* may be the Scottish Gaelic word for 'meadow'[10] but in a later publication she proposed that it may represent a variant spelling of *luan* 'haunch, rump, buttock, hip' and be used figuratively to refer to the hill

7 William Reeves, *Ecclesiastical antiquities of Down, Connor, and Dromore* (Dublin, 1847), p. 6.
8 Ibid.   9 *Gasaitéar na hÉireann/Gazetteer of Ireland* (Dublin, 1989), p. 134.   10 Deirdre Morton, 'Tuath-divisions in the baronies of Belfast and Massereene', *Bulletin of the Ulster Place-Name Society* ser. 1, 5:1 (Spring 1957), p. 8.

known as 'the Malone Ridge'[11] and this is certainly a plausible explanation. Personally I am inclined to believe that the final element of Malone may represent the personal *Luan* which was common at an earlier period and is the basis of the surname *Ó Luain* 'O'Loan(e)'.[12]

The combined *tuatha* of the Falls and Malone comprised the southern portion of the civil parish of Shankill, along with the townlands of Old Forge and Ballyfinaghy and a portion of the townland of Dunmurry which are in the parish of Drumbeg. Its northern boundary was the Blackstaff River which flows into the Lagan a short distance from the bottom of the Ormeau Road. It was also partially bounded by the Forth River which divided it from the neighbouring *tuath* which was named Cinament. The portion of the *tuath* which lay in the parish of Shankill consisted of fifteen full townlands, the names of which are as follows:

> Altigarron, Ballymurphy, Ballygomartin, Ballymagarry, Divis, Black Mountain, Hannahstown, Englishtown, Ballycullo, Tom of the Tae-End, Ballydownfine, Ballymoney, Ballygammon, Malone Upper and Malone Lower.

It also included a portion of the townland of Dunmurry, the remainder of which is in the parish of Drumbeg.

Altigarron. Ir. *Allt na nGearrán* 'glen of the horses or geldings'. This townland consists mainly of moorland on the northern slopes of Divis Mountain. The word *gearrán* 'horse, gelding' may be used figuratively here to refer to megaliths or standing stones. There is a cairn named Carn Sheáin Bhuí 'the cairn of fair-haired Shane' on the boundary between this townland and the townland of Divis. There is also a megalith or 'giant's grave' in Altigarron, while there are standing-stones in the neighbouring townlands of Budore, Tornagrough, Legoniel and Divis. The glen referred to in the first element of the place-name appears to be the glen of the headwaters of the Clady Water which rises here and flows west. Altigarron is not referred to as a townland in seventeenth-century documents, but the Antrim Inquisition of 1605 refers to *the glinn of Barraaltnagarran* (Ir. *Barr Allt na nGearrán* 'top of the glen of the horses or geldings') as a boundary marker of *Tuoghnefall*.[13]

Ballymurphy. Ir. *Baile Uí Mhurchú* 'Murphy's townland'. Ballymurphy is an extemely large townland covering approximately 1,433 acres. Its eastern bound-

11 Deirdre Uí Fhlannagáin, 'Bóthar na bhFál, Maigh Lón, an tSeanchill agus Baile na mBráthar', *An tUltach* (Nollaig 1970), p. 22.   12 Edward MacLysaght, *The surnames of Ireland* (Dublin, 1985), p. 196.   13 'Inquisition taken at Antrim, 12 July 1605' in *26th report of the deputy keeper of the public records in Ireland* (Dublin, 1894), appendix i, p. 48.

ary is the Blackstaff River which runs parallel to Boucher Road, while its western border is the top of the Whiterock Road, on the slopes of Black Mountain and its southern boundary is roughly marked by the upper portion of Kennedy Way. The modern townland of Ballymurphy seems to include a now-obsolete townland which is referred to as *Ballyclony* in seventeenth-century English documents. *Ballyclony* represents the Irish name *Cluanaigh* 'place of meadows' (with the English element *Bally* prefixed to mark it as a townland) and refers to the Beechmount/Bog Meadows district of Belfast, in the angle between the Forth River and the Blackstaff. The lower course of the Forth River is locally called the 'Clowney Water' and the name is officially perpetuated in 'Clowney Street', off Beechmount Avenue. The name of the obsolete townland is also preserved in *Bóthar Chluanaí*, the Irish name of the Springfield Road, most of which is, in fact, in the neighbouring townland of Edenderry!

Ballygomartin. Ir. *Baile Gharraí Mháirtín* 'townland of Martin's garden or enclosed field'. Ballygomartin lies between the Upper Crumlin Road and the slopes of Divis Mountain and includes the Glencairn area of the city.

Ballymagarry. Ir. *Baile an Gharraí* 'townland of the enclosed field'. This townland stretches from St Mary's University College in the east almost to the summit of Divis Mountain on the west. The West Circular Road bisects the townland in a north-south direction.

Townlands of Divis and Black Mountain. The name Divis is derived from Irish *Dubhais* 'black ridge or peak'. The townland takes its name from Divis Mountain (478m) which stands on the boundary with the townland of Altigarron. It includes the neighbouring peak Black Mountain (390m) which is the name of the townland which bounds it on the south. It is possible that the name Black Mountain is in fact a translation of the Irish name *Dubhais* and that originally Divis and Black Mountain were thought of as being all the one mountain, named from its highest peak, *Dubhais*. Quite possibly the peak now known as Black Mountain had an Irish name which has now been lost. There is a summit named Black Hill (360m) on the slopes of the mountain. As the name suggests, the townland of Black Mountain consists mainly of mountain, but it also includes part of the village of Hannahstown, the remainder of which is in the townland of that name.

Hannahstown. Ir. *Baile Haine* in the *Gazetteer of Ireland*.[14] This appears to be a gaelicization of a place-name which was originally coined in the English language. If the place-name were of Gaelic origin one would expect to find it

14 *Gasaitéar na hÉireann*, p. 19.

recorded in the early seventeenth-century documents. The townland probably takes its name from the Hannah family whose ancestors were from
Galloway in Scotland and settled in Ulster between 1640 and 1690.[15]
Ironically, the Scottish surname Hanna appears to go back originally to Irish
Ó hAnnaidh[16] (cf. *Mac Annaidh* 'MacCanny, Canny'). The townland includes
most of the village of Hannahstown. Its western boundary is formed by a portion of the Collin River which flows through Collin Glen.

Englishtown. This place-name is clearly of English origin. There are six other
townlands in Ireland named Englishtown, including one near Coleraine in Co.
Derry and others in Galway, Limerick, Tipperary, Waterford and Wicklow.
In all these place-names the final element is a nationality term rather than
the surname English and I believe this to be also the case with this townland.
Townlands named from nationalities are not uncommon: there are in all
twenty-three townlands named Irishtown, including two in Co. Antrim. It is
possible that Englishtown was named by way of contrast with Hannahstown
which appears to have been settled by Scots. Englishtown includes
Hannahstown Hill on the lower slopes of Black Mountain. Its western boundary is the Collin River and it extends southwards to include the Upper Glen
Road and the village of Suffolk.

Ballycullo. Ir. *Baile Mhic Cú Uladh* 'MacCullagh's/MacCullow's townland'
or, possibly, *Baile Cúile Eo* 'townland of the corner of the yews'. The southern boundary of this townland is marked by the Stewartstown Road at Suffolk,
from where it stretches northwards as far as Collin Glen.

Tom of the Tae-End. This is a small townland of only twenty-three acres which
straddles the Stewartstown Road near Suffolk village. The townland name
appears to represent a slightly adapted form of 'Tam o' tae end', an expression which, according to *The Concise Scottish Dictionary*, signifies 'a kind of
large haggis, *now* the skin in which a haggis is stuffed'.[17] According to
Chambers Scots Dictionary 'Tam o' tae end' is 'a ludicrous designation of the
larger end of the pudding'.[18] The word 'Tam' in the phrase is to be understood as the proper name Tom, used in a jocular sense to signify something
like 'the fellow/the chap' while 'the tae end' means one end of something as
opposed to the other end, hence its use to refer originally to only one end of
the pudding. However, the significance of the use of the phrase as a place-
name is not clear. I can only suggest that the townland has been named for

15 Robert Bell, *The book of Ulster surnames* (Belfast, 1988), p. 89. 16 Ibid. 17 *The Concise Scottish Dictionary*, ed. M. Robinson (Aberdeen, 1985). 18 *Chambers Scots Dictionary*, compiled by A.Warrack (Edinburgh, 1911).

comic effect as there is nothing in its shape or topography which suggests that the name is used symbolically to refer to local conditions.

Ballydownfine. Ir. *Baile Dhún Fionn* 'townland of the white fort'. Interestingly, there is a hostelry named the Whitefort Inn in the townland! The final element of the name of this townland might also be understood as referring to the mythological hero *Fionn mac Cumhail*. Ballydownfine includes part of Andersonstown and also Casement Park. There is no record of any fort in the townland.

Ballymoney. Ir. *Baile Maighe Muine* 'townland of the plain of the thicket'. Ballymoney stretches westwards from where the Blackstaff River meets the Woodlands River, close to Musgrave Park Hospital, to the slopes of Black Mountain. It includes Finaghy Road North, Shaw's Road and St Genevieves's High School (the site of the former St Joseph's Training College).

Ballygammon. Ir. *Baile Ó gComáin* 'townland of the *Ó Comáin* family, anglicized Cummings, Hurly etc.' This is a fairly small townland, consisting of approximately 123 acres and is roughly coextensive with Musgrave Park.

Dunmurry Ir. *Dún Muirígh.* 'Muiríoch's (earlier Muiredach's) fort'. It is possible that Dunmurry is named from *Muiredach* son of *Eochaid* and father of the *Matudán* who gave name to *Benn Matudáin* or Cave Hill (see p. 28 below). The fact that the *Muiredach* in question died in 839 whereas Dunmurry appears to have been named from a Norman *motte* (which still survives) would at first sight seem to rule out this possibility. However, Dunmurry is one of a number of *mottes* in Cos Antrim and Down whose names consist of the native Irish term *dún* 'fort' followed by a Gaelic personal name, possibly as a result of the transfer of the names of native Irish forts to Norman *motte*s constructed on the same sites.[19] The possibility that Dunmurry could have been named from *Muiredach* father of *Matudán* cannot therefore be ruled out, though the fact that *Muiredach* was a popular personal name in early Ireland means that the suggestion can only be regarded as a tentative one. A large portion of the townland of Dunmurry lies in the civil parish of Drumbeg.

Townlands of Malone Lower and Malone Upper. As pointed out above, Malone was not originally a townland name but rather the name of a petty kingdom or territory (see p. 18). The district of Malone included *Ballicromoge, Ballinym Raharr, Ballyodran* and *Ballivally* which are described as townlands in 1605.[20]

---

19 Deirdre Flanagan, 'Common elements in Irish place-names: dún, ráth, lios', *Bulletin of the Ulster Place-Name Society*, ser. 2, vol. 3 (1980–1), 18.   20 Antrim Inquistion of 1605, p. 48.

Ballicromoge is obviously to be identified with Cromac, which is well-known since it has given name to Cromac Street at the bottom of the Ormeau Road but which is no longer recognized as a townland. Its name derives from Irish *Cromóg* 'little bend or turn' and it appears to refer to a bend in the course of the river Lagan which borders it on the east. *Ballinym Raharr* represents Irish *Baile na mBráthar* 'townland of the brothers or friars'. The name survives in the form 'Friars' Bush' which refers to an ancient graveyard near the bottom of the Stranmillis Road. This graveyard is likely to mark the site of a former monastery, possibly the chapel referred to as *Kilpatrick in Malone* in the Antrim Inquisition of 1605.[21] *Ballyodran* represents the southern portion of Malone Upper townland. The name is preserved in 'Ballydrain Lake', the name of a lake in Malone Golf Course which is on the opposite side of Upper Malone Road from Sir Thomas and Lady Dixon Park. It is possible that *Ballyodran* was the original name for the entire townland of Malone Upper. *Ballyodran* may represent Ir. *Baile Uí Dhreáin* '(O')Drain's townland'. Woulfe informs us that the family of Ó Dreáin appear to have been forced to remove from Roscommon to Antrim in the course of the thirteenth and fourteenth centuries.[22] *Ballivallie* is likely to derive from Irish *Baile an Bhealaigh* 'townland of the pass'. It is written as *Ballyvallie al. Ballynvallie al. Toughmanagh* in 1669[23] and the alias name *Toughmanagh* is obviously to be identified with Taughmonagh, the name of a district (and also a housing estate) in the modern townland of Malone Upper. The name Taughmonagh may derive from Irish *Tuath Monach* 'the *tuath* or district of the *Monaigh* (tribe)'. The latter, whose name was also written *Manaigh* and forms the final element of the name of the county of Fermanagh, are said to have been expelled from Leinster in the early Christian period and settled in Fermanagh and also in the east of Co. Down.

Farther down the Lagan, the townland of Malone Lower contains the well-known district of Stranmillis, the name of which derives from Irish *An Sruthán Milis* 'the sweet stream'. There is no stream here and it is likely that this was a local name for the section of the Lagan above the point where the water ceases to be tidal and is therefore fresh or 'sweet'. This seems to be the place referred to in 1644 in Friar Ó Mealláin's diary as *bun a' tSrutháin Mhilis*, where Henry mac Tuathal Ó Néill was sent to plunder the district in the war against the English.[24] Deirdre Flanagan suggests that the element *bun* (literally 'foot') in *bun a' tSrutháin Mhilis* could refer to a ford which is attested on the Lagan at this point.[25]

---

21 Ibid.   22 Patrick Woulfe, *Sloinnte Gaedheal is Gall: Irish names and surnames* (Dublin, 1923), p. 507.   23 'Confirmation of the Chichester patents' in R.M. Young (ed.), *Historical notices of old Belfast and its vicinity* (Belfast, 1895), p. 128.   24 'Cín Lae Ó Mealláin', ed. Tadhg Ó Donnchada, *Analecta Hibernica*, 3 (Dublin, 1931), 29.   25 Uí Fhlannagáin, p. 59.

The Cinament

The word *Cinament* (sometimes written *synament*) is used in seventeenth-century English documents to refer to a smaller-than-average territory or petty kingdom. Its derivation is uncertain but it may have its origin in the Norman period and go back ultimately to Old French *ceignement*, derived from the verb *ceindre* 'to circumscribe, surround'. The district referred to as Cinament comprised the northern portion of the civil parish of Shankill (including the centre of Belfast), along with the townlands of Colinward, Glengormley, Ballygolan and Drumnadrough which are in the parish of Carnmoney. The townlands in the parish of Shankill which were in the district of Cinament are:

> Town Parks, Edenderry, Ballysillan Lower, Ballysillan Upper, Legoniel, Skegoneill, Old Park, Ballyaghagan, Low Wood, Greencastle, Ballyvaston, Ballybought and Ballywonard.

Town Parks. Town Parks is very common as a townland name. It is found as the name of the central portion of many substantial towns and often replaced the name of the original townland, the name of which was then transferred to the town, for example, Town Parks in Ballymena was originally the townland of Ballymena, Town Parks in Ballymoney was originally the townland of Ballymoney. In the case of Belfast, it appears that there was never a townland named Belfast which was renamed Town Parks. The townland of Town Parks is extensive, stretching from Belfast centre to the Waterworks on the north, to the bottom of the Ormeau Road on the south and almost to the top of the Shankill Road on the west. It has clearly absorbed a number of smaller native land divisions. We know that the castle of Belfast which originally stood at the top of High Street was in a townland whose name is variously written *Ballycullcallagy, Ballycoolcallagh, B.coolegaly, B.coolegalgie, B.coolegallagie* and *Ballirecoolegalgie* in seventeenth-century English documents and which consisted of the area between the Farset (marked by High Street) and the Blackstaff (which flows into the Lagan close to the bottom of the Ormeau Road). In English documents of this period the element *Bally-* is often used to mark out a place as a townland and does not always point to the presence of the element *baile* 'townland, settlement' in the original Irish form of the place-name (see *Ballyclony*, p. 20 above). *Ballycullcallagy* etc. may therefore represent either *Baile Chúil Chalgaigh* 'townland of *Calgach*'s corner or nook' or, perhaps more likely, simply *Cúil Chalgaigh* '*Calgach*'s corner or nook'.

Town Parks also includes an obsolete townland named *Ballyculnytry*, from Irish *Cuileanntraigh* 'place abounding in holly', or, possibly, *Baile na Cuileanntrai* 'townland of the place abounding in holly'. This townland was located in the Grosvenor Road area, where there is still a road known as 'Cullingtree Road'. It lay between the townlands of *Ballycullcallagy* and *Ballyclony*.

Edenderry. Ir. *Éadan an Doire* 'hill brow of the oak wood'. Edenderry includes the upper portion of the Shankill Road, comprising the site of the ancient church of Shankill, as well as Ardoyne and the lower portion of the Springfield Road. Its southern boundary is marked by St Mary's University College.

The name Ardoyne derives from Irish *Ard Eoghain* 'Eoghan's height'. It is recorded as 'the half town of Ardoyne' in 1605,[26] the term 'half town' referring to a denomination which had roughly half the acreage of a full townland.

Ballysillan Lower and Ballysillan Upper. Ir. *Baile na Saileán* 'townland of the sally places/willow groves'. Ballysillan Lower stretches from Ardoyne on the east to Legoniel on the west. Ballysillan Upper is extensive but consists mainly of coarse mountain pasture and includes Squire's Hill which stands to the west of the Hightown Road.

Legoniel. Ir. *Lag an Aoil* 'hollow of the lime'. Legoniel (often known as 'Ligoniel') marks the western extremity of the district of Cinament. Here there is a conspicuous valley or hollow where limestone has been extensively quarried. The townland includes Wolf Hill where the last wolf in Ireland is reputed to have been killed.

Skegoneill. Ir. *Sceitheog an Iarla* 'the earl's thorn bush'. According to O'Laverty, the earl in question was William de Burgo, earl of Ulster, and the townland name commemorates the place where he was assassinated in 1333.[27] While this suggestion must be regarded as speculative, it is not at all unlikely that the place has been named from one of the Anglo-Norman earls. The townland is bounded on the south by the Mile Water, a stream which roughly follows the course of the Limestone Road and divides the townland of Skegoneill from Town Parks. On the north, Skegoneill stretches as far as the Fortwilliam roundabout and on the west as far as the North Circular Road.

In the nineteenth century, Skegoneill Avenue was known as 'Buttermilk Loney'. Nowadays, the name 'Buttermilk Lane' is used for Ballysillan Park in the neighbouring townland of Old Park , suggesting that Ballysillan Park may have formed the upper portion of the old Buttermilk Loney. Recently, 'Buttermilk Loney' has been used as the name of a side street off Ballysillan Park.

Old Park. The townland of Old Park extends from the upper lake at the Waterworks to the Horseshoe Bend on the Upper Crumlin Road. The name is well known from the Old Park Road which divides the townland in two. The townland of *Old parke* is first documented in 1659 and refers to a deer

26 Antrim Inquisition of 1605, p. 48.   27 James O'Laverty, *An historical account of the diocese of Down and Connor*, ii (Dublin, 1880), p. 401n.

park enclosed by the English lord deputy Sir Arthur Chichester at the beginning of the seventeenth cetury. It was named 'Old Park' when a new park was created at Parkmount in the nearby townland of Low Wood.[28]

Ballyaghagan. Ir. *Baile Uí Eachagáin* 'O'Haughian's/O'Hagan's townland'. *Ó hEachagáin* represents a variant form of *Ó hEachaidhín/Ó hEachaidhéin* (standard Irish *Ó hEacháin*), one of a number of families who were poets to the O'Neills of Clandeboy until the late seventeenth century.[29] The surname is also shared by a celebrated rapparee of the late seventeenth and early eighteenth century, Naoise *Ó hEacháin*/Ness O'Haughian, whose deed are synonymous with the Belfast mountains.[30] Ballyaghagan runs north-westwards from St Patrick's College (Bearnageeha) on the Antrim Road. It includes the Cave Hill and stretches as far as Belfast Zoo at Bellevue.

Low Wood. Low Wood comprises the area between Cave Hill and the Shore Road. The modern townland is roughly coextensive with the now-obsolete townland of *Listollyard*, the name of which appears to derive from Irish *Lios Tulaí Airde* 'fort of the high mound or hillock'. The fort referred to was a Norman *motte* and stood in the vicinity of the Upper Antrim Road.

Greencastle. This townland extends from the summit of Cave Hill on the west to the shore of Belfast Lough. The castle referred to was a Norman one and it is documented in English documents of the late sixteenth century as *Cloghmalestie/Cloghmycostally*, from Irish *Cloch Mhic Coisteala* 'Costello's stone (castle)'. The final part of the surname *Mac Coisteala* 'Costello' is a development from the personal name *Oisdealbh*, a gaelicization of the Norman personal name Jocelin. The surname is believed to have originated in Connacht with Gilbert, son of Jocelin de Angulo. One branch of the Norman de Angulo family became Costellos; the other branch became Nangles (a corruption of de Angulo).[31] One might ask what an Anglo-Irish surname from Connacht is doing in a place-name here. Perhaps the explanation is that the Connacht branch of the Costellos were connected with the de Burgos who were very prominent in this area. There is now no trace of the castle of Greencastle but it is referred to in 1574 as 'a little pyle belonging to Mr Barkley, an adventurer who came to Ireland with the Earl of Essex'.[32] In 1604 the castle is described as 'ruinous'.[33] It was situated on the Shore Road, close to its junction with Gray's Lane.

---

28 Roddy Hegarty, 'Old Park: an urban townland?', *Due North*, 1:10 (Belfast, Autumn/Winter 2004), 33.   29 Tadhg Ó Donnchadha (eag.), *Leabhar Cloinne Aodha Buidhe* (Dublin 1931), pp xxv–xxx.   30 Cathal O'Byrne, *As I roved out* (Belfast, 1946), pp 313–16.   31 Edward MacLysaght, *Irish families* (Dublin, 1957), p. 95.   32 O'Laverty, p. 452.   33 *Irish patent rolls*

Ballyvaston. Ir. (?) *Baile Bhastúin* 'Weston's townland'. The final element of Ballyvaston appears to be a gaelicization of the Anglo-Norman surname Weston'.[34] Ballyvaston consists largely of uncultivated pasture and moorland and straddles the Hightown Road behind the Cave Hill and the neighbouring Collinward Hill. It contains the site of one of the outlying chapels of the church of Shankill but no trace of this now remains. It is likely to have been in the vicinity of a castle, the ruins of which are referred to in 1605 as 'the ancient stone foundations called *Clogh Ballibaston*'.[35]

Ballybought. Ir. *An Baile Bocht* 'the poor townland'. Ballybought lies to the west of the village of Glengormley. There is some marshy land in the north of the townland and the name may refer to the poor quality of the soil.

Ballywonard. Ir. *Baile an Mhuine Aird* 'townland of the high thicket'. Ballywonard forms the north-western corner of the parish of Shankill and includes the well-known route intersection known as Sandyknowes Roundabout. The *Ordnance Survey Name Book* for the parish of Shankill (*c.*1830) remarks that Ballywonard, Ballybought and Ballyvaston were collectively known as the 'High Towns',[36] hence the name of the Hightown Road which runs through Ballyvaston and Ballybought.

Glengormley (parish of Carnmoney). Glengormley is the name of a townland and village approximately eight kilometres north-west of Belfast city centre, in the civil parish of Carnmoney. The 'official' Irish version of the place-name is *Gleann Ghormlaithe* 'Gormlaith's glen'.[37] However, a sept named *Clann Gormlaithe* 'the descendants of *Gormlaith*', is recorded in a genealogy of the *Dál Fiatach* as being descended from *Muiredach* the father of the ninth-century king *Matudán* (see p. 22 above) and, as pointed out by O'Laverty, the modern name Glengormley clearly represents the name of the ancient sept.[38] The element *glen* in the place-name is therefore a corruption of original Irish *clann* 'family, descendants' and Glengormley is a good example of the transfer of the name of a sept to the district in which they were settled. It also constitutes further evidence of *Dál Fiatach* settlement in the area (see p. 16 above). An interesting point is that *Gormlaith* appears to have been a female personal name, whereas most Gaelic septs are named from male progenitors.

The Cave Hill
The Cave Hill is probably the most distinctive feature of the Belfast landscape, an elongated mountain with sheer rocky precipices which stands a short

of James I: facsimile of the Irish record commissioner's calendar prepared prior to 1830 (Dublin, 1966), p. 49a. **34** MacLysaght (1985), p. 298. **35** Antrim Inquisition of 1605, p. 47. **36** Ordnance Survey name book for the parish of Shankill, *c.*1830 (Book A24); original in National Archives, Dublin. **37** Gasaitéar na hÉireann, p. 112. **38** O'Laverty, p. 453.

distance north-west of the city centre. The modern name Cave Hill appears to be a translation from the original Irish which is documented as *Benn Uamha* 'peak or cliff of the cave' in 1468.[39] At an earlier period the mountain went by the name of *Benn Matudáin* '*Matudán*'s peak or cliff', while a stone promontory fort known as 'McArt's fort', which was spectacularly perched on the edge of the cliff and the last remnants of which are still visible, was formerly known as *Dún Matudáin* '*Matudán's* fort'.[40] The *Matudán* (Mod. Ir. *Madagán*) who gave name to both the Cave Hill and the fort on its summit was an overking of Ulster whose name occurs as *Matudán* son of *Muiredach* son of *Eochaid* in a genealogy of the *Dál Fiatach* and who died in 857.[41] The fact that *Matudán* was able to rule Ulster from his stronghold on Cave Hill in the ninth century proves that by this time the supremacy of the *Dál Fiatach* in the Belfast area had been well-and-truly established and lends further support to the suggestion that it was at Belfast rather than at Toome that they did battle with the *Cruthin* in 668 (see p. 15 above).

The Lagan
The name of the river Lagan is recorded even earlier than that of Belfast itself. It appears on the famous map of the Egyptian geographer Ptolemy which dates from *c.*AD 150 where it is written as *Logia*.[42] This represents Old Irish *Lóeg* 'calf' (Mod. Ir. *laogh* or *lao*). It may strike one as strange that a river should be named from a calf but we must remember that the name precedes Christianity and that the pagan practice of naming rivers from bovine goddesses is well enough attested in Irish place-names, as, for example, in the name of the river Boyne which derives from *Bóinn* (<*bófhinn*) 'cow-white (goddess)' and the Bush, from Ir. *Buais* 'cow-like one'. The word *lao* in Irish means a young, suckling calf and there is no doubt that the name is connected with pagan veneration of the river as the source of new life and fertility. This early name for the Lagan has also given name to Belfast Lough which in Irish is *Loch Lao* 'lough or sea estuary of the river *Lao*'. That the old name for the river was still in use in the fourteenth century is attested by a reference in Heist's *Lives of the Irish Saints* to the Lagan as 'a river named *Locha*',[43] *Locha* representing a later development from the Old Irish form *Lóeg*.

The modern name Lagan has nothing to do with Ptolemy's form *Logia*, even though it bears a superficial resemblance to it. It is from the Irish *Abhainn an Lagáin* which means 'river of the low-lying district', the district in question being the plain through which the river flows, from Moira to its

---

39 *Annals of the kingdom of Ireland, by the Four Masters*, ed. John O'Donovan, 7 vols (Dublin, 1856), iv, p. 1056.   **40** O'Laverty, p. 454.   **41** F.J. Byrne, *Irish Kings and high-kings* (London, 1973), p. 285.   **42** T.F. O'Rahilly, *Early Irish history and mythology* (Dublin, 1946), p. 3.   **43** *Vitae sanctorum Hiberniae ex codice olim Salamanticensi nunc Bruxellensi*, ed. William W. Heist, (Bruxelles, 1965), §6.

mouth at Belfast. This version of the name is of no great antiquity. It is not recorded at all in the Irish language and is not documented in an English source until 1556 when it is referred to as 'a river called *Venelaggan*'[44] which is a corruption of the Irish name *Abhainn an Lagáin*.

The Irish name *Loch Lao* has recently been accepted as the official name of a street in the Short Strand area of the city (see p. 34 below).

The Blackstaff River (Owenvarra)

Ir. *Abhainn Bheara* 'river of the stake'. The Blackstaff rises on the slopes of Black Mountain and flows through Andersonstown and parallel to the MI motorway before being channelled underground until it enters Belfast Lough close to the bottom of the Ormeau Road. Writing in 1880 O'Laverty remarks:

> Down the present Corn Market and William Street there was a passage to the causeway which led over the Owen-Varra –'River of the Stake' – or Black Staff. That causeway was probably bound together by wooden stakes, and the numerous passages for the water were crossed according to the Irish custom by beams of oak stretched from stone to stone; such beams are now generally called *Black Sticks* but more than a century ago they were called *Black Staffs* ... the river, which is now so artificially changed, then fell into the Lagan in Victoria Square and presented a breadth extending from the north side of Victoria Square to far down in the present Joy Street.[45]

The river has given name to Owenvarragh Park and Owenvarragh Gardens adjacent to Casement Park and also to Blackstaff Road and Blackstaff Way in Kennedy Way Industrial Estate.

PLACE-NAMES IN THE CO. DOWN PORTION OF BELFAST

The portion of the city of Belfast which lies east of the river Lagan is entirely in Co. Down and is mainly in the civil parish of Knockbreda with a small portion in the parish of Holywood.

Parish of Knockbreda

If you walk from the city centre across either the Queen's Bridge or the Albert Bridge you find yourself in the townland of Ballymacarret in the parish of Knockbreda in Co. Down. The parish name Knockbreda is a combination of *Knock* and *Breda*, the names of two parishes which were united in 1658 to form the modern civil parish of Knockbreda. The original parish church of

44 *Calendar of the Carew manuscripts*, ed. J.S. Brewer and W. Bullen, i (London, 1867), p. 259.
45 O'Laverty, p. 386.

Knock in the townland of Knock was formerly known as *Knockcolumcille*, from Irish *Cnoc Cholm Cille* '(St) Colmcille's hill'. There are still fragmentary remains of the parish church in a graveyard on a hill in the townland. In the medieval period, the parish church was sometimes known as *the chapel of Dundela*, Dundela being the name of a nearby Norman *motte* which is now known as Shandon Park Mound.

While the name Knock is not recorded in any Irish language source, Breda is recorded *c.*1050 as both *in Bréatach* and *in Brédach* in *Leabhar na gCeart or* the Book of Rights[46] and *c.*1200 as *in Bretach* in 'The history of the descendants of Ir.'[47] In the latter work, which refers back to an earlier period than *Leabhar na gCeart, in Bretach* is described as one of the four chief tribes of the *Monaigh*, a population group who in early Christian times were settled in Fermanagh as well as in east Down and have been referred to above in connection with Taughmonagh on the Co. Antrim side of the Lagan (see p. 23 above). The form of the place-name, which in both sources contains the definite article *in* (Mod. Ir. *an*), suggests that it was originally a territorial name rather than a tribal one. The Old Irish word *brétach* is defined in the *Dictionary of the Irish Language* as 'broken pieces, fragments, breakage' and *in Brétach* (Mod. Ir. *An Bhréadach*) appears to signify something like 'the broken land/fragmented or partitioned land', or possibly 'the cut, the narrow glen'.[48] The fact that it is found as the name of a tribe suggests that in this case the tribe has been named from the territory, whereas in most instances the reverse is the case (see Glengormley, p. 27 above).

The parish church of the former parish of Breda is marked by an old graveyard in the townland of Breda which now forms part of Belvoir Park Forest. Breda has also given name to the village of Newtownbreda which is in the townland of Breda and now forms a suburb of Belfast.

Ballymacarret. Ir. *Baile Mhic Gearóid* 'MacGarrett's or MacCarrett's townland'. *Mac Gearóid* is a rare surname. It means 'son of Gerard', the personal name Gerard having been brought to Ireland by the Normans.[49] Ballymacarret is a large townland which lies on the east bank of the river Lagan. Its eastern boundary is the Conn's Water which flows under the Beersbridge Road, the Newtownards Road and the Sydenham Bypass and also forms part of the boundary between the baronies of Upper and Lower Castlereagh and between the parishes of Newtownbreda and Holywood. Ballymacarret has given name to the townland of Ballymacarret Intake which adjoins it on the north, the element *Intake* referring to land which has been reclaimed from Belfast Lough.

---

46 *Leabhar na gCeart or The Book of Rights*, ed. J. O'Donovan (Dublin, 1947), pp 168 and 172. 47 'The history of the descendants of Ir', ed. M. Dobbs, *Zeitscrift für celtische Philologie*, 14 (1923), 72 and 76.   48 P.W. Joyce, *Irish names of places*, iii (Dublin, 1913) p. 149.   49 Woulfe, p. 365.

Ballynafoy. Ir. *Baile na Faiche* 'townland of the green or lawn'. Ballynafoy is a very large townland which adjoins Ballymacarret on the south. Its western boundary is the Lagan and it extends along the Saintfield Road almost as far as the Forestside Shopping Centre. The name 'Ballynafeigh' is now used for a district within the townland i.e. the area immediately to the south of Ormeau Bridge, but this is obviously merely a variant form of the townland name. The element *faiche* often refers to a lawn or green in front of a fort, but there is no record of any fort in the townland.

Galwally. Galwally is a small townland which adjoins Ballynafoy on the south. Its name goes back to Ir. *Gallbhaile* 'foreigners' town'. In this case, the 'foreigners' referred to are likely to have been the Anglo-Normans.

Breda. The townland of Breda lies on the east bank of the Lagan and includes the village of Newtownbreda. Its name has been discussed above in connection with the parish name Knockbreda (see p. 30 above).

Ballymaconaghy. Ir. *Baile Mhic Dhonnchaidh* 'McConaghy's (McConkey's) (*space added before this*) or (Mac)Donaghy's townland'. The surname *Mac Dhonnchaidh* is normally associated with Scotland and can be anglicized *McConaghy* or *McConkey* (occasionally *Duncan*). It is particularly common in Perthshire where the MacConaghys are a branch of Clan Robertson.[50] However, in this place-name the lenition of the initial *D–* of *Dhonnchaidh* may be due to the fact that the surname is in the genitive case after *Baile* 'townland of ...' It is possible, therefore, that we are dealing with the Irish surname *Mac Donnchaidh* which can be anglicized (*Mac*) *Donaghy*. The townland is bisected by the Knock dual carriageway, to the east of Saintfield Road.

Cregagh. Ir. *An Chreagaigh* 'the rocky place'. The townland of Cregagh includes a road named the Rocky Road and this may reflect the meaning of the place-name. Cregagh lies to the west of Castlereagh.

Lisnasharragh. Ir. *Lios na Searrach* 'fort or enclosure of the foals'. Lisnasharragh borders the Castlereagh Road on the south. There is no record of a fort in the townland.

Carnamuck. The townland of Carnamuck adjoins the townland of Castlereagh on the north-east. Its name derives from Irish *Ceathrú na Muc* 'quarterland of the pigs'.

---

50 Bell, p. 54.

Braniel. Ir. (?)*Broinngheal* 'bright-fronted place'. Braniel is a large townland lying to the east of Castlereagh. It contains a conspicuous hill named Braniel Hill (176m).

Castlereagh. Ir. *An Caisleán Riabhach* 'the grey castle'. The castle (no trace of which remains) was probably described as *riabhach* 'grey' because it was made of stone. It was sometimes known as *Castle Clannaboy* because it was the stronghold of the Clannaboy or Clandeboy O'Neills in the second half of the sixteenth century. It was sold by Sir Conn O'Neill (who gave name to Conn's Water) to Sir Moses Hill in 1616. The site is marked by the Orange Hall close to Castlereagh Presbyterian church on Church Road. Castlereagh formed part of a larger native Irish territory which consisted of eighteen townlands and is referred to as *Castlereagh and Gallowgh* in an Inquisition of 1623.[51] The origin of the name *Gallowgh* is obscure.

Gilnahirk. Gilnahirk borders the townland of Braniel on the east. Seventeenth-century spellings such as *Edengilneherick* point to the derivation *Éadan Ghiolla na hAdhairce* 'the hill brow of the horn bearer'. The element *adharc* 'horn' could conceivably refer to a hunting horn or to a musical horn but seems more likely to denote a drinking horn.

Townlands in the parish of Holywood

Ballyhackamore. The origin of this place-name is obscure. In the *Gazetteer of Ireland* the recommended Irish form is *Baile Hacamar*[52] but the meaning of the final element is unclear. Other suggested interpretations are *Bealach Achomair* 'short cut' and *Baile an Chacamair* 'townland of the slob land or mud flat'. Ballyhackamore now lies inland but prior to land reclamation schemes it may have touched on the shore of Belfast Lough and this may lend support to the last-mentioned interpretation. The townland includes the Upper Newtownards Road.

Strandtown. The name of this townland is recorded as *Ballimachoris* etc. in seventeenth-century documents which appears to suggest *Baile Mhic Fheorais* '(Mac)Corish's townland'. Strandtown formerly bordered on Belfast Lough, hence the English name. Due to land reclamation schemes, it is now a short distance inland. The townland straddles the Holywood Road and its western boundary is the Conn's Water. Its name is documented as *Strandtowne* as early as 1672.

Knocknagoney. Ir. *Cnoc na gCoiníní* 'hill of the rabbits'. Knocknagoney extends from the roundabout at the Holywood end of the Sydenham Bypass to the southern outskirts of the town of Holywood.

51 Lt. Col. Greeves, 'North Down at the beginning of the XVIIth century', *Bulletin of the Ulster Place-Name Society*, ser. 1, 3:2 (Summer 1956), p. 21.   52 *Gasaitéar na hÉireann*, p. 19.

RECENT DEVELOPMENTS

In 1995 the Local Government (Northern Ireland) Order allowed for the erection of bilingual street names in areas where this reflected the will of the local residents. Of course many Irish-language street names had been erected unofficially prior to this but the effect of the 1995 legislation is that for the first time street names which are in a language other than English have been given official recognition. As a result of this, the *Gazetteer* to the Ordnance Survey *Belfast Street Map* of 2000[53] carried a small number of street names (sixteen in all) in both English and Irish. In the latest edition of this map (the 2002 edition) a total of sixty-one bilingual Irish/English street names appears and a significant difference from the earlier edition is that the Irish-language versions of the names are printed on the map itself and not just in the accompanying *Gazetteer*. The bilingual street names appearing on the 2002 *Belfast Street Map*[54] are as follows:

Irish	*English*	*District*
Arda Chluain Ard	Clonard Heights	Clonard
Ardán Mhic an Tiompánaigh	McAtamney Terrace	Short Strand
Ascaill Chluanaí	Springfield Avenue	Springfield
Bóthar Bhaile Andarsan	Andersonstown Road	Andersonstown
Bóthar Chluanaí	Springfield Road	Springfield
Bóthar na bhFál	Falls Road	Falls
Bóthar Thulach Forde	Mountforde Road	Short Strand
Bóthar Thulach Phoitinséir	Mountpottinger Road	Short Strand
Céide Chlann Aodha Buí	Clandeboy Drive	Short Strand
Céide Chluanaí	Springfield Drive	Springfield
Céide na Seileastar	Iris Drive	Falls
Céide Thulach Forde	Mountforde Drive	Short Strand
Clós na Carraige Báine	Whiterock Close	Whiterock
Cnoc na Carraige	Carrick Hill	Carrick Hill
Clós Pholaird	Pollard Close	Springfield
Corrán Bhaile Andarsan	Andersonstown Crescent	Andersonstown
Corrán Chluanaí	Springfield Crescent	Springfield
Corrán Chluain Ard	Clonard Crescent	Clonard
Cúirt Allt an Chairthe	Altcar Court	Short Strand
Cúirt Andarsan	Anderson Court	Short Strand
Cúirt Bholcáin	Vulcan Court	Short Strand
Cúirt Chaibhendis	Cavendish Court	Springfield

53 Ordnance Survey of Northern Ireland, *Belfast Street Map* and *Belfast Street Map Gazetteer* (2000 edition).   54 Ibid. (2002 edition).

Cúirt Chluaidh	Clyde Court	Short Strand
Cúirt Mhaigh Rath	Moira Court	Short Strand
Cúirt Mhic Giolla Stoic	Stockman's Court	Andersonstown
Cúirt na bhFál	Falls Court	Falls Road
Cúirt Naoimh Maitiú	St Matthew's Court	Short Strand
Cúirt Phluincéid	Plunkett Court	Carrick Hill
Cúirt Chnocán Forde	Mountforde Court	Short Strand
Cúirt Shuí Forde	Seaforde Court	Short Strand
Eachlann na Trá	Strand Mews	Short Strand
Gairdíní Bholcáin	Vulcan Gardens	Short Strand
Gairdíní Chlann Aodha Buí	Clandeboy Gardens	Short Strand
Garraithe Chnocán Forde	Mountforde Gardens	Short Strand
Loch Lao	Lough Lea	Short Strand
Lúb Bholcáin	Vulcan Link	Short Strand
Lúb Thulach Poitinséir	Mountpottinger Link	Short Strand
Mala Chluain Ard	Clonard Rise	Clonard
Páirc Bhaile Andarsan	Andersonstown Park	Andersonstown
Plás Chluain Ard	Clonard Place	Clonard
Sráid an Bhalla	Wall Street	Carrick Hill
Sráid Árann	Arran Street	Short Strand
Sráid Bharda Chollan	Colinward Street	Springfield
Sráid Bholcáin	Vulcan Street	Short Strand
Sráid Chill Dara	Kildare Street	Carrick Hill
Sráid Chnoc an Phiobair	Pepper Hill Street	Carrick Hill
Sráid Earnáin	Arnon Street	Carrick Hill
Sráid Elswick	Elswick Street	Springfield
Sráid Fothar Faire	Forfar Street	Springfield
Sráid Loch Altáin	Alton Street	Carrick Hill
Sráid na gCeimiceán	Chemical Street	Short Strand
Sráid na Ríona	Regent Street	Carrick Hill
Sráid Odása	Odessa Street	Clonard
Sráid Pháirc Chollan	Colinpark Street	Springfield
Sráid Pháirc na Feá	Beechfield Street	Short Strand
Sráid Pholaird	Pollard Street	Springfield
Sráid Radharc Chollan	Colinview Street	Springfield
Sráid Ríona Íochtair	Lower Regent Street	Carrick Hill
Sráid Seibheástopol	Sevastopol Street	Clonard
Sráid Shuí Forde	Seaforde Street	Short Strand
Sráid Thír Eoghain	Tyrone Street	Carrick Hill

In addition, the following Irish-language street names have been supplied to Belfast City Council by the Northern Ireland Place-Name Project and have been erected on bilingual street signage. Presumably they will appear on the next edition of the Ordnance Survey *Belfast Street Map*.

Irish	English	District
Ardán Radharc an Ghleanna	Glenview Terrace	Andersonstown
Bóthar na Carraige Báine	Whiterock Road	Whiterock
Céide Éadan Mór	Edenmore Drive	Andersonstown
Clós Thaobh an Ghleanna	Valleyside Close	Springfield
Corrán Inis Mór	Inishmore Crescent	Andersonstown
Corrán Shruthán na Coille	Woodbourne Crescent	Andersonstown
Cúirt Árann	Arran Court	Short Strand
Gairdíní an Chabháin Mhóir	Cavanmore Gardens	Andersonstown
Gairdíní Ghlasmhulláin	Glasmullin Gardens	Andersonstown
Sráid Chúbar	Cupar Street	Springfield
Sráid Stanhóip	Stanhope Street	Carrick Hill

Postal addresses

Another encouraging development is the recent decision by the Department of Culture, Arts and Leisure to include townland names in postal addresses. Under the new policy the official version of every postal address will include a townland name as well as a house number and road or street name. This decision will be especially warmly welcomed in rural areas, where the removal of townland names from addresses in the late 1970s rendered many historical place-names redundant. In the case of Belfast addresses, the vast majority of which did not originally include a townland name, the issue is obviously less relevant. Nonetheless, many people in the city will welcome the fact that the new address database will include the names of historical urban townlands such as Ballydownfine, Ballyaghagan and Ballymaconaghy and will be happy to include them as part of their postal addresses.

The Irish language in Belfast until
the eighteenth cenury

AODÁN MAC PÓILIN

In 1603, the castle of Belfast was granted to Sir Arthur Chichester, who soon began to fortify the surrounding settlement. When he was made lord lieutenant of Ireland the following year he undertook, with energy and some relish, 'first to plough and break up those barbarous people [the native Irish] and then to sow them with seeds of civility'.[1] Chichester's Belfast was a frontier settlement, an English speaking Protestant community set in the middle of an area that was overwhelmingly Catholic in religion and Gaelic in culture. It guarded a strategic ford between Antrim and Down, and provided a beachhead for what the English crown hoped would be the final pacification of Ulster. The cluster of dwellings which comprised the town were given a charter in 1613, not because it had grown to any significant extent, but in response to a political and religious imperative; it was one of forty new boroughs established to ensure a Protestant majority in the Irish parliament. As in most colonising projects, there was also a cultural aspect to the conquest; the 'civility' which was to be sown involved not only the introduction of Protestantism, but the destruction of Gaelic society, culture and language. Belfast town under Chichester was deliberately designed as a node of anglicization.

Given its later history, it is apt that the earliest reference to Belfast is in the context of a territorial struggle: '*665 AD, the Battle of Farset between the Ulaidh [Ulstermen] and the Cruithin, where Cathasach, son of Laircine, was slain*'.[2] By the late seventh century the Ulaidh, who had once controlled most of Ulster, had been forced back to what is now Co. Down. Every so often they managed to extend their territory. At one stage, Fiachna dubh drocheach – Fiachna of the black bridges – who became king of the Ulaidh in 750, extended their territory across the Lagan, building a bridge known as Droichead na Feirsi – the bridge of the Farset.[3] There was not to be another bridge at Belfast for a long time.

The last chiefs of the Ulaidh, the Dunleaveys, were eventually defeated and found a new vocation as hereditary physicians to various Gaelic families

---

1 Breandán Ó Buachalla, *I mBéal Feirste Cois Cuain* (Dublin 1968), 3.　2 D.J. Owen, *History of Belfast* (Belfast 1921), p. 5. This reference is from the seventeenth-century Annals of Donegal. Other annals date the battle to 666, 667 and 668.　3 Thomas McErlean, Rosemary McConkey, Wes Forsythe, *Strangford Lough: an archaeological survey of the maritime cultural landscape* (Belfast, 2002), pp 59–60.

in Ireland and Scotland – Doctor Livingstone of the Congo came from a Scottish branch of the family. Their opponents, the elusive Cruithin, were soon to be written out of history when Gaelic ideologues created a unified racial origin-myth in the eighth century. In a bizarre act of repossession, both the Cruithin and the Ulaidh were re-incarnated as the basis for a unionist origin-myth in the cultural wars of the late twentieth century.

The oldest stratum of Gaelic Belfast survives in the palimpsest of its place-names. Some older townland names, such as Multyhogy and Bally-downfine, survive only on property deeds, and the splendidly named Ballyroculgalgalgie – the townland in which the castle stood – has disappeared. Many of these place-names are descriptive; Cromac, for instance, refers to a bend in the Lagan, and Legoniel means the hollow of the lime, but others have historic resonances. Among these latter is Knockbreda, the hill of the Bréadach, a people of Cruithin origin whose annual tribute of a hundred cows, sheep and pigs to the Ulaidh is recorded in a Gaelic poem in the eleventh-century Book of Rights. Baile na mBráthar, the original name for Friars' Bush, is likely to refer to an old monastery, and Shankill, the name of the parish in which Belfast was set, means 'old church'.[4]

A castle guarded the ford from the twelfth century, but we have no idea when or by whom it was built. Hugh de Lacey captured or re-captured it late in the century, and it appears in various annals at later dates, always in the context of being taken or destroyed by someone – O'Donnell, Edward the Bruce, the earl of Kildare, the earl of Essex, and above all the O'Neills. In the last half of the sixteenth century it changed hands up to a dozen times.

In this period a great swathe of land in south Antrim and north Down, with the exception of the garrison town of Carrickfergus and – intermittently – Belfast Castle itself, was held by the O'Neills of Clandeboy, an offshoot of the great O'Neill family, who had exploited the power vacuum left by the retreat of the Norman earldom of Ulster to expand to the east. This family maintained the traditional way of life of the Gaelic aristocracy, including the maintenance of hereditary bards, such as the Ó hEacháin family (from whom the townland of Ballyaghagan on the Antrim Road is probably named) and the Ó Gnímh family of Larne.

The first mention of the Farset in Irish poetry dates from 1573, when the earl of Essex, lord lieutenant of Ireland, who had been granted most of Antrim and Down by Queen Elizabeth, appeared in Belfast to make his claim. Neither Sir Brian O'Neill, chief of Lower (northern) Clandeboy, nor Brian Ó Gnímh, his chief poet, were particularly happy with this development, and Ó Gnímh wrote a poem urging his patron to attack and kill the upstart Saxon.

4 Deirdre Uí Fhlannagáin, 'Béal Feirste agus Áitainmneacha Laistigh', in B.S. Mac Aodha (ed.), *Topothesia* (Galway, 1982).

Bardic poems, composed by the professional poet in a dark cell with a boulder on his stomach and his head wrapped in a plaid, are elegant artefacts, marshalling a dense, formal and archaic linguistic register and frighteningly complex metres which could be mastered only after years of study. To modern taste they are usually unreadable, and this one is as turgid as any; its main interest for us is that it praises the Farset, now a sluggish and foetid seugh, for the beauty of its water.[5]

O'Neill, who had become chief of Lower Clandeboy mainly through his ostentatious loyalty to the crown, took Ó Gnímh's advice and resisted Essex for about six months. Although defeated near the ford, he retained possession of the castle. There are two accounts, at least one of which must be fiction, of what happened the following year in the castle of 'Belfyrst' as Essex calls it in his contemporary if self-serving version. The other, given below, was written in Irish in the mid-seventeenth-century document popularly known as the Annals of the Four Masters:

> Peace and friendship were established between Brian the son of Felim Bacagh O'Neill and the Earl of Essex, and a feast was afterwards prepared by Brian to which the Lord Justice and the chiefs of his people were invited, and they spent three days and three nights pleasantly and cheerfully. At the end of this time, however, while they were drinking companionably and making merry, Brian, his brother and his wife were seized by the Earl, and all his people, men, women, youths and maidens, put unsparingly to the sword in Brian's own presence. Brian, his brother and wife were afterwards sent to Dublin, where they were cut in quarters, and this is how their feast ended. This unexpected massacre, this vile and treacherous murder of the lord of the race of Hugh Boy O'Neill, head and principal of the race of Eoghan, son of Niall of the Nine Hostages, and of all the Gaels, except a few, gave the Irish sufficient grounds for hatred and outrage.[6]

According to Essex, being aware that Brian was secretly conspiring to rebellion, and suspicious of his 'lewd practices', he ordered his arrest, but as Brian's followers in the town resisted, 115 of them were slain.[7] Evidently some form of settlement already existed thirty years before Chichester's time, and we know from contemporary maps that a church stood on the site of the present St George's in High Street. In 1574 the inhabitants of the 'town' of Belfast were undoubtedly Irish speakers.

5 Tadhg Ó Donnchadha (ed.), *Leabhar Cloinne Aodha Buidhe* (Dublin, 1931), p. 89.   6 *Annala Rioghachta Eireann / The Annals of the Kingdom of Ireland*, v, ed. J. O'Donovan (Dublin 1855), 1674–6.   7 Owen, *History of Belfast*, p. 15.

Chichester had also been granted 52 townlands of O'Neill land in south Antrim, which he tried to plant exclusively with English settlers. He disliked and mistrusted both lowland and highland Scots, but the accession of James VI of Scotland to the English crown gave the Scots a power-base. Conn, the feckless chief of the southern Clandeboy territories, was tricked out of two thirds of the 60,000 acres he still controlled in north Down by two Scotsmen – an extended drinking session, Belfast Castle and a brawl played a part in this also – and soon tricked himself out of most of the remaining third. This area was heavily settled by lowland Scots, who then began to settle in Antrim. In the immediate vicinity of Belfast Chichester and Sir Moses Hill managed to bring a number of English settlers, who then began to expand west along the Lagan valley. The population of Belfast in the early 1600s thus reflected both incoming communities, but the native Irish were thin on the ground when the Plantation Commissioners visited in 1611: 'The town of Belfast is plotted out in good forme wherein are many famelyes of English, Scotish and some Manksmen already inhabitinge of which some are good artificers who have buylte good tymber houses with chimneyes after the fashion of the English palle.'[8] Curiously, the Protestant Manxmen were almost certain to have been Gaelic speakers.

No urban settlement exists in isolation from its hinterland, even if it wants to, and Gaelic culture continued to survive outside the town walls. There is strong evidence of the survival of Irish in the immediate locality. According to G.B. Adams, the Petty Census of 1659 indicates that more than 40 percent of the population of the barony of Castlereagh was Irish speaking; 20 to 50 percent of those who lived in what is now east Belfast were native Irish, and there were areas within a couple of miles of the town in which the proportion rose to over 80 percent.[9] The Belfast market was commonly referred to as the 'margymore' (*margadh mór*/great market) into the eighteenth century.[10]

Surprisingly, the native high culture was maintained for some considerable time in pockets in the surrounding area. Fearflatha Ó Gnímh, who was still making poems for the O'Neills of Clandeboy in 1638, composed a long lament on the downfall of Gaelic society. The bardic poems of the seventeenth century are often deeply felt and powerful; far closer to what we now think of as poetry than the elaborate clichés of most of the earlier work: 'It is not the English who are the intruders, but the Gaels who are aliens,' he said: 'If it be fated for her to become a new England called Ireland, for ever in the hands of her foes, then it would be better to leave this island.'[11] Ó

---

8 George Benn, *A history of the town of Belfast from the earliest times to the close of the 18th century* (Belfast, 1877), i, p. 86. 9 G.B.Adams, 'Aspects of monoglottism in Ulster', in Michael Barry and Phillip Tilling (eds), *The English dialects of Ulster* (Cultra, Co. Down, 1986). 10 Kennedy (1967: 43). Jonathan Bardon, *Belfast: an illustrated history* (Belfast, 1982), p. 28. 11 Róis Ní Ógáin, *Duanaire III* (Dublin, no date), pp 23–5; 104–6.

Gnímh was among the first to compare the Gaels in their disaster with the Israelites in captivity. Another poem by him laments the decline of learned Gaelic families such as O'Higgins, Ward, McNamee and Daly: 'I am blinded with tears and a mist of grief at how few are still alive of the professors, prophets and seer-poets.'[12] In yet another poem he notes that because the honour of the poetic craft was gone, the learned classes would be better off as 'husbandmen of the ploughland'.[13]

We have other tantalizing glimpses of the survival of cultivated literature in Belfast's hinterland. Two Gaelic poets from Co. Down, for example, composed poems of exile during the Cromwellian Wars. One of these was Feardorcha Ó Mealláin, a Catholic priest, who reflects fatalistically on the banishment to Connacht, like Ó Gnímh comparing the Gaels to the Israelites in the time of Moses. He has no expectation of earthly deliverance, but comforts his dispossessed flock with the thought that 'heaven alone is their native soil'.[14] The other, Pádraig Mac Donnagáin (Patrick Dunkin), not only had a technical mastery of classical Gaelic metre, but was also a Trinity-educated Anglican clergyman. He was a Royalist who had been forced by three Puritans he describes as 'roundhead thugs' to flee to the Isle of Man. He curses them roundly for destroying St Patrick's faith and inventing a 'religion without authority', and laments through six verses that the heroes of old were not there to defend their people. It is interesting that, as well as Cú Chulainn and eight named individuals or branches of the O'Neill family, Dunkin also refers to the Norman families of Savage and Russell as defenders of the Gael.[15]

As late as 1680, Cormac O'Neill, a descendant of Sir Brian, married to one of his Castlereagh O'Neill cousins and living in Broughshane in mid-Antrim, commissioned the Book of Clandeboy, an anthology of prose and poetry relating to his family. The collection includes a poem praising his own father, Art Óg, as a Gaelic poet, and another, written by one of the Ward family during the Cromwellian Wars, urging him to take up arms. There are also a number of more recently composed poems to Cormac himself. These are not particularly successful, and it is typical of the unreality of the tail end of the bardic tradition that, at a time when Belfast had been lost to the family for generations, one poem refers to Cormac as 'the dragon of the Farset'.[16]

In the years 1700–1, when the Welsh scholar Edward Lhyud toured Ireland in search of Gaelic manuscripts, Belfast was still a village of no more than a couple of thousand inhabitants, only a tiny proportion of whom were Catholics – as few as seven in 1708.[17] This does not of course mean that there

12 Láimhbheartach Mac Cionnaith, *Dioghluim Dána* (Dublin 1938), p. 399.   13 Osborn Bergin, *Irish bardic poetry* (Dublin 1970), p. 267.   14 Seán Ó Tuama and Thomas Kinsella, *An Duanaire: poems of the dispossessed* (Dublin, 1981), pp 106–7.   15 Éinrí Ó Muirgheasa, *Dhá Chéad de Cheoltaibh Uladh* (Dublin 1934), pp 13–15.   16 Ó Donnchadha , 274.   17 Report from George McCartney, Sovereign of Belfast, cited in Bardon, *Belfast*, p. 25.

were no Protestant Gaelic speakers among them, as the Reformation had had considerable success in east Ulster, and it is also possible that some of the incoming Scots could speak Gaelic, which was still strong in Argyll and had survived in pockets of Ayrshire and Galloway. However, the orientation of the town would have been strongly anglophone at his stage.

Lhyud leaves us a glimpse of the native learned class in their final degradation. In Larne he came upon one of the Ó Gnímh family who had obviously taken the advice of Fearflatha to become a husbandman of the plough: 'I met Eoin Agniw, whose ancestors had been hereditary poets for many generations to the O Neals; but the lands they held thereby being taken away from his father, he had forsaken the Muses and betaken himself to the plow; so we made an easy purchase of about a dozen ancient manuscripts on parchment.'[18] In Lurgan, Lhuyd also met Arthur Brownlow, alias Chamberlain, alias Mac Artúir, a Protestant landlord who owned an impressive collection of manuscripts. Brownlow, whose family was raised to the aristocracy as the Lurgan family, was a Gaelic scholar, and a patron of poets and scribes. His collection included the Book of Clandeboy – Cormac O'Neill, the dragon of the Farset, had taken the losing side in the Williamite Wars and fled to France – and the priceless Book of Armagh, obtained from its last hereditary custodian, Flann Mac Maoir, who had pledged it for £5 so that he could travel to London to give evidence against Oliver Plunkett.

Some hereditary learned families in the vicinity held on to their patrimony much longer, although through time they too became gradually reduced in circumstances. 'Clog an Uachta' reputedly the Bell of St Patrick, had been in the keeping of two learned families, the Mallons and the Mulhollands, since about 1100, but had disappeared from view in 1446. On his deathbed sometime before 1819, an old schoolmaster called Henry Mulhollan, living in Edenduffcarrick near the seat of the O'Neills of Shane's Castle, directed one of his ex-pupils to dig up and keep the contents of an old oak box in his garden. The box contained St Patrick's Bell and its shrine, along with a copy of Bedell's Irish translation of the Bible.[19]

Belfast at the time of Lhuyd's visit was an unlikely setting in which the Irish language could thrive. However, an unbroken thread of Irish language activity in the town began within a couple of decades. The initial impetus was to evangelize the Catholic Irish through the language. James Blow, the Belfast printer, had already published the first English language Bible in Ireland and a collection of Scots poetry when in 1722 he also printed a bilingual Catechism directed at the people of Rathlin Island. This work was commissioned by John

---

18 Nessa Ní Sheaghdha, *Collectors of Irish manuscripts: motives and methods* (Dublin, 1985), pp 9–10. 19 James O'Laverty, *A digest of the historical account of the diocese of Down and Connor* (Dublin, 1879–85), iii, pp 321–4.

Hutchinson, Anglican bishop of Down and Connor, an Englishman with a scholarly and evangelical bent. Few of the inhabitants of Rathlin could speak any English, and although there was 'neither Protestant minister nor Popish Priest as yet settled amongst them' they were, according to Hutchinson 'well disposed towards religion, and very capable of civil improvements'.[20] It was intended to promote civility by not only converting the islanders to Protestantism, but using Gaelic to enable them to learn English.

The 1720s also saw the publication in Dublin of the first major collection of Irish music, and about the same time a Belfastman called Mulholland began to make a collection of Irish songs, the airs of which were published by his son nearly ninety years later, in 1810, under the title *A Collection of Ancient Irish Airs*.[21] It is not clear whether or not the words were also collected, but in the published work, all the titles are given in Irish. While Mulholland was clearly of Irish Gaelic stock, we know nothing else about him. However, as we shall see, a significant core of Protestant middle-class Irish speakers began to develop in Belfast during the eighteenth century, and it is likely, although I have found no documentation to prove this before the last decades of the century, that Catholic native speakers of a lower social class were also beginning to settle in the town.

Mulholland's work foreshadowed one of the most significant cultural events of Belfast in any period, the Belfast Harp Festival of 1792. We tend to imagine cities, like characters in novels, in the context of a critical defining moment. In Belfast this period was comparatively short, and barely extended beyond the 1790s, but those years mark the period in which an earnest market town became the meeting-place for a number of critical streams in Irish society; political, social, religious, intellectual, economic, cultural – and linguistic. It is certain that the Irish language was an integral part of the life of Belfast at this time, and continued to be so for a considerable time.

---

20 Nicholas Williams, *I bPrionta i Leabhar: Na Protastúin agus Prós na Gaeilge, 1567–1724* (Dublin 1986), p. 121.   21 John Mulholland, *Collection of ancient Irish airs* (Belfast 1810).

Robert MacAdam and the nineteenth-century Irish language revival

A.J. HUGHES

The radical politics so beloved of the mainly Presbyterian middle-class of Belfast in the late eighteenth century seem, in some measure, to have been succeeded by an equally passionate concern for cultural antiquarianism and a desire to secure and promote the use of the Irish language in the early nineteenth century. The progress of this cultural activity is reflected most clearly in the life and work of Robert MacAdam (1808–95) and it is MacAdam's contribution to the Irish language revival which provides the framework for both this chapter and the following chapter.

BELFAST: THE EMERGING CITY

Robert MacAdam was born in Belfast in 1808 when, with a population of 20,000, it had yet to witness the remarkable expansion of population which occurred before the end of his life, when this prosperous and tidy town had become a large industrialized city. Although small by today's standards, the early nineteenth-century town had already evolved considerably from the urban centre,[1] which had been very much in the shade of Carrickfergus from the twelfth to the seventeenth centuries.[2]

In the medieval period Belfast was noted only for its small castle at a ford which marked the crossing point between the counties of Antrim and Down.[3] It developed slowly as a plantation town under the ownership of the Chichester family and by the seventeenth century Belfast had acquired a charter as a town. The surname MacAdam featured among the arrivals to the town during that period; the nineteenth-century historian, Benn, includes an account by a 'Captain John MacAdam' of the capture of Belfast by the Scotch in 1641.[4]

---

1 On the encroachment of many areas of the modern city districts on former townlands, see Deirdre Flanagan, in Hughes (1992). For the industrial development of Belfast, see Bardon (1982: chapters 4–6), Maguire (1993), and Agnew (1996). 2 *Cen. Ire. 1659*, p. 8 lists 589 inhabitants in Belfast (366 English and 223 Irish) with a further 120 inhabitants in the 'towne lands' belonging to Belfast. Robinson (1986: 9 §8) puts the population of Carrickfergus at 596 for this year noted for its small castle at the ford, a crossing point between what is modern counties Antrim and Down. 3 In the medieval period Belfast was only Down. Thus in a pipe roll of Henry III (AD 1262) Belfast is referred to as 'Castle of the Ford' while in 1533 the town is styled 'Bealefarst, an old castle standing on a ford'. See Hughes (1992: 81–2). 4 Benn (1877: 108–9).

By the middle of the eighteenth century many of the townspeople of Belfast were complaining about the rundown nature of the town, which they felt was a result of the short leases and tenancies issued by the Chichester family (now the earls of Donegall), whereby no obligation to carry out improvements was required. Around this time the fifth earl of Donegall granted new 99-year leases which, twinned with the eventual demise of the property holdings of the Chichester family, paved the way for the more rapid rise in population and industry in Belfast. Nevertheless, the conditions of some of the later leases granted by the fifth earl, which were considered as overbearing and excessive by some of his tenants, precipitated disturbances in Belfast and the surrounding rural hinterland by the 'Hearts of Steel', a movement of agrarian protesters. The assertion of rights by the Presbyterian middle classes, who challenged the monopolizing stranglehold of the old Ascendancy, meant that 'Belfast had the reputation of being the most radical and seditious centre in Ireland'.[5] The new lease conditions and the consequent upsurge in industry saw Belfast's population expand from 8,500 in 1757 and 13,000 in 1782. Although, in a marginal note in the manuscript of his Irish dictionary, Robert MacAdam commented 'Belfast is not equal to Limerick in size,'[6] the reputation of Belfast had been spreading as the nineteenth century wore on. One commentator wrote in 1833 in the *Dublin Penny Journal*: 'Of the other towns in Ireland, Cork is spirited and contains an intelligent and reading population; and the same remark applies to Limerick. But neither Limerick or Cork or Waterford can compare with Belfast.'[7]

THE MacADAM FAMILY BUSINESS: THE SOHO FOUNDRY

Robert MacAdam was born into the enterprising and commercially successful middle-class Presbyterian community of Belfast, which was poised on the brink of phenomenal expansion. His father James MacAdam (1755–1821) was a hardware merchant who had a shop in Belfast and the young Robert Shipboy MacAdam bore the maiden surname of his mother Jane Shipboy (1774–1827), a native of Coleraine in Co. Derry. An obituary published in the year of his death, 1895, stated that:

> Robert Shipboy MacAdam was born in Belfast in 1808, at his father's residence in High St., two doors from Bridge St., on the Castle Place side. He was educated at the Royal Academical Institution, and early in life entered his father's hardware business.[8]

---

5 Bardon (1982: 31).   6 MS p. 160.   7 *Dublin Penny Journal*, 23 March 1833, p. 310, cited in Ó Buachalla (1968: 46).   8 'In Memoriam Robert S. MacAdam', *Ulster Journal of Archaeology*, 2nd series, 1 (1895) 152.

On the death of James MacAdam Senior, his sons James (1801–61) and Robert continued and developed the family's commercial interests.⁹ Thanks to the MacAdam brothers' joint endeavours business improved briskly.

By 1833 they were able to move from High Street¹⁰ to a private residence in what was steadily becoming a more select area of town, 18 College Square East. Around 1834 they established the Soho Foundry with other business associates.¹¹ It eventually employed more than 250 workers producing a variety of iron products and turbine engines. The MacAdam brothers were to the fore in recognizing a niche for such a foundry to supply the needs of emerging industries:

> The textile trade brought in its wake a need for iron-foundries primarily to supply textile machinery. The first opened in 1792; a number of others over the next few years. Macadam's Soho Foundry, opened in Townsend Street about 1834, is still partly standing; the street front is another of the vernacular classical style. It has a simple monumental brick façade, designed to impress with the strength and solidity of the manufacture. The lower windows to the street are blank, the upper ones heavily pedimented, all admirably proportioned. The gateway is flanked by enormous (and very practical) iron bollards. Later on this factory participated in the boom in prefabricated ironwork; and in 1849 exported to Cairo a set of large cast-iron windows for the palace of an Egyptian prince.¹²

DR JAMES MacDONNELL (1763–1845)

One of the most influential figures in Robert MacAdam's life was Dr James MacDonnell, who also happened to be one of the most prominent individuals involved in the establishment of schools, libraries, hospitals and learned and literary societies in mid nineteenth-century Belfast. A native of the Glens of Antrim, and son of a Catholic father and a Presbyterian mother, MacDonnell was educated in a hedge school in one of the caves at Red Bay quite near to his family home.¹³ Later on, he was sent to the David Manson school in

9 According to Beckett (1995: 3), there were three other MacAdam siblings who died at an early age. 10 For a plan and sketch of High Street Belfast in the late eighteenth century see Elliot (1989: plates 19 and 20, p. 180). 11 Ó Buachalla (1968: 101) refuted the 1838 date proposed in the *Centenary Volume* of The Belfast Natural History and Philosophical Society, p. 90, as there is a reference to the Soho Foundry in *Matier's Belfast Directory, 1835–6*. Brett (1895: 18) suggested that this business opened 'about 1834'. 12 Brett (1985: 18, who also further refers (n. 36) to H.-R. Hitchcock, *Early Victorian archictecture*, London, 1954, p. 527). 13 For a summary of his life cf. Ó Buachalla (1968: 17–19, esp. p. 18 n. 7), Benn (ii, pp 157–61) and Anderson (1888: 32–4 for a summary and plate of a bust, plus a photograph of his grave

Clugston's Entry, Belfast where he was a classmate of Mary Ann and Frank McCracken (siblings of the United Irishman, Henry Joy McCracken).[14] James McDonnell then went to Edinburgh to study medicine and on his return to Belfast in 1784 he set up practice in Donegall Place where he was to earn himself a reputation as a first-rate physician. His social conscience and Christian charity, however, were reflected in his untiring efforts for the less fortunate people of Belfast, and among his great achievements was his involvement in the setting-up of the Belfast Dispensary in 1792, the Belfast Fever Hospital in 1797 and the General Hospital in 1801, which later became the Royal Victoria Hospital. Indeed, Sir William Whitla attributed to him the foundation of the Belfast Medical School (which ultimately became the Faculty of Medicine at Queen's University Belfast): 'If any one name is to be singled out from the founders of the Belfast Medical School ... it must be that of MacDonnell.'[15]

In addition to his medical career MacDonnell was also a leading member of the literary and cultural circles of his day. He was one of the founding members of the Belfast Library and Society for Promoting Knowledge and he was also to feature prominently in the Literary Society and other similar Belfast-based societies of the period. An Irish speaker from an early age, MacDonnell was also deeply interested in Gaelic language, literature and music, particularly the harp.

THE BELFAST HARP FESTIVAL 1792

James MacDonnell, and his two brothers Randal and Alexander, had, for a period of two years, the services of a blind Tyrone harper called Art O'Neill (*c.*1734–1815) in their father's house in the Glens of Antrim. When one considers this formative musical training which the MacDonnell children received in their early youth from Art O'Neill, it is not surprising to learn that Dr James MacDonnell was the author of the following circular issued in 1791:

> Some inhabitants of Belfast, feeling themselves interested in everything which relates to the Honor, as well as to the Prosperity of their country; propose to open a subscription which they intend to apply in attempting to revive and perpetuate THE ANCIENT MUSIC AND POETRY OF IRELAND. They are solicitous to preserve from oblivion the few fragments, which have been *permitted* to remain as Monuments to the refined taste and Genius of their Ancestors.

in Layd Graveyard, Cushendall facing p. 60). The house where he was brought up still stands on the coast road between Waterfoot and Cushendall where a commemorative plaque, in Irish, has recently been erected.   14 On the career of Mary Ann McCracken see McNeill (1960).   15 Cited Ó Buachalla (1968: 77).

In order to carry this project into execution, it must appear obvious to those acquainted with the situation of this Country, that it will be necessary to assemble the Harpers, almost exclusively possessed of all the remains of the MUSIC, POETRY and ORAL TRADITIONS of Ireland.

It is proposed, that the Harpers should be induced to assemble in Belfast (suppose on the 1st of July next) by the distribution of such prizes as may seem adequate to the subscribers: And that a person well versed in the Language and Antiquities of the Nation, should attend, with a skillful musician to transcribe and arrange the most beautiful and interesting parts of their knowledge.

An undertaking of this nature, will undoubtedly meet the approbation of Men of Refinement and Erudition in every country: And when it is considered how ultimately the SPIRIT and CHARACTER of a people are connected with their NATIONAL POETRY and MUSIC it is presumed that the Irish Patriot and Politician, will not deem it an object unworthy of his patronage and Protection.[16]

An account of the opening concert of this festival which took place in Belfast on Wednesday 11 July 1792 describes the excitement of this important event. The performers, each normally playing three tunes, were: Dennis Dempsey [Hempson] (aged 68, blind), Co. Derry, Arthur O'Neill (55, blind) Co. Tyrone, Charles Fanning (56), Co. Cavan – winner of first prize, Daniel Black (75, blind), Co. Derry, Charles Byrne (80), Co. Leitrim, Hugh Higgins (55, blind), Co. Mayo, Paddy Quin (70, blind), Co. Armagh, William Carr (15), Co. Armagh (only one tune), Rose Mooney (blind), Co. Meath, and James Duncan (45), Co. Down.[17]

EDWARD BUNTING (1773–1843)

The task of transcribing the melodies played by the various harpists at the Belfast Harp Festival fell to a young Co. Armagh man, Edward Bunting, the son of an English engineer. As a musical child prodigy he came to Belfast at the age of 11 as assistant organist at St Anne's Parish Church[18] and as his reputation grew he was known throughout Belfast as a professor of Music. He lived in the inn run by the McCracken family in Rosemary Lane for almost thirty years. Here Edward Bunting grew up in the company of the

---

16 Introduction to Bunting's *A general collection of the ancient Irish music.*   17 Young, R. 1894–5: 'The Irish Harpers in Belfast in 1792', *Ulster Journal of Archaeology*, 2nd series, 1 (1895), 120–7 See also Hayward (1952: 71–4).   18 Now St Anne's Cathedral in Donegal Street.

McCracken children John, Mary Ann, William, Frank and Henry Joy who was later to become a leader of the United Irishmen and eventually executed in 1798. Bunting was also part of a circle of celebrated habitués of the McCracken establishment such as Wolfe Tone,[19] Thomas Russell ('The Man from God Knows Where')[20] and Dr James MacDonnell. It would appear that the young Bunting enjoyed, if not revelled in, the status of an *enfant gâté*:

> He became a professor on his own account and abilities as a performer had become developed, his company was courted by the higher class of Belfast citizens, as well as by the gentry of its neighbourhood and in short the boy prodigy became an idol among them ... courted, caressed, flattered and humoured as he was ... wayward and pettish he remained through life, and, for a long period at least, occasionally idle and we fear dissipated for hard drinking was the habit of the Belfastians in those days.[21]

Bunting's fondness for the high life did not inhibit him from producing the important three-volume work, *A General Collection of Irish Music*, the first volume of which appeared in 1796, the second in 1809 and the third in 1840. Here, however, one can detect the steadying hand of Dr James MacDonnell who, along with the McCracken family, advised and encouraged Bunting until he married and moved to Dublin in 1819. Following the publication of the first volume of *A General Collection of Irish Music* in 1796, Bunting went to the countryside to collect more tunes throughout Ulster and Connaught and as far south as Co. Tipperary. As he did not have an accurate knowledge of written Irish (although it would seem inconceivable that he did not possess a reasonable amount of conversational Irish), the Co. Down schoolteacher Patrick Lynch (Pádraig Ó Loingsigh) was financed by the McCracken family to go into Connacht and transcribe the Irish words of the song tunes recorded by Bunting.

Lynch was the same scholar employed to teach the Irish language in the Belfast Academy. One of his pupils in Belfast was Thomas Russell, then librarian in the Linen Hall Library. Lynch also produced a Gaelic magazine, *Bolg an tSolair*, which was printed in Belfast by the *Northern Star* in 1795.[22] Employment was also forthcoming for Lynch from the senior churchman and Trinity College academic, Whitley Stokes who commissioned an Irish translation, in a script adapted for those more familiar with English orthography, of the Gospel according to St Luke and the Acts of the Apostles: *An Soisgeal*

---

19 Elliot (1989).   20 Carroll (1995).   21 *Dublin University Magazine* 29 (1847) 67, cited in Ó Buachalla (1968: 23).   22 *Bolg an tSolair or Gaelic Magazine* described by Ó Snodaigh (1995: 63–4) as 'an 120–page miscellany of dialogue, poetry, translations, prayers and vocabulary. Lynch and Russell seem to have been its main begetters'. Unfortunately this publication only survived through a single issue. A limited edition was reproduced by the Linen Hall Library in 1995.

do réir Lucais, agus Gniovarha na Neasbol (Dublin 1799).[23] We also learn that Samuel Coulter of Dundalk paid Lynch 13*d.* per page for copying manuscripts relating to Ulster Gaelic poets Peadar Ó Doirnín (*c.*1704–69)[24] and Pádraig Ó Prontaigh (the original family name of the Brontë sisters).[25]

Lynch has left some animated accounts of his wanderings through Connacht in search of Irish songs, which survive as part of his correspondence with the McCracken family of Belfast, his patrons for these expeditions:

> I made good progress in Castlebar. I got forty seven songs in it, having stayed ten days, it cost me just two guineas ... I walked the town not knowing whom to apply to and passing by a brogue-maker's shop I heard him singing an Irish song. I stepped in and asked him if he would take a pot of beer. He came with me to the house of John McAvilly, a jolly publican, who sang well, and was acquainted with all good singers in town. Under Tuesday I found out a hairdresser, a shoemaker, a mason and a fiddler – all good singers ... I send you here a list of 150 songs with the names of the persons and places where I got them for Mr Bunting's use ... I heard of a blind piper Billy O'Maily, who had the greatest variety of Irish songs ... Paid my bill 2*s.* 2*d.*, and went to the house were I had seen Blind Billy yesterday, sent for him, gave him a shilling and grog, took down six good songs, cost me 2*s.* 8½*d.* My money is near gone ... I have made good progress – 177 songs ... My dear Miss Mary I have been very attentive, very zealous, and very diligent in this business. I have near 200 songs. I have done all I could yet I am detained for want of travelling charges.[26]

THE BRYSON FAMILY: JAMES, ANDREW AND SAMUEL

In 1774 James Bryson, a 44-year-old Presbyterian minister from Holywood, Co. Down, was appointed as third minister in succession of the Second Presbyterian Church (Rosemary Street) in Belfast and in 1778 he became the first minister of the Donegall Street congregation. James Bryson was to become a committee and honorary member of the Linen Hall Library[27] and was highly respected in the Belfast of his day. Although a member of the Masons, he was also active in the United Irishmen[28] and presided, as chairman, when a motion

---

23 Ó Casaide (1930: 15ff). 24 For details on this poet see Hughes (1987). 25 Chitham (1986). 26 Lynch to Mary Ann McCracken in Bunting MSS, Main Library Queen's University Belfast, cited Ó Buachalla (1968: 38–9). 27 Anderson (1888: 32). Cf. also on 5 October 1793 'That the Revd Jas Bryson and Doctor M'Donnell be requested to solicit Donations of Books from such persons as they think proper', ibid., p. 18. 28 On the links between freemasons and the United Irishmen see Smyth (1993).

was passed in the Linen Hall Library on 17 January 1792 on the 'propriety of their publicly declaring their sentiments on the great important question of admitting the Roman Catholics to a full and immediate participation of the rights enjoyed by their fellow-citizens and countrymen'.[29]

One of James' sons Andrew was a Presbyterian minister in Dundalk where he more often than not preached in Irish.[30] Another son was Samuel (1778–1853) who trained in the medical profession and was listed as Assistant Surgeon in the 32nd Regiment and also recorded as 'apothecary and surgeon' of both 96 High Street and Ballymacarret.[31] This same Samuel Bryson, under the Gaelic form of his name Somhairle Mac Brise, produced careful copies of eight Irish-language manuscripts which contained many of the essentials of early Irish literature such as: The Cattle Raid of Cooley (*Táin Bó Cuailnge*), The Children of Lir (*Oidhe Chloinne Lir*), The Tale of Deirdre and the Slaughter of the Sons of Uisneach (*Imtheacht Dheirdre agus Oidhe Chloinne Uisnigh*),[32] The Life of St Patrick (*Beatha Phádraig*), etc.[33] Indeed Aodh Mac Domhnaill (Hugh McDonnell), the Co. Meath scribe employed by Robert MacAdam to copy Irish manuscripts also composed a six-verse poem in the Irish language singing the praises of Samuel Bryson's skills as a physician after he had treated him successfully.[34]

THE REVD WILLIAM NEILSON (1774–1821)

Another Presbyterian very much to the fore in Irish language circles in Belfast at this time was the Revd William Neilson, the son of Dr Moses Neilson of Rademon in Co. Down. Moses Neilson opened an academy in Rademon which, in addition to educating the sons of members of his own congregation, also 'prepared young men intended for the Catholic priesthood in Latin and Greek'.[35] Fr Luke Walsh, from the same area, set out in his 1844 work, *The Home Mission Unmasked*, to expose, what he viewed as: 'the frauds, deceptions and falsehoods practised by the agents of the Home Mission of the General Assembly of the Presbyterian Church in Ireland', could only but applaud the generosity and unwavering uprightness of William's father: 'I was educated myself by a Presbyterian Clergyman, a man of as great moral worth and sterling integrity as Ireland could boast of – the Dr Moses Neilson of Rademon in the Co. Down.'[36]

---

29 Anderson (1888: 91). **30** Fortunately four of his sermons have survived, Ó Snodaigh (1995: 55). **31** Ó Buachalla (1968: 55). **32** For the English translation of Bryson's version of the Deirdre story see Hughes & McDaniel (1988-9). **33** Ó Buachalla (1968: 54). For details of the Irish manuscript collection in Belfast Public Library see the catalogue compiled by Ó Buachalla (1962) and Appendix A in Ó Buachalla (1968: 275). **34** Details in Ó Buachalla (1968: 56–7). **35** Ó Snodaigh (1995: 57, citing Magee 56). **36** Walsh (1844: 146).

In summing up William Neilson's career, Breandán Ó Buachalla, concludes that William inherited many of the virtues of his father Moses.[37] It is not clear whether or not William was a native Irish speaker although his excellent command of the language would suggest that he was. Ciarán Ó Duibhín points out that his father Moses Neilson was an Irish speaker[38] who used Irish in his sermons at Rademon, and Ó Duibhín goes on to cite a late eighteenth-century source which implied that Irish was the language of both communities in this part of Co. Down at the time: 'The Dissenters and Papists of this parish mostly speak in that language [Irish], and his [Revd Moses Neilson's] prayers and discourses are made in it.'[39]

At any rate, William Neilson's attendance at the hedge school run by the Ó Loingsigh (Lynch) family of Loughinisland, Co. Down, where Patrick Lynch – future teacher of Irish at the Belfast Academy – was to be his tutor would have ensured a solid grounding in Irish at an early age. This was certainly an important prerequisite for the successor of the Revd Andrew Bryson at the Dundalk Presbyterian Church where 'it was considered that the minister of this congregation should be able to speak Irish'.[40] It is hardly surprising, therefore, that William Neilson should have slotted so admirably into this vacant position in 1795. Indeed the Revd William Neilson's oratory skills in Irish were not confined to Dundalk, as the *Belfast Newsletter* reported, on 9 July 1805, how he preached sermons in Irish in Belfast 'to a numerous and respectable audience', while the *Hibernian Magazine* in September 1805 refers to the fact that he was on a tour throughout Ulster 'preaching in Irish'.

As a scholar and linguist William Neilson demonstrated outstanding ability. In his student years he wrote an English grammar which became a standard text-book in many Ulster schools. He built a fine reputation as a classical scholar, due to publications such as his *Greek Exercises in Syntax, Ellipsis, Dialects Prosody and Metaphrasis* (Dundalk 1804), which went into eight editions by 1842; *Greek Idioms* (Dublin 1810); and *Elementa Linguae Graecae* in 1820. He was elected to the chair of Greek in the University of Glasgow in 1821 but died before taking up the post.[41] He was also a Hebrew scholar.

In 1808 he published *An Introduction to the Irish Language in three parts: I. An original and comprehensive grammar; II. Familiar phrases and dialogues; III. Extracts from Irish books manuscripts, in the original character with copious tables of the contractions.*[42] This work may well have contributed to Rev Neilson's election as a member of the Royal Irish Academy in Dublin and it would also have assisted his appointment to future teaching posts. He also

---

37 Ó Buachalla (1968: 59–64). 38 Moses Neilson was a native of Castlederg in Co. Tyrone, according to Ó Snodaigh (1995: 57). 39 Dr Ó Duibhín has since informed me that this was cited by Robb (1946). 40 Jamieson (1959: 40). 41 Brady & Cleeve (1985: 320). 42 Originally printed in Dublin (P. Wogan) this work has been reprinted (with a bilingual foreword by R. Ó Bléine/Blaney) by Iontabhas Ulatch/Ultach Trust (Belfast 1990).

had valuable teaching experience from his days as a minister in Dundalk where he helped set up a school which was 'attended by all denominations and from it has sent students for TCD, Maynooth and the Scotch Universities'.[43] In his *Introduction to the Irish Language* Neilson was quick to point out not merely the importance of Irish from a philological and historical perspective but also its worth and beauty as a spoken language in the Ireland of his day:

> That the Irish is the best preserved dialect of the ancient and exten-
> sive Celtic language, is allowed by the most liberal and enlightened
> antiquarians. To the general scholar, therefore, a knowledge of it is
> of great importance; as it will enable him to trace the origin of names
> and customs, which he would seek in vain in any other tongue. To
> the inhabitant of Ireland it is doubly interesting. In this language are
> preserved the venerable annals of our country, with as much fidelity,
> as is usually found in the primitive records of any nation; while the
> poetic and romantic compositions, with which the Irish manuscripts
> abound, afford the finest specimens, of elegant taste and luxuriant
> imagination. But it is, particularly, from the *absolute necessity* of under-
> standing this language, in order to converse with the natives of a great
> part of Ireland, that the study of it is indispensable. If Irish be no
> longer the language of the court, or the senate, yet the bar and the
> pulpit require the use of it; and he that would communicate moral
> instruction, or investigate the claims of justice, must be versed in the
> native tongue if he expects to be generally understood, or to succeed
> in his researches. In travelling, and the common occurrences of agri-
> culture and rural traffic, a knowledge of Irish is also absolutely nec-
> essary ... it is surely reasonable and desirable, that every person
> should be able to hold converse with his country men; as well as to
> taste and admire the beauties of one of the most expressive, philo-
> sophically accurate, and polished languages that has ever existed.[44]

In 1818 William Neilson was elected to the Belfast Academical Institution as 'Head-master of the Classical school' where he was professor of Irish, Greek, Latin, Hebrew and Oriental languages – a position he maintained until his death three years later. Irish was already taught in the Belfast Academy by Patrick Lynch and with people such as Dr James MacDonnell among the founders of the Belfast Academical Institution, it is hardly surprising that the authorities at the Institution proved similarly receptive to the inclusion of Irish on the school's curriculum. Campbell, in his treatment of the role of the Belfast Academical Institution, sums up its aims and functions as follows:

---

43 Ó Snodaigh (1995: 56).   44 Neilson (1808: ix–x).

This school was planned to serve the needs of Belfast's expanding business and professional classes. It also had the function of educating potential Presbyterian ministers. It was predominantly Nonconformist in enrolment but also took some episcopalian and Catholic pupils. It was an unusual organization in so far that it was both a school and a college. In contrast to the universities of England and Scotland it imposed no religious test on its entrants.[45]

Considering the role which this institution had in the preparation of candidates for the Presbyterian ministry, and the need for a command of the Irish language which the Synod felt to be necessary for ministers in Ulster at this period, an accomplished grammarian such as Neilson, was eminently suitable as an Irish teacher.

THE BELFAST ACADEMY AND THE BELFAST ACADEMICAL INSTITUTION

While industrial Belfast began to prosper at the end of the eighteenth century, similar progress was made in the provision of institutions for education, literature and the arts. Both of the MacAdam brothers had received their education at the Belfast Academical Institution and they, in their turn, would come to the forefront in such activities. The aims of the Institution, as set out at its establishment, serve to underline the liberal and tolerant quality of the Presbyterian ethos in Belfast, at this time:

The object of the Academical Institution was and is, shortly and simply this – to diffuse as widely as possible throughout the province and population of Ulster the benefits of education both useful and liberal and by that the means to prevent the hard and disgraceful necessity, in such a great and prosperous community, in sending their children to seek in other countries, with much risk to their health and morals, for that instruction and those literary qualifications and honours which might equally be obtained at home ... Of nothing are the Boards more desirous than that pupils of all religious denominations should communicate by frequent and friendly intercourse in the common business of education, by which means a new turn must be given to the national character and habits, and all the children of Ireland should know and love each other.[46]

45 Campbell (1991: 125).   **46** Fisher and Robb (eds), *The Book of the Royal Belfast Academical Institution*, pp 203–5, cited in Ó Buachalla (1968: 47).

Known today as the Royal Belfast Academical Institution and still occupying its original site in the city centre, the Belfast Academical Institution was established in 1810, to cope with the increased demand for education in Belfast.[47] It was preceded by the Belfast Academy, founded in 1785 and still in existence to this day as the Belfast Royal Academy – now on the Cliftonville Road in North Belfast – although Academy Street near St Anne's Cathedral bears witness to its original site in the city centre.[48]

In both these schools the Irish language and its literature were regarded as important and actively promoted. Pádraig Ó Loingsigh (Patrick Lynch), the Irish scholar from Loughinisland in Co. Down, offered his services in the *Northern Star*, on 16–20 April 1794:

Irish Language

An attempt to revive the grammatical and critical knowledge of the Irish language in this town is generously made by Mr Lynch: he teaches publically in the Academy and privately in several families. This language recommends itself to us, by the advantages it affords the students of Irish and Eastern Antiquities, especially to those who wish to acquire the knowledge of Druidical Theology and worship, as sketched by Cæsar and Tacitus.

It is particularly interesting to all who wish for the improvement and Union of this neglected and divided Kingdom. By our understanding and speaking it we could more easily and effectually communicate our sentiments and instructions to all our Countrymen; and thus mutually improve and conciliate each other's affections.

The merchant and artist would reap great benefit from the knowledge of it. They would then be qualified for carrying on Trade and Manufactures in every part of their native country.

Such knowledge, we understand, could easily be acquired in three or four months by the assistance of Mr Lynch.[49]

The Academy was by no means the only institution in Belfast promoting the Irish language and Gaelic literature and music in the late eighteenth century. By 1788, the Belfast Reading Society had been established from which sprang

47 For a history of this school see Jamieson (1960). The word 'Royal' was inserted into the title in 1830, apparently in recognition of the restoration of a government grant in 1827. The initial grant was removed in 1816 when a number of the teaching staff toasted the success of the French Revolution as part of their St Patrick's Day celebrations. When this was reported to the government authorities they offered an ultimatum that the Academical Institution would have to chose between its freedom of conscience or its financial aid – the Institution opted for the former! *The book of the RBAI*, p. 63.   48 For a history of the Academy, see Shearman (1935).
49 Cited by Ó Buachalla (1968: 30) and Ó Snodaigh (1995: 63).

the Belfast Library and Society for Promoting Knowledge (now known as the Linen Hall Library).[50] In 1798 a full list of members included 'Jas M'Adam'[51] (the father of Robert Shipboy and James) and he was also listed as a member of the committee in 1803 and 1810.[52] It was unsurprising therefore, that his sons James and Robert served as committee members in later years.

In the *Belfast Newsletter*, 22 May 1818, the following appeared:

The Irish Language

Doctor Neilson proposes to open a class for teaching Irish in the Belfast Academical Institution on Monday next 25th inst., at seven o'clock in the evening. The class will meet every Monday, Wednesday and Friday. Terms: One Guinea per Quarter.

THE MACADAM BROTHERS AT THE
BELFAST ACADEMICAL INSTITUTION

Ó Buachalla gives the roll of names of those attending Neilson's Irish class in May 1819, found in the personal copy of Neilson's *An Introduction to the Irish Language* which belonged to R.J. Tennent, an old boy of the Belfast Academical Institution and former Belfast MP between 1847 to 1852: 'Irish Class List, May 1819: R. Carlisle, J. Mac Adam, R. Tennent, Wm. Simms, R. Vance, Jas. Gibson, Francis Ward, Sam. Coulter, Edmund Hayes, R.J. Tennent'.[53]

The 'J. MacAdam' in question was probably James, elder brother of Robert. Born in 1801 he received his education at the Belfast Academical Institution before going on to Trinity College Dublin. James' main pursuits were of a scientific nature. He took advantage of the opportunities afforded by the construction of the Irish railway system to study the geology of the country and was elected a Fellow of the Royal Geological Society and amassed quite a collection of exhibits in his home.[54] He was appointed as first Librarian to the Queen's College in 1849 although he relinquished this post after one year as it apparently hindered his other activities.[55] While he had the joint responsibility of running the Soho Foundry, James, like his younger brother and partner Robert, wished to indulge his academic pursuits: 'This is by no means the life that I should wish to lead but I am bound to assist my brother

50 On the history of this illustrious institution see Anderson (1888) and Killen (1990). 51 Anderson (1888: 35). 52 Ibid., 95 & 42. 53 R.J. Tennent's copy of this book is preserved in the Library of the Royal Belfast Academical Institution. 54 'He had a private museum of geological specimens which was regarded as the best in Ireland'. Newmann (1993: 143). 55 'The first two librarians were ... James MacAdam, who stayed only one year before deciding he could not afford the time the post demanded, and the Reverend George Hill, who was Librarian for thirty years and in many ways the founder of the Library'. Walker & McCreary (1994: 87).

with a hope of occasionally getting away on scientific matters.'[56] James
MacAdam's contribution to learning has been summed up as follows:

> The librarian James MacAdam, an alumnus of the Institution [Belfast
> Academical Institution] and of Trinity College, Dublin, was an excel-
> lent example of a Belfast type in which the pursuit of business and
> devotion to learning were successfully combined. He was one of the
> founders of the Botanic Gardens and an amateur geologist of some
> distinction. He had been assistant secretary of the Institution and in
> that capacity had been responsible for the management of its library;
> and he had been a candidate for the chair of mineralogy and geology
> in the new college.[57]

ROBERT MacADAM'S FIRST INVOLVEMENT WITH THE IRISH LANGUAGE

Although there is no roll extant which confirms that Robert MacAdam
attended the classes of the Revd William Neilson at the Belfast Academical
Institution, it seems a reasonable assumption that he did. Robert would have
been 13 years old when Neilson died – a hypothesis supported by the fact
that the name of Robert MacAdam appears in the register of the Academical
Institution in the year 1818,[58] the same year of William Neilson's appointment. That the MacAdam brothers should have gone to the Belfast
Academical Institution to be educated was a logical progression given the
establishment's proximity to their home and the fact that their father James
was also a founder member of the Institution.[59] What is more debatable, however, is whether or not the Belfast Academical Institution would have been
young Robert's first exposure to the Irish language.

Ó Buachalla points out that there was a Robert MacAdam Senior living in
Belfast in the late eighteenth and early nineteenth century who was a collector
of Gaelic songs, some of which have turned up in the manuscripts which were
in the possession of Robert Shipboy MacAdam. For example, on page 40 of
Belfast Public Library Irish MS XXXI, Robert Shipboy states that the forego-
ing poems and songs 'were collected by R. Mac Adam Sen.'[60] Robert Senior
was also a committee member of the Linen Hall Library in 1813[61] and was earlier listed on the music committee of the Irish Harp Society, a body established

---

56 Young MS 9/3 Queen's University Belfast, cited in Ó Buachalla (1968: 179).   57 Moody
& Beckett (1959: 122).   58 Fisher & Robb (1913: 246).   59 'Another founder with similar [i.e.
liberal and tolerant] views was James MacAdam, a prosperous iron-founder in the city, and
father of the Gaelic scholar Robert MacAdam'. Campbell (1991: 125).   60 Ó Buachalla (1962:
27).   61 Anderson (1888: 95).

by Dr James MacDonnell and Edward Bunting in Belfast in 1808 'primarily to provide blind boys and girls with the means of earning a living by teaching them the harp; secondarily to promote the study of the Irish language, history and antiquities'. In the light of this family connection with Irish music, Robert Shipboy MacAdam's first exposure to the Gaelic language may not have been through the classroom, it is likely that young Robert's tuition by the Revd William Neilson at the Belfast Academical Institution would have contributed greatly to his enthusiasm for the Irish language and laid the foundations for his later expertise in the subject. In the foreword to the first volume of the *Ulster Journal of Archaeology*, which Robert launched and edited in 1853, he paid homage to Neilson's work in the sphere of the Irish language, placing his name among the leading luminaries of his age: 'nor must we omit that of our townsman, Dr Neilson, to whose exertions, at a critical moment, we are perhaps, indebted for a renewed interest in the ancient language of Ireland'.

There is no doubt that Robert MacAdam would have been attracted to the cultural, literary and artistic aspects of the language, but Irish was also still very much a functional language in widespread daily use at this point. As the Revd Neilson said in outlining his reasons for introducing Irish into the curriculum of the Belfast Academical Institution:

> it is surely reasonable and desirable, that every person should be able to hold converse with his country men; as well as to taste and admire the beauties of one of the most expressive, philosophically accurate, and polished languages that has ever existed.

Aside from its aesthetic qualities, then, there were practical reasons for learning the Irish language which would have been spoken quite extensively in rural Ulster at this time, and would have been heard in the streets of Belfast at market or in the taverns where visitors or recent arrivals to town would have gathered.

IRISH AS A SPOKEN LANGUAGE IN RURAL ULSTER IN THE EARLY NINETEENTH CENTURY

When Swiss-born scholar Heinrich Wagner began his four-volume *Linguistic Atlas and Survey of Irish Dialects* in the 1950s, most of his Ulster material was collected from Co. Donegal – where Gaeltacht areas still exist – although he did manage to locate native speakers of Irish in counties Cavan, Tyrone and Rathlin Island, Co. Antrim,[62] in addition to Omeath, Co. Louth.[63]

---

62 Rathlin Gaelic was a variety of Scottish Gaelic apparently introduced post-1575: 'Rathlin was depopulated in 1575, when the inhabitants (Gaelic speaking Scots) were massacred by English soldiers under John Norris, so that the present dialect was introduced since that date'.

Between the beginning of the twentieth century and the time of Wagner's fieldwork of the 1950s, native speakers of Irish were also found in the Glens of Antrim, and in counties of Derry, Monaghan and Armagh.[64] G.B. Adams, in his in-depth analysis of the returns to the question on the use of the Irish language for the six northern counties from the 1911 *Census of Ireland*, concluded that while the overall figure represented 2.3 percent of the total population, some areas of the six counties had returned figures of 20–30 percent Irish speaking.[65]

If one goes back further to pre-Famine rural Ulster in which Robert MacAdam grew up, one finds that the numbers of Irish speakers increase dramatically. We know, for example, that when the Kilkenny-born Irish-language scholar John O'Donovan (1806–61) began fieldwork for the first Ordnance Survey of Ireland in the 1830s he was to encounter Irish speakers in virtually all of the counties in Ireland. O'Donovan's official task was to standardize the anglicized spellings of, in the main, the *c*.65,000 townlands of Ireland, although in the *Ordnance Survey Name Books* he often entered what he considered to be the original Irish forms of the name in question.[66] In many instances O'Donovan recorded the Irish names of the townlands from speakers of Irish in the locality. For example, in Downpatrick he recorded the Irish name for Saul (a parish in the barony of Lecale, Co. Down) as *Sabhall Phádraig*, from an old local man, Luke Killen. *Sabhall* is an Irish word for 'barn' which is borrowed from Latin *staballum* (as in the English *stable*). The form *Sabhall Phádraig*, preserved by Killen, can be traced back as far as the text of the Tripartite Life of St Patrick, compiled nearly 1000 years earlier in *c*.AD 900.[67]

A significant part of the colossal Ordnance Survey of Ireland at six inches to the mile in the first half of the nineteenth century, in its early stages, included an accompanying set of memoirs. It was unfortunate that this aspect of the project had to be abandoned after Ulster was surveyed, as the extant material on the northern counties constitutes an invaluable detailed portrait of Irish parish life before the Great Famine.[68] From this source it is clear that Irish speakers were to be found throughout the length and breadth of Ulster, although some areas contained many more than others. The mountainous districts and those removed from the main towns proved particularly disposed

O'Rahilly (1932: 164 n. 2).   **63** Wagner (1958, esp. xx–xxi) and Wagner & Ó Baoill (1969) which covered Ulster, Scotland and the Isle of Man. See also map in Hughes (1994: 610).   **64** Bibliographical details in Hughes (1994: 619–20).   **65** G.B. Adams (1964).   **66** For details of this large-scale nineteenth-century Ordnance Survey, see Andrews (1974) , Ó Maolfabhail (1989) and Hughes (1991: 121–2).   **67** See Hughes (1999) – although for the corruption of modern Killinchy (Co. Down) from its original Irish *Cill Duinsighe* 'Church of St Duinseach' to local Irish *Cill Inse* 'Church of the Island', see Hughes ibid.   **68** Nevertheless the Ordnance Survey memoirs for Ulster have been published by the Institute of Irish Studies, Queen's University Belfast, see Day (1986).

to the preservation of Irish. Although O'Donovan was able to find Irish speakers among the older generation in Lecale, Co. Down, his contemporary on the survey, Lieutenant T.H. Rimmington observed, in January 1835, of the parish of Ardglass: 'the English language is entirely spoken, the Irish having quite fallen into disuse'.[69] Similarly, in letters written during the course of the Ordnance Survey in the Newry area, O'Donovan records his difficulty in locating a local informant who spoke Irish, before being led by the Revd Mr Glenny to the octogenarian 'Old MacGilvoy'.[70] Of course, the central area for Irish speaking in Co. Down at this period was around Castlewellan, an area which Mícheál Ó Mainnín suggests 'seems to have included the [civil] parishes of Clonduff, Drumgath, Drumballyroney, Drumgooland, Kilcoo, Maghera, Kilmegan, Loughinisland and Down'.[71] The reference to Loughinisland, of course, reminds one of the Irish-language school which was run there, and the presence of scholars such as the family of Pádraig Ó Loingsigh (Patrick Lynch, the Irish-language teacher in the Belfast Academy in the late eighteenth century), and Revds Moses and William Neilson.

In addition to the accounts by John O'Donovan, and by other personnel involved in the Ordnance Survey, one can find further corroboratory accounts of other contemporary commentators. Abraham Hume, compiling a report for the British Association in 1874, pronounced that 'as late as 1820 ... the Irish language was spoken along with English from Ballynahinch to near Newry'; while Christopher Anderson in his *Historical Sketches of the Native Irish* estimated that 93,000 out of a total population of 325,410 for Co. Down were Irish speakers.[72]

There were several surveys of the level of Irish spoken in Co. Tyrone in the eighteenth century. One estimate put the figure at two-thirds of the population while a 50 percent figure was cited in a tract published by Dr Whitley Stokes of Trinity College Dublin in 1806 'on the prevailing language in most counties of Ireland'.[73] Stokes' figure was more or less confirmed by the slightly later investigation conducted, in the late 1820s, by Christopher Anderson in his *Historical Sketches of the Native Irish* which estimated that around 140,000 out of the total of 261,865 inhabitants of that county, returned for the 1821 census, spoke Irish.[74] It is also of note that an Irish-language devotional work was published in Dublin in 1849 entitled *The Story of the Life and Passion of Our Lord and Saviour Jesus Christ* which was aimed specifically for 'the use of Ulster folk in Derry and Tyrone in their own provincial language'.[75] This

69 *OSM*, vol. 17, p. 4.   **70** *OSL Down*, p. 46. On the reasonable quality of this speaker's Irish cf. Toner/Ó Mainnín (1992: 2–3).   **71** Ó Mainnín (1992: 11).   **72** Cited Ó Casaide (1930: 54ff).   **73** Ó Tuathail (1933: xi).   **74** *Historical sketches of the native Irish* in 1830. It would be true to say that Irish speaking continued more vibrantly in Tyrone than any other area of the six counties in the twentieth century, with the possible exception of the Glens of Antrim. For a detailed discussion of Irish in Co. Tyrone in the current century see Ó Conluain (1989).   **75** *Sgéul fa*

work was signed 'R Ua C' which Ó Tuathail has successfully identified as Ristéard Ó Cionga, or the Revd Richard King.

Richard King (1815–1900), a native of Cork, was educated at Trinity College Dublin and ordained a Church of Ireland minister in 1841. Between the years 1851 and 1858 he was curate at Armagh before moving on to Ballymena Diocesan School where he served as principal until the year of his death. King was a prolific scholar and his books included many devotional works in English, a catechism and a life of Christ, plus a three-volume *History of the Church of Ireland* and a *Memoir of the Primacy of Armagh*. Kate Newmann notes that he 'was a devoted scholar of the Irish language, and published an Irish translation of the Book of Common Prayer'.[76]

Nearer Belfast, in rural Co. Antrim, the Irish language would also have been heard in many areas. Thomas Fagan, in his fair sheets for the Ordnance Survey Memoir of the Parish of Aghagallon, in south-west Co. Antrim on the shores of Lough Neagh, wrote that 'The Irish language too prevailed to a great extent throughout the period about 40 years back, particularly in the Montiaghs. A few settlers from other districts still speak Irish fluently but none of the natives of the parish.' [77] Further north in Co. Antrim, Lieutenant J. Greatorex in his Statistical Account of the Parish of Loughguile, September 1833, remarked of the '6,889 souls' in the parish:

> They are a mixture of the Scotch and English emigrants, with the primitive inhabitants. The pure race of the latter are to be found in the mountainous range of the parish, and the Irish language made use of to this day, but very partially.[78]

The Glens remained a bastion of Irish language and lore and was explored by Robert MacAdam in the 1830s for the purposes of recording Gaelic songs, and folk stories.

THE IRISH LANGUAGE IN TRADE AND COMMUNICATION IN NINETEENTH-CENTURY ULSTER

In the advertisement for Irish classes to be given by Patrick Lynch, placed in the *Northern Star* 16–20 April 1794, pains were taken to point out that one of the incentives listed for learning Irish was that the 'merchant and artist would reap great benefit from the knowledge of it. They would then be qual-

bheatha agus pháis ár dTighearna agus ár Slánuightheora, Íosa Críost. Le h-ághaidh úsáide na nUlltach a n-Doire agus a d-Tír Eoghain, an a dteangaidh cuigeadhaigh féinn – cited in Ó Tuathail (1933: xii). 76 Newmann (1993: 127). 77 Parish of Aghagallon, Co. Antrim Fair Sheets 1838, *OSM*, vol. 21, p. 22. 78 *OSM*, vol. 13, p. 58.

ified for carrying on Trade and Manufactures in every part of their native country'. The Rev William Neilson made a similar point in his outline of the various reasons why Irish was going to be offered as a subject on the curriculum of the Belfast Academical Institution:

> But it is, particularly, from the *absolute necessity* of understanding this language, in order to converse with the natives of a great part of Ireland, that the study of it is indispensable. If Irish be no longer the language of the court, or the senate, yet the bar and the pulpit require the use of it; and he that would communicate moral instruction, or investigate the claims of justice, must be versed in the native tongue if he expects to be generally understood, or to succeed in his researches. In travelling, and the common occurrences of agriculture and rural traffic, a knowledge of Irish is also absolutely necessary.[79]

As an example of the need that would have been felt by English-, or Scots-, speaking settlers in nineteenth-century Ulster to acquire a knowledge of Irish for commercial purposes, one can cite the account by J. Stokes in the Ordnance Survey Memoirs for the parish of Drumachose in Co. Derry:

> The parishioners are very anxious to obtain books from the Irish Bible Society.[80] They have also a wish for some acquaintance with the Irish language, as they feel their ignorance of it highly inconvenient, not only in their intercourse with some parts of the county, but also on visiting other counties to purchase goods. In the markets where Irish is spoken those unacquainted with the language are regarded as foreigners, and to cheat them is considered a praiseworthy deed. This wish to acquire the language prevails in all the surrounding parishes.[81]

In counties Down and Armagh one can adduce an identical use of Irish at fair and market, as W.H. Patterson received the following information from a correspondent 'from the mountainous district in the South of Down' in 1880:

> There are a good many Irish speaking people in the neighbourhood of Hilltown, but I think nearly all of them can speak English; when, however, they frequent fairs in the upper parts of the Co. Armagh for instance at Newtownhamilton or Crossmaglen, they meet num-

---

79 Neilson (1808: ix–x).   80 On the work of societies such as the Hibernian Bible Society, the Irish Evangelical Society (1814), the Irish Society for Promoting Education of the Native Irish through the Medium of their own Language (1818), see Hempton & Hill (1992: 52ff).   81 *OSM*, vol. 9, p. 84.

bers of people who speak English very imperfectly, and with these people the Down men converse altogether in Irish.[82]

It is worthwhile recalling that, in addition to trade with Britain and further afield, the MacAdam family business at home (an ironworks and saddlers) relied on local trade with both town and countryside in Ulster. The evidence of Robert MacAdam's correspondence clearly shows that travel throughout the rural areas formed a central part of the family business commitments and there would, therefore, have been a commercial advantage in having a command of Irish, at that time, in order to facilitate and successfully carry out such trade.

ROBERT MacADAM'S EARLY INVOLVEMENT WITH LANGUAGE AND LITERARY SOCIETIES

While a knowledge of Irish was commercially useful for conducting business in some parts of rural Ulster, the language was clearly not seen by Robert as a mere vehicle for conducting transactions. For him, the language was much more – it was a mode of expression which he sought to use and propagate at any available opportunity. Indeed one may well assume that as much, if not more, of his energies and talents were spent in promoting and fostering the arts and amassing his Irish-language collection in Belfast than in furthering his business enterprises, although he pursued both with a great deal of success from the 1830s to the 1860s.

The literary historian, Breandán Ó Buachalla, draws our attention to the fact that Samuel Bryson was a neighbour of the MacAdam family in High Street and the Bryson boys would have been contemporaries of Robert MacAdam at school and, presumably, play. Nearby was McCracken's inn in Rosemary Lane, for so long Edward Bunting's lodgings, and a focal point in the heart of the town for social and cultural intercourse. Dr James MacDonnell's house in Donegall Place was also in the immediate vicinity, and it is noteworthy that in 1828 both the senior Dr MacDonnell and the young 18-year-old Robert MacAdam appeared as lecturers on the same evening of a meeting of the Natural History Society.

Dr MacDonnell was a highly respected figure in the MacAdam household. Publically, he was renowned for his Herculean work in Belfast health provision and his organization of the Harp Festival in 1792, but he was also a close acquaintance of Robert Shipboy's father. Both the Doctor and James MacAdam Senior were founder members of the Belfast Academical Institution (1810) and both served on the Board of the Linen Hall Library – two institutions which would each become the future *alma mater*, and place of leisure reading and learning for R.S. MacAdam and his older brother James.

82 Cited in Ó Casaide (1930: 56f).

Robert Shipboy MacAdam, then, was a product of the era of great liberal and intellectual development in Belfast, coming a generation after solid foundations had been laid by the likes of James MacDonnell, Mary Ann McCracken, his own father and others. Through time Robert himself was to play a pivotal role in continuing to support the cultural and intellectual well-being of Belfast, and in facing up to the responsibility of ensuring that these same institutions and societies could be sustained, enjoyed by, and of benefit to, future generations in the emerging city. From an early age he became actively involved at committee level in the societies which had been established in his native city in the decades leading up to and following his birth. In later years MacAdam was to become President of the Belfast Literary Society for two terms of office, 1846–7 and 1856–7.[83]

Robert MacAdam formed a close friendship with Dr MacDonnell which remained constant from the time of Robert's début on the social and intellectual scene in Belfast as a young man in the late 1820s until James MacDonnell's death in 1845.

During the 1790s, Dr James MacDonnell was a regular visitor to McCracken's tavern in Rosemary Lane, or at least up until the period following the aftermath of the hanging of Henry Joy McCracken in 1798, when the doctor refused a request from Mary Ann McCracken to come and try to revive the body of her dead brother. James MacDonnell was later pressured into adding his signature to a document, in 1803, which sought the arrest of United Irishman Thomas Russell. In a later letter MacDonnell conceded, 'I had not done it an hour until I wished of all things it was undone.'[84] His marginal involvement with Russell's arrest and subsequent execution at Downpatrick gaol was sufficient to ensure that Mary Ann McCracken would not speak to her childhood friend for the next twenty years, while well-known botanist and founding member of the Belfast Academical Institution John Templeton (1766–1825)[85] withdrew his membership of the Literary Society 'to avoid his former friend McDonnell', although a reconciliation between the two appears to have been brokered in later years by Mary Ann McCracken.[86] Similarly, Belfast luminary, founder member of the United Irishmen and founder member of the Belfast Academical Institution Dr William Drennan (1754–1820) described James MacDonnell as a 'Contemptible cold-blooded Judas' and 'the Brutus of Belfast'.[87]

However, the rapport between the senior doctor and Robert MacAdam did not suffer from the events of surrounding 1798 as they had, after all, tran-

83 Smith (1902). 84 Madden (1846: vol. 2, pp 230–1, cited in Ó Buachalla 1968: 40). 85 Newmann (1993: 250). 86 '*John Templeton*, one of Russell's sincerest friends, lived until 1825. He continued his scientific work and maintained his interest in Dublin's Botanic Gardens. Just before his death he was reconciled with Dr McDonnell through the intermediacy of Mary Ann McCracken'. Carroll (1995: 224). 87 Chart (1931: 333). On the career of William Drennan, son of Presbyterian minister Revd Thomas Drennan, see Hayward (1952: 45–8).

spired five years before MacAdam's birth, and the bond of friendship between them strengthened after their joint lecture evening in 1828. One common interest shared by both men was their fluency in Irish and their keenness to promote the language. It was significant that Dr MacDonnell employed Irish-speaking nurses to look after his children in Belfast.[88] As a logical extension, then, of their linguistic interests and aspirations Dr MacDonnell and the young MacAdam, in collaboration with Dr Reuben J Bryce, were to set the seeds for Cuideacht Gaedhilge Uladh, or the Ulster Gaelic Society.

88 One is reminded here of the British prime minister Lloyd George who employed Welsh-speaking nannies in London for his children.

The Ulster Gaelic Society and the work of MacAdam's Irish scribes

A.J. HUGHES

'CUIDEACHT GAEDHILGE ULADH': THE ULSTER GAELIC SOCIETY

The publication of Christopher Anderson's *Historical Sketches of the Native Irish* was to act as a catalyst in the founding of the Ulster Gaelic Society in 1830. Anderson assessed the contemporary state of the Irish language and its literature, and as part of his treatment of this subject, the author urged that the language should not be left to perish without anything being done to preserve it. Instead, Anderson went on to suggest how the Irish speaking population could be educated in their native tongue. *Historical Sketches of the Native Irish* had an immediate impact on Lord Downshire, the fourth marquis of Down, a wealthy landlord who possessed holdings of over 100,000 acres of estate in King's Co. (modern Offaly), Wicklow, Antrim and Down. His father, the third marquis, had acted as patron of the Harp Festival in 1792, while the fourth marquis himself was welcomed with *Céad Míle Fáilte* ('A Hundred Thousand Welcomes') by his tenants in his Hillsborough estate in 1833. The fourth marquis' brother, Lord George Hill, was a fluent speaker of the language and a collector of Irish manuscripts.[1]

On reading a substantial portion of Anderson's 1829 book, Lord Downshire, sent a copy to Dr James MacDonnell urging him that some action be taken:

> I have not yet read the book through, but I have been led to think from the portion which I have perused, that 'The Ancient Irish Literature' ought no longer to remain in the obscurity in which it has laid for so many centuries. I should wish to see this object treated as a foundation for further enquiry and proceedings ... Such an undertaking would be serviceable in many ways and tend to drive men's minds from speculative discussions and political disputations from which this country has suffered so much to a subject well worthy of attention and well calculated to replace Ireland in the station she formerly held among Nations as a nursery of learning and the resort of pious and learned men.[2]

1 McCall (1881: 52, 90, 110, 117, cited in Ó Buachalla 1968: 75–6). 2 Public Record Office Northern Ireland D671/Bundle C.235, cited by Ó Buachalla (1968: 73).

James MacDonnell duly responded (28 January 1830), thanking Lord Downshire for lending him Anderson's *Sketches of the Native Irish*,[3] and confided:

> [what Anderson] proposes to do is what several people *here* have been wishing for and attempting to do altho' none of us have seen it in so clear and comprehensive a manner. We have a small society and a subscription for keeping up a class of Irish Scholars ... [4]

As early as 1828 we have evidence of MacAdam sending a native Irish-speaking scholar, Tomás Ó Fiannachta (Thomas Feenachty) to Ballinascreen in Co. Derry with a view to setting up Irish schools in the district.[5] This scheme identifies MacAdam as a forward-thinking theorist in educational practice for his time, ahead even of the insightful Scottish Presbyterian commentator Christopher Anderson: 'He [MacAdam] was a personal friend of several hedge-schoolmasters and, in contradiction to the trend towards teaching English in schools, he favoured the teaching of Irish to children in those areas where the language was widely spoken.'[6]

In his response to Lord Downshire Dr MacDonnell's letter also included a printed 'Statement of the objects of the Belfast Gaelic Society' for the former's perusal. On 7 February 1830 Downshire concluded his response to Dr MacDonnell in encouraging and enthusiastic terms:

> I like the plan of the Society as explained in the 'Statement' referred to and I will thank you to let me know who the subscribers to the Society are besides yourself and what contributions are required. I imagine the Irish Celtic Society in Dublin is founded upon the same principles and for the same object and I hope one day to see the funds so enlarged as to enable the two societies to rescue the ancient Literature and History of Ireland from the obscurity in which it has too long remained. At the time of my writing to you the letter to

---

3 Dr MacDonnell praised Anderson for his scholarly objectivity and balanced approach: 'The Book which your Lordship sent me is written with great prudence and circumspection for altho' the author be a Scotch Presbyterian yet one can never discern from his work to what sect he belongs. There is none of those absurd reproaches cast upon Papists, no predictions of their conversion, nothing said about Antichrist, the Babylonesh Lady and the beast with the ten horns.'   4 Ibid., p. 74.   5 Ó Buachalla (1968: 71–2) reproduces the text of a copy of a letter (written in English and dated Ballynascreen, 21 July 1828) from Feenachty to MacAdam on a report of his progress on this project: 'Now unless this recommendation from the clergy [= "Mr Murphy the Parish Priest"] induce the people to come forward and attend we can do nothing else to render our endeavours successful. The truth is the people in general are so poor and distressed that they have not time to attend. They tell me that Winter would be the only time here for such an undertaking ...'   6 Campbell (1991: 230).

which you have replied I was not aware that a Society had already
been formed in Belfast. The object is worthy of the generous feelings
which so usefully animate the minds of many respectable and learned
individuals like yourself and I request that you will lay my first letter before the Society.

I remain, Dear Sir,

Your faithful and obedient servant.

Downshire.[7]

This offer of support and encouragement from Lord Downshire was a timely
one for MacDonnell and his junior collaborators MacAdam and Reuben Bryce.
In the same year the Ulster Gaelic Society came into being, with Lord
Downshire as president, Dr MacDonnell as chairman and MacAdam and
Bryce as co-secretaries. The Revd R.J. Bryce LLD (1797–1888), a professor
of mathematics and eventual principal at the Belfast Academy, was yet another
of the leading Presbyterian figures in Belfast at this time. Like MacDonnell
he was a member of the board of the Linen Hall Library, and Anderson
relates that Bryce was 'Principal of the Belfast Academy, and Minister of the
United Presbyterian Congregation, York Street; also author of several valuable books'.[8]

Reuben Bryce was also a personal friend of English-born Anglo-Irish novelist Maria Edgeworth (1767–1849) whose *Castle Rackrent* won her universal
acclaim in 1800. The first publication of the Ulster Gaelic Society was an
Irish translation by Tomás Ó Fiannachta in 1833, of Maria Edgeworth's works
Forgive and Forget, and *Rosanna*. The book was dedicated to Lord Downshire,
and in their foreword (written in Irish) the secretaries stated how they hoped
that the publication would facilitate the reader to learn Irish, and also
expressed a desire that its contents would be of moral sustenance to the reader:

We hope that many who shall read this short book will follow the
fine example of hard-working farmer Rosanna, so that they might lead
a life of happiness and fulfilment. It is also our hope that all malice
and evil intention which has beleaguered and disgraced our country
can be banished; and that the reader will follow, on every occasion,
the adage of Morris, i.e. 'Forgive and Forget'.

We remain, Esteemed Reader

Your humble and ever-faithful servants

R. Æ Brise

R.S. Mac Adaimh Secretaries of the Society.[9]

7 Cited Ó Buachalla (1968: 74).   8 Deane (1924: 65). On the Revd R.J. Bryce, see the relevant section of Blaney (1996: 133–43).   9 Original Irish cited in Ó Buachalla (1968: 86), my translation.

In the same year Irish was reintroduced in the Royal Belfast Academical Institution, under the recommendation of the Board which was chaired by Dr MacDonnell and had as secretary Robert MacAdam's older brother James. Irish scholar Tomás Ó Fiannachta was appointed professor of Irish, and as Ó Buachalla points out, the main interest in reopening this post was to aid candidates preparing for the Presbyterian ministry: 'The Synod of Ulster have passed a law making the study of Irish *imperative* for holy orders. They will not now ordain without that qualification.'

At the same time as these Belfast developments, Philip Barron was coming to the fore as a language revivalist in Co. Waterford, where he founded an Irish-language college in Bonmahon, Co. Waterford, in 1835.[10] He launched a magazine, *Ancient Ireland*, which ran from January to May of that year: 'a weekly magazine established for the purpose of reviving and the cultivation of the Irish language'. This magazine was to sell over 30,000 copies but it did not last more than a year and the apparently disheartened Barron subsequently left the country – although we have evidence of MacAdam entering into correspondence with him in 1836. Nevertheless, during the short existence of *Ancient Ireland* many contributions were submitted to it from members of the Ulster Gaelic Society. The president, Lord Downshire, wrote to Barron congratulating him on his achievement and aims:

> I enter very fully into your views respecting ancient Irish literature. I am not myself the possessor of any Irish manuscripts but my brother Lord George Hill, has paid attention to the subject and desires me to say that he will be very happy to promote your views – and that whenever you should happen to be in Dublin if you will call upon him at the castle, he will show you some manuscripts which he has, and which are rather curious.[11]

Downshire continued, drawing Barron's attention to the fact that there 'is an Irish Society in Belfast, to which my brother and I subscribe – Dr McDonnell and Dr Bryce are at the head of it – and I shall submit your letter to Dr McDonnell.'

In a separate submission to *Ancient Ireland*, Thomas Feenachty bemoaned the shortage of textbooks in Irish as an acute problem: 'The Irish Professorship in the Belfast College, is, as yet, but an experiment. In the article of class-books, a great want exists. The chief obstacle to reviving the cultivation of the Irish language is the want of elementary books.'[12] It was obvious that Feenachty himself was taking practical measures to rectify this

---

10 Ó hAilín (1969: 94). He was a brother of Sir Henry Winston Barron, MP for Waterford. 11 *Ancient Ireland*, vol. 1, no. 1, pp 5–6 (cited in Ó Buachalla 1968: 76).   12 *Ancient Ireland*, vol. 1, Prospectus (cited in Ó Buachalla 1968: 87).

situation, for in addition to his translation of *Forgive and Forget* (*Maith agus Dearmad*), both he and Robert MacAdam combined to produce: *An Introduction to the Irish Language intended for the Use of the Irish Classes in the Royal Belfast Academical Institution.*[13] As further evidence of the urgency felt concerning the provision of suitable textbooks, MacAdam (writing to Barron, 20 June 1836, in relation to printing and character sets), reiterated sentiments similar to those expressed by Feenachty: 'the outcry for "Books, Books" is very great indeed and let us not allow the enthusiasm to evaporate lest in might be difficult to revive'.[14]

In addition to his unstinting efforts on behalf of the Ulster Gaelic Society, Robert MacAdam was particularly active in another of the great cultural institutions of the day, the Belfast Natural History and Philosophical Society, founded in 1821.[15] MacAdam served as secretary for the years 1832–3, 1834–5, 1837–8; treasurer 1867–71; vice-president 1851–6, 1871–3, 1881–6. While in office, Mac Adam would doubtless have enjoyed the support and encouragement of Dr MacDonnell in his early years in the BNHPS as the Glensman was among the founders of that society. MacAdam rightfully regarded Dr James MacDonnell as 'an intellectual giant of his day' and when he died in 1845 MacAdam paid respectful homage to his social mentor's achievements:

> For half a century he [Dr MacDonnell] was the centre of literary and scientific matters in Belfast. He was a medical man of extensive practice but his taste collected round him all those who cultivated science or literature in the Province. He had a great library and collection of Irish antiquities and was uniformly the person to whom all travellers of distinction were introduced when coming to Belfast. I have met many foreigners at his home.[16]

Members of the committee of the Ulster Gaelic Society felt free to draw each other's attention to any visiting scholars or luminaries who happened to be in town, and to arrange for social visits and introductions. For example, MacAdam in sending a subscription to Philip Barron (20 June 1836) asked: 'Are there any subscriptions which I can receive for you here [Belfast]? I wish to send you Dr McDonnell's and my own.'

When the redoubtable John O'Donovan, visited Belfast during the course of the Ordnance Survey in the mid 1830s, he records: 'I was introduced by McAdam to Dr MacDonnell and Dr Bryce.' O'Donovan wrote glowingly of

---

13 Although the work (which resembles Neilson's grammar of 1808) is anonymous Ó Buachalla points out that the Queen's University copy includes a dedication 'To Prof. Stevelly from Robt. MacAdam one of the compilers', and he adduces evidence for Feenachty's part in the work from other sources.   14 The text of this letter (Nat. Lib. G702) has been reproduced in Ó Buachalla (1968: 88).   15 Deane (1924).   16 R. MacAdam to John Windele MS 4B6 RIA, pp 181–2, cited in Ó Buachalla (1968: 78).

Dr MacDonnell and the welcome he received at his home, but it would appear that O'Donovan did not take as kindly to Robert MacAdam, initially, at any rate. O'Donovan found MacAdam somewhat possessive of his manuscripts, although O'Donovan himself does not seem to have treated MacAdam with due courtesy on this occasion:

> I can never forget the kindness with which he [Dr MacDonnell] received me, and the trouble he took to direct me in my object ... I breakfasted this morning with Doctor McDonnell in whose posses-sion the original manuscript is. It is well written and I find that in McAdam's copy several mistakes have been committed in lengthen-ing out the contractions ... When I told McAdam that Mr Petrie had taken a copy of it he did not seem altogether satisfied ... I have thought it better to get the thing thus managed than be under a com-pliment to McAdam who is very jealous of his manuscripts'.[17]

ROBERT MacADAM AS A COLLECTOR OF IRISH MANUSCRIPTS AND FOLKLORE

So far, we have a picture of Robert MacAdam emerging from a successful Belfast Presbyterian commercial class which was equally concerned with the provision of a liberal education and health-care for all classes and creeds. Preoccupation with intellectual pursuits and the arts was also an integral part of their everyday lives.

The family business passed from James MacAdam (*d.*1821) to his sons James and Robert Shipboy who developed the foundry which traded in Ireland, Britain, Europe and beyond. Success in business did not absorb all their ener-gies, and each, in their own individual way, continued to build on the educa-tion they had received at the Belfast Academical Institution. Similarly both became involved with the cultural societies of the era and made major contri-butions to the quality of life and ambience of their native town which William Thackeray, following his visit to Belfast in 1842, declared to be 'as neat, pros-perous, and handsome a city as need be seen. It looked hearty thriving and prosperous as if it had money in its pocket and roast beef for dinner.'[18]

The MacAdam brothers, in their new abode in the fashionable College Square East, were part and parcel of the Belfast described by Thackeray. Even so, Robert also ventured deep into the Ulster countryside whenever it was possible. On these visits he delighted in speaking Irish and he recorded folk-lore and sayings, and bought, or arranged to have copied, any Irish manu-

---

17 *OSL Co. Down*, p. 5. However, Robert MacAdam published many of O'Donovan's lectures in the *Ulster Journal of Archaeology* in the 1850s.   18 *Irish Sketch Book* (London 1843), cited in Walker & McCreary (1995: 2).

scripts he might come across. Time and time again, we find references to him corresponding about these with local people. One typical example of his mixing of business and pleasure is his letter to one of the Liffin brothers, of Inishowen in Co. Donegal, which contains an apology for not being able to visit them as business matters called him back to Belfast from Derry:

> Derry
> 7th September 1833

Sir,

When I came from Belfast about a week ago I fully intended to have paid a visit to Carn and Clonmany and to have done myself the pleasure of calling on you and your brother; but on my arrival here to-day I found letters waiting for me which recall me home sooner than I expected. I am thus disappointed of the gratification I had hoped for and of the information I was sure of receiving from you on different matters relating to Irish Literature. I must therefore defer my visit for some time longer and in the meantime you will be good enough to accept from me the accompanying little publication in Irish, being the first book printed by the Ulster Gaelic Society to which I belong.[19] If you would not think it too much trouble I would feel greatly obliged by your writing to me some time during the next month or two and letting me know whether you think Irish schools would be encouraged in Innishowen, or whether anything of the kind is already established. You were good enough in a former letter to mention that some old people in your neighbourhood were able to repeat old poems and Fenian tales. I am particularly desirous to see these preserved and published and shall willingly take an opportunity of going down to Innishowen for the purpose of writing them down with you and your brother's assistance. During last week I was several days engaged in that manner in the Glens of County Antrim and succeeded in writing a good number from the old people there.

When you see your brother, Mr. Con Liffin you will please remember me to him. Tell him that I am taking ever care of the Irish books he lent me and that some of them are partly copied. If he would have no objection to part with them and would put a value on them I would be glad if you would mention it in your letter.

Hoping to hear from you,
I am Sir,
Your obedient Servant,
Robt. S. McAdam.[20]

---

19 *Maith agus Dearmad* the Irish translation of Maria Edgeworth's *Forgive and Forget.*   20 Nat.

We are also made aware in this letter that Robert MacAdam visited the Glens of Antrim to record lore from old local Gaelic storytellers. In May 1835 James Boyle, an employee engaged on Ordnance Survey Memoir work, passed comment not only on the predominance of Irish in the parish of Layd but also on the fact that, as one of its sons, Dr James MacDonnell, was given pride of place with regard to the collection of local traditions or the acquisition of manuscripts:

> Many of the lower orders in the Glens neither speak nor understand a word of English, and most of their stories are recited in Irish; to these the people are very fond of listening. Many of the old people who used to tell them are now dead. There are not now any old manuscripts in the Glens; they used to abound but Dr McDonnell of Belfast (whose connections live in this parish) has collected them all, and to no-one else would the people give them.[21]

MacAdam's friendship with Dr MacDonnell may have helped to open doors in the Glens. It also emerges from Boyle's memoir for the same parish that MacAdam would have found plenty of Gaelic lore in the Glens:

> There are many old persons who do little but recite tales and stories about ghosts, fairies, enchantments and the wonderful doings of Ossian, Fin McCoul and a great many other giants who made Lurigethan hill the scene of their fabled exploits. The people are also very superstitious, having a firm belief in all manner of charms, goblins etc. There are not now any clan marches, but many beautiful Irish airs are sung in both the English and Irish language, particularly in Glenariff.

This strong Gaelic tradition continued on into the current century as Glensman and renowned international folklorist James Hamilton Delargy or Séamus Ó Duilearga (1899–1980)[22] recorded Irish-language material from local *seanchaí* Barney Bhriain MacAulay of Glenariff in the 1920s.[23]

MacAdam's excursions were not confined to Inishowen or the Glens of Antrim. Even in Belfast, we have evidence of him taking down folklore and songs from individuals who were reared in Gaelic-speaking areas but who had come into the town in search of work. One prime example of such collection was his acquaintance with a blacksmith from Co. Louth:

Lib. G702, cited in Ó Buachalla (1968: 96). 21 *OSM*, vol. 13, p. 52. 22 For details see Newmann (1993: 60–1) and Whitaker (1982). A biography of Delargy is in preparation by Prof. S. Ó Catháin, Department of Irish Folklore, University College Dublin. 23 For an edition of this valuable material see Watson (1984 & 1987). According to Watson (1984: 77) Barney Bhriain

This story was taken verbatim from a blacksmith in Belfast about the year 1830. He had been a rebel in '98, made prisoner at Tara and according to the humanity of the officer on guard was suffered to run away while exhibiting an action of great muscular strength.[24]

In 1833 a 'James Maguire of Ballinamore, County Leitrim' wrote to MacAdam from Enniskillen seeking a pound for two boards of 'backgammon (or the playing tables) or in Irish *tamhlisc*'. In the course of the letter it emerges that books, or manuscripts had previously changed hands between Maguire and MacAdam as the former makes reference to 'the reign of Cairbre Lifeachair a gabrael of the Liffey. He reigned 37 years and that is 38 generations from me. You will find this King's reign in the last book I gave you.'[25] As late as 1854 we see MacAdam continually on the lookout for an opportunity to combine a business trip with the chance to extend his Irish collection, as he wrote to Corkman John Windele, a similarly-minded antiquarian and language revivalist who also employed scribes and collected manuscripts:[26]

I find that I have a number of duplicate Irish manuscripts and it occurs to me that if you have any such we might make exchanges and thus benefit both collections. If you have, let me know and as I shall be in Cork once or twice in Spring on business I would bring my duplicate manuscripts along with me to show you.[27]

In the same letter MacAdam informs Windele:

I was in London for a few weeks lately and spent a good many agreeable days in the Library of the British Museum. Among the Irish manuscripts I observed a copy of the Moy Tuireadh. I shall be there soon again and if there is any passage you wish copied I will do it for you.

THE HOME MISSION AND THE 'BIBLE WAR' IN THE GLENS OF ANTRIM, 1842–4

Of the various religious bodies to emerge in the nineteenth century to provide religious instruction for Ireland's poor, it has been argued that 'The Irish Society had a greater emphasis on the Irish language, and was therefore more

MacAulay, 75 years old in August 1925, was 'born in Baile Ímonn, reared in Clonriach'. For a recording of this speaker see Ó Duibhín (forthcoming). **24** University College Galway Irish MS 66 p. 5, cited in Ó Buachalla (1968: 97). **25** Cited in Ó Buachalla (1968: 99). **26** On John Windele (1801–86), see *Journal of the Cork Historical and Archaeological Society* 4 (1900) 35–9. **27** Cited Ó Buachalla (1968: 240).

involved with Roman Catholic areas of Ireland'.[28] As part of its plan to widen the availability of Irish-language versions of the scriptures in Ireland, the Irish Society, under the direction of the Presbyterian Synod of Ulster, set up an organization entitled the Home Mission in 1836. This latter educational body set up schools to provide schoolchildren with a grounding in the bible and by 1844 Henry Joseph Monck Mason, in *History of the Origin and Progress of the Irish Society*, declared: 'more interesting scenes I have never witnessed than the triumphs of the Irish Bible in the dark mountains of Ulster'.

In 1841 George Field (under an Irish form of his name which he rendered Seorsa Ó Mhachaire)[29] issued a book intended as 'a footway' to the Irish language:

> *Casán na Gaedhilge, An Introduction to the Irish Language*; compiled at the request of the Irish Teachers; under the patronage of the General Assembly of Ireland, And Dedicated to them as a tribute of their esteem for their zeal in preserving and extending their Mother-tongue, By their friend and countryman, S. ÓM.

Field, who lived in Castle Place, Belfast, had written to Robert MacAdam, in Irish, giving him the words of a song, *Feadag an Iolaire* 'The Eagle's Whistle'.[30] In addition to stating in the preface, that his grammar 'has been compiled for the use of the Native Irish and for those who wish to acquire a knowledge of our sweet and venerable mother tongue', Field also acknowledged the contribution to his work by the authors of past grammars – such as those of the Revd William Neilson (1808) and Thomas Feenachty (1835) – and continued: 'I have likewise to acknowledge the assistance and instruction afforded by Michael McNulty, Hugh Gordon, Hugh McDonnell, Michael Branagan and other native Irishmen'.

These Irish speakers were all teachers: Michael McNulty taught in Co. Leitrim and Hugh Gordon in Loughinisland, Co. Down during 1824–7 before going on to become an Irish scripture reader in Kerry 1843.[31] In a letter to Robert MacAdam, dated 8 May 1844, Brian MacGucian requested work for his own son and for a 'Mícheál A. Bhrangan'.[32] Hugh McDonnell, the third party mentioned by Field – and a future close companion to Robert MacAdam – was to play a significant part in the controversy surrounding the Home Mission in the Glens of Antrim which erupted in long-running, vitriolic correspondences in the Catholic periodical the *Vindicator* and a Protestant publication of the period *Banner of Ulster*.[33]

---

28 Hempton & Mill (1992: 56).   29 *Seoirse Ó Mhachaire*, literally 'George from (the) Plain/Field'. The Ó of surnames, which means 'descendant, or grandson', should not cause aspiration to the following word.   30 Ó Buachalla (1968: 100ff). For further details on Field see R. Blaney (1996).   31 Ó Casaide (1930: 66).   32 Ó Buachalla (1968: 120–1).   33 In the

The issues of contention centred on accusations of proselytism and around whether or not the schools in question had actually been established or whether the roll books had been falsified in order 'to take the money which the Synod gave us for doing nothing', as four teachers were to write in the *Vindicator* in 1842. The teachers and inspectors (salaried by the Home Mission) contradicted both each other and even themselves in a series of published letters and statements, although a glimpse of the probable reality emerged when Fr Luke Walsh, PP of Culfeightrin, using testimony which he had obtained from Hugh McDonnell,[34] seemed to soften and admit that there were schools of this nature for a short time but after their closure, the teachers continued to claim payment for bogus instruction. The curate also stated that any monies received fraudulently from this programme had been returned to him. For their roles as inspectors, Hugh McDonnell and his predecessor, Mr Moloney, came in for cutting criticism from the Culfeightrin PP, who described them as 'renegade' and as being prepared to sell the birthright 'for a mess of potage'.

Accusation upon counter-accusation followed. At one point Fr Walsh demanded to see the text of a letter from McDonnell in order to verify the handwriting, and furiously proclaimed:

> When I had satisfied myself that proselytism was the object of your mission and not teaching the vernacular, from a love of the Irish language, I first suspended them – that is I suppressed your schools, and when I found out that those teachers were humbugging you, and taking your money for *doing nothing*, and practising a fraud, I then suspended them – that is to say I denied them Christian rites until they would desist and promise to give to the poor of God the wages of their sin.

This latter, rather coded reference to a donation 'to the poor of God' seems to partly, but most indirectly, answer the question as to what Fr Walsh did with the money he recovered from the repentant teachers. The financial arrangements for the teachers were '1 shilling each for every person they taught to read the primer; 1s. 6d. each for teaching the Gospel; and 2s. for teaching to read the epistles'.[35]

---

remainder of this section on the 'Bible War' in Co. Antrim, citations are taken from O'Laverty, vol. 5, pp 500ff and Ó Buachalla (1968: 103–13). 34 'I was obliged to make false reports of their schools to the Directors as it was altogether falsehood from beginning to end as I thought the more we could take off them the better as St Paul said he robbed other sects to establish his own'. 35 According to the *Belfast Newsletter*, 4 March 1852. In his work *The Home Mission unmasked* Walsh (1844: 90) estimated that the total costs of the Home Mission's operation was somewhere in the region of £4,000 per annum.

The Revd Robert Allen (1789–1865), the director of the Home Mission, still resisted, arguing that some of the teachers 'have been tempted to deny to the priest that they were teaching for fear of his displeasure and the persecution that would thence arise'.[36] Fr Walsh returned to the fray with a letter to the *Banner of Ulster*, three to the Directory of the Home Mission and an open letter to 'The Presbyterians of Ireland' which he sent to the Presbyterian Moderator Dr Stewart. Very much forced onto the defensive, Revd Allen tried to appeal to logic by asking if these schools did not exist:

> Then I ask why is the good man [Fr Walsh] so uneasy – why waste so much time, and trouble, and paper, and virtuous wrath about a non-entity? Can a thing that is merely fictitious – that has no existence – do him or others any harm?

In terrier-like fashion Fr Walsh embarked upon a total review of all the matters involved and in a seeming *coup de grâce* he published a letter from Hugh McDonnell, which declared that he had given false returns in order to keep his position and satisfy his employers and implying that the superintendent was aware of the situation.

As a sting in the tail of the 'Bible War' saga, Charles McLoughlin, a miller by trade but erstwhile teacher for the Home Mission, won £70.00 compensation as damages for loss of earnings in a legal action he took against Fr Luke Walsh.

The work of the Home Mission, the controversy surrounding it and resistance to proselytism, was to have a significant role in creating suspicion against the involvement of outsiders in the preservation of the Gaelic language.

MacADAM'S IRISH SCRIBE: AODH MAC DOMHNAILL OR
HUGH McDONNELL OF CO. MEATH

The Hugh McDonnell at the centre of the Glens of Antrim 'Bible War' was a native Irish speaker, Aodh Mac Domhnaill, who was born in the townland of Lower Drumgill, near Dromcondra in north-east Co. Meath. On 7 February 1827, there is a record of his marriage to Bridget Roe in Ardee, Co. Louth. Breandán Ó Buachalla is of the opinion that he remained in Co. Meath until the death of his wife Bridget, aged 34, in 1836,[37] and Colm Beckett surmises that he was the 'Hugh McDaniel, Carrickleck' whose name appears among the subscribers to M. Clarke's *Man's Final End* and who was also attached to the Irish Society for Promoting the Education of the native Irish

---

36 On the Revd Allen, see Blaney (1996: 86–9).   37 Beckett (1967: 1). On the manuscript in question, see Ó Buachalla (1968: 114).

through the Medium of their Own Language under the auspices of the Church of Ireland.[38] Beckett also points out that a teacher named Owen McDaniel (possibly a relation of Hugh's) was teaching in Carrickleck for the Kildare Place Society in 1823 but was later killed as a result of disturbances in 1830 in relation to the bible teaching which erupted in 1830. Following Hugh McDonnell's removal to Co. Antrim, first as teacher and then as an inspector for the Home Mission, and the subsequent termination of his three-year period in the latter post from 1839 to 1842, we find that he has secured employment in a much more convivial environment and in more private and less contentious circumstances with Robert MacAdam.

Beckett suggests that Robert MacAdam may first have come into contact with the McDonnell family of Co. Meath through Hugh's father James, as MacAdam, in a marginal note in manuscript XXXI in the Belfast Public Library, records the phrase 'Repeated to me by Old McDonal 1831'.[39] Leaving aside any judgment of Hugh McDonnell's worth as an inspector from the sorry saga of his Home Mission years, where Fr Luke Walsh had castigated him as a member of the 'set of abandoned and unprincipled swindlers', Hugh's reputation as an Irish scholar was fairly solid. His credentials, would have been enhanced, by George Field's acknowledgment of him in his 1841 book *Casán na Gaedhilge: An Introduction to the Irish Language*. In any case, when the unemployed Hugh McDonnell came to Belfast in search of work, following his sojourn as a Home Mission inspector in the Glens of Antrim, Robert MacAdam was to come to his aid. From the years 1842–56 his services as an Irish scribe, folklore collector and manuscript copyist were secured on a full-time basis by Robert MacAdam in Belfast. In return for these services Hugh was provided with lodgings and a salary, and according to Beckett, Hugh McDonnell lived at 88 Millfield, five minutes' walk from MacAdam's home in College Square.[40]

One of Hugh McDonnell's initial duties was to go out into the rural areas of counties Louth, Armagh and Donegal to collect songs, folklore, manuscripts and other Irish language materials. On his travels McDonnell would explain that he came on behalf of Robert MacAdam of Belfast, and Ó Buachalla quotes from letters MacAdam received from a variety of Irish scholars scattered throughout the countryside: Michael Levins of Drogheda, offered a manuscript of Keating's seventeenth-century *History of Ireland* and 'three Ogham's with instructions for reading them'; P. McGahan, from Dongooly, Co. Louth, sent in stories; while Patrick McGeough of Lurgankeel (whose forwarding address was c/o Michael Coburn, Publican, Dundalk) expressed doubts as to the *bona fide* nature of McDonnell's mission:

> I beg leave to state that in the month of December last I was visited by a man of the name of Hugh McDonald who stated to me that he

38 Beckett (1987: 10).   39 Ó Buachalla (1962: 29).   40 Beckett (1995: 4).

was by your order and direction collecting Irish manuscripts for the purposes of publishing them in print. Some of them he was purchasing for ready money and some for love of returning them ... I lent him a valuable Irish manuscript so I request that you'll have the kindness to let me know by letter whether these promises may prove effective or not that myself and others may be satisfied by your favourite reply, or that we may understand was he an impostor.[41]

Many correspondents appeared to have had designs on the role which McDonnell was undertaking. For example, Brian McGucian proposed the services of both his own son and those of Mícheál Ó Brannagáin (a former Home Mission teacher); while Bernard Tumalty recommended the services of Co. Louth scholar Nicholas Ó Cearnaigh (c.1802–65)[42] and criticized the scholarship of Peter Gallegan.[43]

Despite these advances it would appear that Robert MacAdam was satisfied with McDonnell's services and he continued to employ him for over a decade and a half.

PEADAR Ó GEALACÁIN OR PETER GALLEGAN (1792–1860)

When a second scribe was required, MacAdam called on Peter Gallegan (Peadar Ó Gealacáin). Born in Monnterconaught, Co. Cavan, Peter Gallegan had been an old friend of Hugh McDonnell's and composed an Irish lament on the death of Hugh's wife Bridget in 1836. He had been a hedge-school master and took up a teaching post for a while with the Irish Society in Co. Meath where he described the resulting tension between the Catholic and Presbyterian churches, similar to that witnessed in Co. Antrim, only that the depth of feeling in the Meath case was dramatically illustrated by the tragic murder of one of the teachers, Owen McDaniel, in 1830.

As a scribe, he was a prolific copyist with a neat and accurate hand. Furthermore, he was evidently filled with a deep love for his subject: 'O Heavens! was there ever anything half so sweet or to be compared to our dear but neglected Irish language'.[44] In 1844 Peter Gallegan began his first Irish manuscript for Robert MacAdam, a text containing the life of St Maodhóg, with a second following shortly after, 300 pages on the works of blind Co. Louth poet Séamus Mac Cuarta (c.1647–1729).[45] Peter Gallegan was to describe Robert MacAdam (Maighistir Roibeart Mhac Adhaimh) as the

---

41 Cited in Ó Buachalla (1968: 115, 117, 120–1). 42 On the career of this colourful character, prone to presenting his own compositions to earlier Gaelic poets, see Duffy (1989). 43 Ó Buachalla (1968: 120, 119). 44 Ó Buachalla (1968: 132). 45 Both survive in the Belfast Public Library as MSS XXIII and XXIV, Ó Buachalla (1962: 17–20).

'defender of the Old Irish tongue' (*cosantóir na Sean-Ghaoidheilge*), and their relations remained on a solid footing until just before Peter's death in 1860. In 1851 Peter wrote to MacAdam:

> Sir
> I have taken a little turn at the harvest here just in order to save a trifle to buy some linen as I was totally run out of shirts last summer which often grieved me that I could not save one half-crown the whole time in Belfast after spending near four months there. I received a note from Hugh McDonnell in which he stated that he had some conversation with you previous to that and that you remarked to him that you had two years work for me in the writing business. I suppose now, Sir, at the very lowest calculation I think that about five shillings a week would not be unreasonable for me to get in order to pay for my lodging and to live as frugal as possible.
>
> As I began your books, of course, I should wish to finish them and other things which I remarked to you in your office.
>
> I was lately requested by a schoolmaster who holds a National school to take on as usher which would bring me five shillings a week but I would rather go to you at the same rate of payment. I have a great many Irish scraps and poems that you never met with as yet. There are also some old men in this neighbourhood who have some songs which I could not meet with in your collections but on hearing that I was on the mission of providing Irish songs and poems I could not get anything from them unless I made them some little remuneration and it very often happens that my little earning was too scanty for myself much less to graze their hand with a fool's token which they required of me and scarce as my cash was I bribed some for their songs.[46]

From the reference to 'your office' we know that Gallegan – who usually transcribed from his home in Co. Meath – had visited Belfast and the Soho Foundry. A lively account of Peter Gallegan's month-long stay in Belfast survives an Irish-language poem which recounts the exploits of a country-loving small farmer in the big city, describing his virtual petrification on beholding the mechanized engine-filled busy shopfloor of the foundry which he likened to an inferno where the workers' faces were smeared with oil as black as the berry on the sloe, wheels turning and a clamour which drained his

---

46 Letter printed in Ó Buachalla (1968: 213–14). See also pp 276–81 for an impressive list of the total MSS transcribed by Peadar Ó Gealacáin, and for a recent account of Ó Gealacáin's career, see Dawson (1992).

limbs of all courage.[47] The folklorist and collector Henry Morris, who translated portions of this long poem into English, comments that Gallegan 'was
quite bewildered by a visit to MacAdam's ironworks – the Soho Foundry, in
Townsend Street, Belfast; and he describes the workers as a lot of black
demons under the command of arch-demon, Joe English, the foreman'. While
Henry Morris attributed the poem to Gallegan himself, Colm Beckett prefers
to interpret it as a composition of Hugh McDonnell's.

The poem alludes to the warm generosity of MacAdam and to his unstinting support for the Gaelic cause:

> For a manly man is MacAdam, who highly esteems the Gaelic,
> And who is friendly to, and beloved by all its bards and poets.
> 'Tis our hope that the High-King will shower luck on him in this
>   world,
> And, after death, elevate him to the skies.
> And as regards the famed fount of the muses,
> By my conscience, methinks he has drained it dry.
> For in the language of authors and a study of their verses
> I should not compare with him any other man whether of Ulster or
>   Leinster.[48]

Daunting as the floor of the Soho Foundry proved for Gallegan himself, it
was later to provide a means of living for his son, also christened Peter. In a
letter to Robert MacAdam, dated 12 April 1854 and signed 'Peter Gallegan
Senr.', he sent MacAdam a catalogue of books and manuscripts for his perusal.
As a postscript he added:

> I am anxious to know whether my son Peter (who works in the
> Foundry) will go to America at present as I gave him the preference
> to go on my pass and that I would remain till sent for as it is not safe
> to remain in Belfast there being so many cases of Cholera.[49]

ARMAGH SCRIBE: ART MacBIONAID OR ARTHUR BENNETT
(1793–1879)

One of MacAdam's other correspondents at this time was Bryan Sharkey, of
Rothbody, who wrote to MacAdam in May 1845 to arrange to send material

---

47 The full text of this long piece, *Fáilte Pheadair Uí Ghealacáin lena Eachtra agus lena Ráflaigh*
('A welcome to Peter Gallegan and the accounts of his rambles'), has been edited by Beckett
(1987: 84–115).   48 English translation by Morris (1921: 5).   49 Letter in Ó Buachalla (1968:
242–3).

about Art Mac Cumhaigh (*c.*1738–73), a poet of the parish of Creggan (counties Armagh and Louth): 'I was very busy heretofore with agriculture and I had no time to write until now and I will send you by degrees all that I have.'[50] Another was Patrick Higgins, a police sergeant, stationed in Ballyshannon, Co. Donegal, who MacAdam had visited on his tour throughout Ulster. In September 1845 Higgins wrote to MacAdam:

> I send you *Cáineadh Whaley* [ie 'Whaley's Complaint'] and a few other short verses. I am very glad to hear that you succeeded so well on your Northern excursion and that you arrived safe at home ... I cannot omit stating that I never met any man so fit to spell the language and lay it down on paper so correctly as yourself upon which I congratulate you.[51]

Another Irish scholar, Arthur Bennett, or Art MacBionaid lived in the townland of Ballykeel, near Forkill in south Armagh. His father, John Bennett (b. 1760), was an Irish teacher. Although Art was a stonemason by trade, he was also well-versed in Irish language, history and related matters. He began sending Robert MacAdam songs and poems to Belfast in 1844, but by October of the same year a degree of tension was discernible. Art acknowledged the receipt of an order for 9*s.* 6*d.*, the price MacAdam deemed reasonable for material that had been obtained for him in the south Armagh area by Bennett, but added bluntly in his letter to MacAdam: 'The proprietor of that money felt deeply indignant at you and me.' Further on in the same letter Art also added a self-composed verse in Irish complaining of a lack of ink, paper, snuff, or candles and entreating MacAdam to win his favour by sending him the required items.[52]

After an interlude in Art's communication to Belfast, Robert MacAdam asked Hugh McDonnell to write a poem in Irish appealing to Art to resume as before and on receipt of McDonnell's verses MacAdam duly sent them off to Ballykeel. Although MacAdam and McDonnell imagined this poem would be well received, nothing could have been further from the truth. In reply, Art returned a stinging Irish-language satire lambasting McDonnell for such audacity: 'Reflections upon Hugh MacDonnell's conduct for assuming the name of a poet'.[53] Many more exchanges were to follow before Art mellowed. In the meantime Art had managed to secure patronage as a scribe from south Armagh priest and Gaelic scholar Fr Patrick Lamb (1790–1860), although Fr Lamb warned John O'Daly – his colleague in a project to publish the life and work of Ulster Gaelic poet Peadar Ó Doirnín (*c.*1704–68) – that Bennett 'is of very singular and odd disposition. I consider he is very fond of his own

50 Ó Buachalla (1968: 163).   51 Ó Buachalla (1968: 171).   52 Ó Buachalla (1968: 138).   53 Ibid., 140–1.

opinion and would withdraw both from you and me his contribution if we once displeased him'.[54]

A reconciliation was eventually achieved between Bennett and the Belfast-based duo, MacAdam and McDonnell – at the fourth attempt. Relations settled down, for a time at least, so that in years to come Bennett would describe Hugh McDonnell as 'a sharp-edged, erudite poet' (*file faobhrach focalcheart*). However, in 1850 when Bennett proposed to MacAdam the compilation of an extended history of Ireland, Art wanted to write this in English while Robert MacAdam was quite insistent that it be undertaken in Irish. Bennett remained equally intransigent: 'As for the compiling of the Elizabethan Wars etc. in Irish, I would not undertake it upon any consideration.'

Despite the heated language of this letter, the postscript which Bennett appended to it affords an insight into how MacAdam conducted his meetings with these rural Irish-language scholars whose main sources of livelihood were a variety of more mundane occupations and trades. These included: Sergeant Higgins, of Ballyshannon; farm labourer Peter Gallegan taking 'a little turn at the harvest'; and farmer Bryan Sharkey. On this occasion, Art Bennett invited MacAdam, if he was passing by Newry on business, to come and interrupt him at his work as a stonemason so that both could discuss matters of Irish antiquity:

> P.S. As I am cribbing a footpath on the new road round by the Poorhouse of Newry since Decr. last, and will till April next, should you come to Newry at any time you could see me every dry day, but I come home at night. I am very glad that poor Hugh McDonnell is cleverly recovered from his illness.[55]

Eventually MacAdam's hard-headed resolution, as potential patron of the work, held sway and Art began his proposed history in Irish and forwarded an initial excerpt to Belfast. MacAdam, however, did not find the first sample of the work to his liking, and when he responded in early March, with a token remuneration, the South Armagh scribe was incensed and promptly returned a letter to Belfast, dated 20 March 1850, which began:

> I acknowledge the receipt of your letter inclosing a few sheets of paper and *2s. 6d.* I can't say (altogether) that you made little of my pro-

54 Hedge-school educated John O'Daly (1800–78) of Co. Waterford became a teacher of Irish in the Wesleyan College, Kilkenny, before moving to Dublin to set up as a bookseller and publisher. In addition he also wrote many books of interest to the revival of the Irish language, including *Reliques of Irish Jacobite poetry* (1844) and *The poets and poetry of Munster* (1849). See Brady/Cleeve (1985: 184) and Welch (1996: 420).   55 For this correspondence see Ó Buachalla (1968: 194).

posed work. It was as much as the Redeemer of the World was sold for. I anticipated the result.[56]

Unsurprisingly, communications between the two soon ground to a halt and Art Bennett would eventually find an alternative patron in the form of Newry stationer Edward Augustus Maginnis (1822–77). It seems ironically fortunate that Art would see his way to penning this project in Irish despite his earlier assertions to MacAdam that this would not be undertaken 'upon any consideration', Unfortunately, however, Art Bennett's substantial history would not appear in book form until well over a century following his death, although the full printed Irish text of Bennett's 'History of the Gael with the Foreigner' has been recently published under the editorship of Monsignor Réamonn Ó Muirí.[57]

PLANS FOR A GAELIC NEWSPAPER AND MACADAM'S ENGLISH–IRISH DICTIONARY

Robert MacAdam's Irish-language interest was not confined to Ulster and he corresponded on several issues with the Cork Irish-language publisher Thomas Swanton. In 1845 MacAdam wrote to Swanton requesting 'an improved Irish *current handwriting* fit for business and the like', but, as was his wont, the Belfastman also took the opportunity to enquire in the same letter, as to the salient linguistic features of the dialect of Irish spoken in Munster. Later on, in 1851, we find MacAdam airing the idea of a weekly national newspaper in Irish with his friend Swanton:

> Shaoil me go minic da m-beidheadh páipear-nuaidheacht Gaoidheilg ag dul thart na tíre gach seachtmhain, mur ata na páipeair Béurla, go d-tuigeadh muintir na h-Éirinn go h-uile é faoi bheagan aimsire, ge b'é air bith cóigeadh da'r beathuigheadh iad ...
>
> ... Da mbeidheadh na h-aimsireadha beagán níos fearr, agus an ghorta as cuimhne na n-daoine, saoilim go m'b'éidir linn páipear Gaoidheilg fhaghail suas uair 'sa t-seachdmhain. Cuingbhigh so ann do mheabhair ...
>
> I have often thought that if there were an Irish-language newspaper circulating the entire country on a weekly basis, after the fashion of English-language papers, that the entire population of Ireland, no matter what province they may be from, could understand it in a short space of time ...

---

56 Ibid., 198. 57 For a detailed treatment of Art Bennett's life, literary work and patrons see Ó Muirí (1994: 3–114). For an edition of his Irish-language poems see Ó Fiaich & Ó Caithnia (1979).

> ... If times were to improve somewhat and the memory of the
> famine[58] were erased from people's memory, I think we could estab-
> lish an Irish-language weekly. Please bear this in mind ...[59]

In the meantime, we have evidence that MacAdam was taking very practical
steps to improve the position of the language in his attempt to compile a substantial English-Irish dictionary. Unfortunately, the dictionary has not, of yet,
been published but the manuscript survives in the Main Library, Queen's
University Belfast as MS1/153, Hibernica ('Henry') Collection, where it is
described as 'Collection of materials for an English-Irish Dictionary of Ulster
Irish 23 portfolios, wanting letter F, c. 1830'. Colm Beckett dates the compilation of the work to the years 1842–56 on the basis of internal evidence
such as half a dozen references to Daniel O'Connell and the mentioning of
the railway which, as Beckett points out, was completed between Belfast and
Lurgan in 1841, Portadown 1842, Armagh 1848, Dublin 1853.[60]

The surviving manuscript consists of 1,145 pages (11.5 x 14.5 inches)
with three columns of $1^{13}/_{16}$ inches and a fourth wide column of $4^{2}/_{10}$ inches.
In addition to the loss of volume F, the beginning of G is also missing, as is
the introduction (*Díonbhrollach*) although we are fortunate in that, rather mys-
teriously, a microfilm copy survives of the latter. The introduction, in Irish,
is in the hand of Hugh McDonnell,[61] although Beckett suspects that this may
have been taken down from Robert MacAdam's dictation. Beckett also inter-
prets the word-order in the dictionary as resembling the text of Samuel
Johnson's English dictionary which was reprinted in Dublin in 1798. From
the outset, MacAdam gives a clear indication of his motives for undertaking
this mammoth work: 'I assure you it is a measure of the extent of my fondness for my native land and for my glowing love of the language ...'[62]
However, he also outlined reasons why his dictionary was based on the language of the ordinary people, and these included the fact that the language
of many of the Irish dictionaries previously published tended towards the erudite and were removed from common speech.[63] He did not refrain from con-

---

58 This is a relatively rare mention of MacAdam to the Famine, although there are a few mentions of it in sentences in his dictionary, e.g. *Is mór an dul chun deiridh ata a mbarr na prátuidh
a mbliadhna* (D24); *Thug an ghorta so dha thoradh maith* (P81). On the other hand, Hugh
McDonnell treats the famine in some detail as may be seen from his letter (reproduced by
Beckett (1967: 291–3)) and in an Irish poem on the potato blight, Beckett (1987: 46 ff., poem
11). Beckett (1987: 19–20) discusses McDonnell and the Famine, as does Mac Lochlainn (1995).
59 Ó Buachalla (1968: 174–5 & 215–16), my translation.   60 Beckett (1995: 8–9).   61 The full
text of the Introduction is given by Beckett (1995: 14–23).   62 From his Introduction (my
translation): *nuar a dhearfam dobh gur le mead mo ghean air mo thier dhuchais 7 le tesghra don
teanguidh*, cited Beckett (1995: 14).   63 Beckett lists the likely dictionaries which MacAdam
had in mind: O'Reilly, *Irish-English dictionary* (Dublin, 1817); McCurtin *An Foclóir Bearla
Gaoidheilge* (Paris, 1732); O'Brien, *Irish-English dictionary* (Paris, 1768); Foley, *English-Irish dic-*

troversy in reminding his potential readers that 'the Catholic church does not preach in Irish despite that fact that the Irish language has been the guardian of the faith this past three centuries. But what can I say here!'[64] It is obvious that the welfare of the Irish language was MacAdam's chief concern:

> And as a result of these past hardships we see day by day that her indignant uncertain children are forsaking her [the Irish language], with the result that she now resembles a terminally ill patient whose condition has only been worsened by any prescribed medicine or cure.

It is quite clear that MacAdam's main collaborator in the compilation of the English-Irish dictionary was his Meath scribe Hugh McDonnell. MacAdam was evidently sensitive to any potential accusation that might be levelled against himself personally for undertaking such a task – as he was not a native speaker of the language – and in anticipation of such criticism he declared:

> The scripture says that a man must not wage war or build a house without first reckoning his household and counting his money, I have done likewise, I did not begin this work until I secured for myself a trusty assistant, namely Hugh McDonnell, a native speaker of Irish from his youth who has comprehensively studied Gaelic authors and as well as being a poet in his own right he is esteemed by one and all throughout Ireland on account of his expertise in the native language.[65]

The following, then, are some examples I have selected randomly from fascicule A of MacAdam's English-Irish dictionary to give an example of its layout and its potential as a source for Irish lexicography:

| Abolish | | *do dheanamh air shiubhal le, do sgrios, do chur air neimhnidh, do chur a g-crích, do chur ar g-cúl.* | He abolished the law altogether. *Rinn se air siubhal leis an dlíghe go huile.* They abolished the privileges of the clergy. *Rinn siad air siubhal le ceart na h-eaglaise* |
| Abuse v.a. | to make an ill use of | *baoith-chaitheamh, droch-úsaid a dheánadh, droch-bhail a thabhairt air.* | He abused his property. *Thug sé droch-bhail air a mhaoin.* He abuses the talents that God has given him. *Ghnidh se droch-úsaid de na tiodhlaca a thug Dia dó.* |

tionary (Dublin, 1855); Thaddeus Connellan, *An English-Irish dictionary intended for use of schools* (Dublin, 1814) and *Irish-English guide* (London, 1824). **64** Cited Beckett (1995: 14–15). **65** My translation – original in Beckett (1995: 16): mur deir an scripture nach ar choir do neach dol chun cogaidh nó a thogbhal taoidh gan a mhuintir do aireamh 7 a chuid argid a chontas mar sin damhsa nir thinnsgan me an obair so go bhfuair me damh fein mur fhear cuidigh Aodh

	to deceive		He abused your good nature by asking you too often for money. *Ghlac se buntaiste air do nádur mhaith ag íarraidh airgid ro-mhinic ort.*
	to reproach rudely	*do sgolladh,*	She stood and abused me for half an hour. *Sheas si do mo sgolladh air feadh leath-uaire.* He abused me like a pick-pocket. *Sgoll se me mur bheidheadh fear piocadh pócaidh.*
		do mhasladh,	
		droch-chaint a thabhairt,	
		do dhibliughadh,	
		do dhi-moladh.	
		do bhualadh,	
	to beat brutally	*droch-úsaid a thabhairt*	He abused his horse dreadfully. *Thug se droch-úsaid an-mheasardha do n-a ghearran.*
	to maltreat		
Accede v.a.		*do theacht le,*	After some conversation they acceded to my terms. *Tar éis beagan comhráidh thug siad a steach do m'fhuráil.* Do you think he will accede to your terms? *Measann tu a d-tiocaidh se air aon inntin leat?* or *Measann tu a d-tiobhraidh se a steach ann san nidh a ta tu íarraidh?*
		do thabhairt isteach.	
Accumulate	to collect	*do chnuasadh,*	
	to assemble	*do chruinniughadh,*	accumulated *'n-a charthaidh*
	to heap up	*do bhailiughadh,*	
		do charnadh,	The snow is accumulated in the valley. *Ta an sneachta na charthaidh (na charnán) sa n-gleann*
		do chruachadh.	
Accurate	exact	*fíor-cheart,*	He gave me assistance. *Thug se cuidiughadh damh.* He called out for assistance. *Sgairt se a mach air chuidiughadh.* We all went to his assistance. *Chuaidh sinn uile ann a chonganta (thartháil).* Patrick came to my assistance like a man. *Thainig Pádraig ann cúnganta liom mur bheidheadh fear ann.*
	precise	*lán-cheart,*	
		beacht,	
		dearbhtha.	
Assistance		*cuidiughadh*	
		congnadh (or *cúngnadh*)	
		furtachd	
		fóir	
Atone		*sasadh thabhairt,*	He atoned for his bad conduct by working hard. *Thug se sasadh ann a dhroch-ghníomhaibh le h-obair chruaidh.*
		cúitiughadh thabhairt.	
		do chur le (chéile),	They attached a string to the end of it. *Ghreamuigh siad sriongan do n-a chionn.* He attached it to the wood with glue. *Ghreamuigh se don adhmad é le gliú.*
		do chur an aice.	
			His friends are all greatly attached to him. *Ta a cháirde uile docra ceangailte dhó.* The Irish are greatly attached to their country. *Tá speis mhór aige na h-Eirionnaigh ann a dtír féin.*

Audible	*so-chloiste*	Your voice is hardly audible. *Cha mhó ná go g-cluintear do ghlór (Ní mó ná go g-cluintear do ghlór).*
August adj	*uasal, onórach, ard-fhuilteach.*	
Awhile	*tamull; air feadh tamuill, seall, sealad.*	Wait a while *Fuirigh* (and *Fuirigh go fóill).*

BRITISH ASSOCIATION EXHIBITION, BELFAST, 1852 AND THE 'ULSTER JOURNAL OF ARCHAEOLOGY'

In the midst of this frenetic activity on the cultivation of the Irish language in the 1840s, the Soho Foundry was also in need of constant attention. MacAdam wrote to Cork Irish-language and manuscript collector John Windele (1801–86):

> I have been so busy a man for some time looking after the grosser matters of this life that I could not get a moment to open my mind's eyes. I always go on hoping that I will some time have leisure but like the Repeal I see no immediate prospect of it.[66]

The Soho Foundry had a workforce of somewhere between 200 and 250 full-time staff, and among the manuscripts, now preserved in the Library of Queen's University Belfast, there are two receipt books in Robert MacAdam's hand containing details of transactions with customers in Leeds, London, Liverpool and places further afield such as Paris and Cairo.[67]

As if his business and Irish-language pursuits were not enough, Robert MacAdam also undertook the vice-presidency of the Belfast Natural History and Philosophical Society in 1852. In the same year his brother James and he were invited to organize a major exhibition in Belfast for the British Association for the Advancement of Science, and in a letter dated 31 August 1852, James explains how Robert and he were too preoccupied preparing for the exhibition (to be staged during the arrival in Belfast of the British Association for the Advancement of Science in 1852) to attend the opening

mhac domhnaill noch a labhair an geilge ona óge 7 rinne stedair cinnte de na hudair mur aon le bheith na bhard 7 fa mheis aige uasal 7 iosal air feith na heirinne fa na eoluis a dteanguidh a mhathara.   66 Ó Buachalla (1968: 179). The 'Repeal' is a reference by MacAdam to 'The Repeal of the Union', the topical debate of the day. On Hugh McDonnell's Irish-language compositions in relation to the Repeal of the Union and Daniel O'Connell (including 'O'Connell's Welcome to Dundalk', in 1843 and a lament on his death) see Beckett (1987: 17–18).   67 QUB McAdam MSS 1/1108–9, cited in Ó Buachalla (1968: 102 n. 4).

ceremony in the presence of the lord lieutenant on 1 September: 'I and my brother were invited but did not go, being too busy at the Museum, I at the minerals and he at the antiquities.'[68]

This exhibition took up so much of Robert MacAdam's time that his momentary silence somewhat perplexed his Cork friends Thomas Swanton and John Windele who wondered what had become of him. Swanton in particular had been writing urging MacAdam to set up a 'monthly Iberno-Celtic magazine' and reproached his Belfast fellow revivalist commenting:

> I am sorry you do not give yourself more leisure for Gaelic subjects. Hibernia in her present state demands the public services of all her efficient sons ... I shall be happy to see you and discuss and consider your plan for printing Irish in English types and a spelling which will be as simple as can be required.

Swanton then resorted to writing to Windele: 'Have you heard of or from Robert MacAdam? I wrote twice or thrice and have not a line – he was the only man in Ireland who could do much for our ancient tongue in its modern form'.[69]

Through time, MacAdam was to write to Windele to thank him for the Ogham stones which he had sent to Belfast for the exhibition: 'The Oghams which you sent have caused much wonder here and there is an anxiety to know more on the subject. We have nothing of this kind in the North.' If one examines the distribution of the available corpus of Ogham stones in Ireland it can be seen that MacAdam was certainly justified in his comment as, three-fifths of these are concentrated in south-west Munster (Counties Cork and Kerry) with only a handful in the north.[70] MacAdam also explained in this same letter how business commitments and the effort required to organize the British Association exhibition had been absorbing his time:

> Until the affairs connected with the Exhibition are over I shall be a bad correspondent. The average number of letters I have to write daily in the way of business is very large and when I attend to the concerns of 200 workmen and do all the talking as is required I assure you even in ordinary times I cannot find a great deal of leisure for lighter work. Then when in addition to this the whole labour of getting up an extensive exhibition which of itself causes a pretty considerable amount of letter writing devolves on me you will pause for a moment before you set me down as a hopeless correspondent.[71]

68 Young MS 9/4.   69 Cited in Ó Buachalla (1968: 222).   70 McManus (1991: 46 and 48). 71 Ó Buachalla (1968: 223-4).

In his *Descriptive Catalogue of the Collection Antiquities* accompanying the 1852 Exhibition it was clearly stated that a central aim was to 'enable strangers from other countries to judge for themselves of the nature and extent of our ancient civilization', with an aspiration that an upshot of the whole would be 'an impulse given to the study of Archaeology and the preservation of antiquities in Ireland'. This promotion of the Gaelic element of Irish culture, old and modern, was in keeping with Robert MacAdam's mottoes for the visit of Queen Victoria to Belfast three years earlier in 1849, when she was welcomed in Irish:

> *Do mhíle fáilte a Bhanríoghain Éire*
> *Go cathraigh éigseach chríche Uladh.*
> *Mas fuar síon ar mhullaigh a sliabh*
> *Is grádhach díolos croidhe a bunadh.*
>
> 1000 welcomes Oh Queen of Ireland
> to the poetic city of the land of Ulster.
> If cold be the wind on its mountain-tops,
> its people's hearts are warm and loyal.[72]

Among the items on display at the exhibition were Irish manuscripts belonging to Samuel Bryson, Lord George Hill of Gweedore, Co. Donegal, and a large selection of Robert MacAdam's personal collection. There were also harps belonging to O'Kelly, O'Neill and Hempson; two bells, one from Bangor monastery, the other associated with St Muran: 'A most remarkable object; it is encased in silver, elaborately ornamented and set with precious stones. Found in the hut of a poor fisherman in Innishowen, Co. Donegal in 1850'. Further exhibits included: leather sandals recovered from bogs; flint arrowheads, bronze swords and rings, a Tara brooch, pikes, bagpipes, rectangular *methers*, or wooden drinking vessels; an old wooden cup 'said to be that of Con O'Neil'; 'Turlough O'Neill's silver seal with the "bloody hand of Ulster" attached'; and perhaps the most bizarre item of all the 'Skull of Carolan, the celebrated Irish bard'.

Judging by the mood of MacAdam's letter, sent to Windele in Cork, the exhibition proved well worthy of his time and efforts:

> We have got the bustle of the Association work over and are now opening our Exhibition of Antiquities to the general public. It has been a most successful experiment as every visitor assures us. Never before in Ireland was such a collection of antiquities brought together. If at all possible you ought to take a run down and see it – I enclose you an exhibitor's ticket hoping you may really come. The antiquar-

72 Verse cited in Ó Buachalla (1968: 220), my translation.

ian spirit seems to be roused among us and finding so many persons
in the Country taking an interest in such matters we have decided on
trying a 'Journal of Archaeology' to appear quarterly ...[73]

Industrious as ever, MacAdam kept to his promise and the following year
witnessed the appearance of the first volume of the *Ulster Journal of
Archaeology* with him as editor. This journal survives until the present day,
although it has experienced lacunae in its publication during its existence over
practically the last 150 years. Currently, the journal is in its third series but
the issues of the *Ulster Journal of Archaeology* in this latter series are much
more strictly archaeological in content – in the more narrow sense of the modern discipline. In MacAdam's reign as editor, from 1853 to 1862, the journal
was much more wide-ranging and interdisciplinary, and sometimes, anecdotal
in nature:

> The Study of Archaeology is daily becoming more attractive to all
> persons of education and taste. Combining as it now does, a wide
> range of subjects connected with literature and art, it affords materi-
> als for the exercise of almost every kind of talent. Not merely the his-
> torian, and professed antiquary, but also the geographer, the painter,
> the architect, the linguist and all the numberous class of explorers in
> the nooks and crannies of knowledge, may be each of them in this
> way, votaries of Archaeology.[74]

This period around the mid nineteenth century could be regarded as a zenith
in Robert MacAdam's achievements and the *Ulster Journal of Archaeology*
reflected this, attracting contributions from many of the leading and most
eminent scholars in the country, and beyond.

JOHN O'DONOVAN AS PROFESSOR OF CELTIC STUDIES AT QUEEN'S COLLEGE BELFAST

In 1849 a chair of Celtic Studies was created at Queen's College Belfast which
had itself been recently established in 1845. The first appointee, on a salary
of £100 per annum, was John O'Donovan:

> Another self-taught scholar was a pioneer, whose work has proved of
> permanent value, was the Professor of Celtic languages, John

73 Royal Irish Academy MS 4B12 p. 999, cited in Ó Buachalla (1968: 226).   74 Robert
MacAdam in his opening passage of volume 1 of the *Ulster Journal of Archaeology* in 1852.

O'Donovan (aged 40). As an official in the historical department of the ordnance survey of Ireland he had acquired an unrivalled knowledge of Irish topography, both through research in ancient Irish manuscripts and through field-work; and he had a large share in fixing the forms of Irish place-names that were incorporated in the first ordnance-survey maps. He had published a *Grammar of the Irish Language* (1845), and his authoritative editions of important historical texts in Irish had culminated in his monumental work on the Annals of the Four Masters, of which three volumes had appeared in 1848. The closing-down of the historical department of the ordnance survey in 1842 had left O'Donovan with no regular source of income, so that his appointment to the chair at Belfast of which the teaching duties were certain to be slight came as a timely relief for a harassed scholar.[75]

Not having any full-time students, O'Donovan's principal teaching duties in Belfast consisted of six lectures during the summer term on a variety of subjects relating to early Irish language, literature and history.[76] Among those attending O'Donovan's summer lecture courses was Robert MacAdam, and on 8 May 1851 he wrote to his Cork correspondent Thomas Swanton. The letter, written in Irish, expressed delight that Cork had appointed a professor of Irish[77] and then went on to deal mostly with details of O'Donovan's activities in Belfast:

> Our Professor, O'Donovan, arrived here a day or two ago and plans to address us, twice a week in the College, on the origins of the Irish language and its relationship to other languages. When he has done that I shall send you an account. I am glad to see that these sages are coming to life somewhat as I was beginning to think that they had either passed away or fallen asleep! O'Donovan tells me that he knows you from letters he has received from you but that he has not met you in person.

75 Moody & Beckett (1959: 116).   76 'The professorship of the Celtic languages was held by O'Donovan till the latter's death in 1861, at the age of fifty-two. Having no students to teach, he spent most of his time in Dublin, translating the ancient laws of Ireland. But each summer term he came to Belfast and delivered six evening lectures open without fee to the public, on the language, manners, laws, and customs of the ancient Irish. Though the College could ill afford the luxury of a professor without students, both the president and the vice-president expressed to the 1857 commission their appreciation of O'Donovan's eminence as a scholar'. Moody and Beckett (1959: 170).   77 The professor of Irish at Cork was Owen Connellan, a convert to Protestantism who was appointed ahead of the dithering O'Donovan – Boyne (1987: 92–3). Beckett (1995: 10) reveals that Sligo-born Owen Connellan (1800–69), worked for twenty years in the Royal Irish Academy before becoming professor in Cork. His publications included an English translation of the Annals of the Four Masters (1846), although this version is much inferior to the magnificent edition published by O'Donovan.

I have been trying to encourage him to start up an Irish-language monthly along the lines of *Chamber's Journal*, but he is extremely occupied with other matters and is not enthusiastic to risk becoming involved with such an undertaking. He works a great deal on ancient sources preserved in Dublin and publishes them under the patronage of the *Irish Archaeological Society*. He is a most accomplished scholar in this regard and I doubt if there is another scholar alive who can decipher these old manuscripts as comprehensively as he. He tells me there is an antiquaries society in Kilkenny and that it can boast of two or three Irish scholars among its members.[78] Perhaps you are aware of these people, I should certainly like to make contact ...[79]

While it would appear that no ideological meeting of minds occurred between O'Donovan and MacAdam – at least regarding the propagation of the spoken language, where O'Donovan seemed markedly less enthusiastic than MacAdam – it is likely that their relationship remained fairly cordial as MacAdam was to publish articles by the recently appointed professor of Celtic in the *Ulster Journal of Archaeology*. Indeed, Patricia Boyne points out that when O'Donovan began his summer lectures in the Spring of 1850:

He was dissatisfied with the coverage of his lectures in the Belfast papers, and decided to give copies of the lectures to the *Ulster Journal of Archaeology*, which proved a good friend and published twelve features from his pen during the years 1857 to 1861.[80]

MACADAM'S LATER MORE RECLUSIVE YEARS: 'OISÍN I NDÉIDH NA FÉINNE'

Boundless and indefatigable as Robert MacAdam's energy may have appeared, the combined pressures of business at the Soho Foundry, mounting the 1852 British Association Exhibition in Belfast, and the publication of the first issue of the *Ulster Journal of Archaeology* in spring 1853, took a temporary toll on his health, resulting in a suspension of his commercial duties. He spent some time in Scotland recuperating, and later rested near Holywood, Co. Down.

---

78 The society in question was doubtless the *Kilkenny Archaeological Society* which began publishing its own journal *Transactions of the Kilkenny Archaeological Society*, vols 1–2 (1849–53). The publication still continues as *Journal of the Royal Society of Antiquaries of Ireland*; see Hughes & Hannan (1992: 262–3) for details.   79 Irish letter cited in Ó Buachalla (1968: 238–9), my translation.   80 Boyne (1987: 93). Boyne also informs us that O'Donovan was appointed as examiner in Celtic languages in 1855 'at an additional salary of £20 a year'. For a text of the first examination set by O'Donovan see Boyne, pp 133–5 (Appendix 1).

On 29 December 1853 James MacAdam wrote:

> My brother's state of health has been a great source of anxiety to me.
> He had always been a hard worker but he has overexerted himself in
> getting up the exhibition of Irish antiquities at the meeting of the
> British Association here last year and he had no relaxation afterwards.
> His health became very bad in Summer, however he is now nearly
> recovered. As the most important parts of the business devolve upon
> him I was greatly annoyed by his unavoidable absence.[81]

Despite this lapse in Robert's health, he was to continue with his duties as
editor of the *Ulster Journal of Archaeology* for a further ten years. Nevertheless,
by the time the first series of the *Ulster Journal of Archaeology* had come to
an end in 1863, he was quite a solitary figure. As a confirmed bachelor he
had devoted his life to business, his Irish language pursuits and his antiquarian
and literary societies. He had been involved in scholarly and cultural pursuits
from an early age and so he was now beginning to outlive many of his former friends and mentors.

Dr James MacDonnell passed away on 8 April 1845, fittingly lamented
in a moving elegy composed, in Irish, by MacAdam's scribe Hugh
McDonnell.[82] His funeral was one of the largest attended at the time with the
city's rich and poor lining the streets in their thousands to pay farewell to
him as his funeral cortège left Belfast for his native Cushendall.[83] James
MacDonnell's efforts over the previous half a century meant that the town
of Belfast was now equipped with schools, libraries and societies which supported the Irish language and its associated culture and interests. In many
ways MacAdam could be regarded as a successor to MacDonnell, as it was
he who was to become the central figure in Belfast literary and antiquarian
circles following MacDonnell's death.

For fifteen years MacAdam donned this mantle of leadership, gathering
around him a body of scribes and scholars who were at the forefront of work
on the Irish language, literature and antiquities. Through time, however, casu-
alties were sustained such as the loss, in 1853, of surgeon and Irish manuscript compiler Samuel Bryson – and we have already seen how the strain of
managing the Irish antiquities section of the British Association Exhibition,
almost single-handedly, had proved detrimental to MacAdam's physical state
of health in the same year. One of MacAdam's copyists, Peter Gallegan,

81 Young MS 9/4, Queen's University Belfast, cited in Ó Buachalla (1968: 232).   82 For the
full text of this poem see Beckett (1987: 76–9).   83 His tombstone in Layd graveyard begins:
'Erected in Memory of James M'Donnell of Belfast and of Murlough, in this county – a
Physician whose abilities and greater benevolence made him venerated in the Glens of Antrim,
where he was born; and in Belfast where he died 1845 in his eighty second year ...'

appears to have produced little for him after 1854,[84] while another loyal scribe and Irish-language advisor of sixteen years' standing, Hugh McDonnell, left Belfast in 1856 to take up residence with his daughter near Bunbeg in Co. Donegal, where he found employment, through the offices of his son-in-law, as a teacher with the Island and Coast Society schools. Hugh was never to return to Belfast and remained in Donegal until his death in 1867.[85]

The year 1861 brought personal sadness for Robert MacAdam with the death of his brother James. Writing afterwards, to Windele in Cork, Robert put a brave face on things explaining:

> I found so many matters pressing on my attention after my brother's death that I considered it more judicious to lay aside all less impor-tant things for a year. I am gradually getting things into satisfactory order and intend resuming publication of the *Journal* in May ... I hope I am not lost to Archaeology yet ... I am glad to tell you that that I have the *Journal* underway once more.

In spite of this positive attitude, MacAdam did take stock of what had hap-pened in Irish scholarly circles, as 1861 was also the year John O'Donovan died, while Eugene O'Curry, O'Donovan's brother-in-law, died in 1862. These two men were widely recognized as among the most brilliant authorities on ancient Irish sources:

> But what losses we have experienced even since I published the last no. of the *Journal*! I really do not see how we shall ever fill the places of O'Donovan and O'Curry. Several archaeological friends, too, in the North have gone, who assisted me with their pen and their kind encouragement. However I shall go a while longer.[86]

Clare-born O'Curry (1794–1862) was also self-educated before taking up a post in the historical department of the Ordnance Survey alongside O'Donovan and was a scholar of similar ability and expertise as O'Donovan. One of his many great works, *Manuscript Materials of Ancient Irish History*,

---

84 Ó Buachalla (1968: 252) points out that, in 1855, Peter Gallegan gave Eugene Gilbert Finnerty sixteen of his Irish manuscripts in return for kindness the latter had shown to Peter and his remaining family: 'He lived near Kells, in the Co. of Meath and was very thankful to me for some little kindness which I conferred on him and on his only relative a niece since dead ... He was one of the most noble-minded men, and honourable men that I have ever met.' 85 He died in a poorhouse on 31 March 1867, and is buried in Moyra graveyard near Falcarragh. His son-in-law wrote to MacAdam, 14 July 1867, thanking him 'for contributing £1 to the obse-quies of poor Hugh'. Ó Buachalla (1968: 258 n. 37). For an account of his teaching career see de Brún (1987: 81–3). 86 MacAdam to Windele RIA MS 4B22, cited in Ó Buachalla (1968: 255–6).

had just been published in 1861 and was to prove a seminal work in Irish literary history.[87] In saluting the work of O'Donovan[88] and Eugene O'Curry, MacAdam showed an insightful appreciation of two great scholars of the age, later echoed by Lady Gregory in the early twentieth century:

> Through all those years we had thought so barren, a group of scholars had gone on with their work, the translation of the old Irish manuscripts. O'Curry in his *Manners and Customs of Ancient Ireland* had given fine pages of history and romance. O'Donovan and O'Daly did the same.[89]

Try as he might, the valiant MacAdam could only sustain the expensively produced *Ulster Journal of Archaeology* (of which he was both editor and proprietor) through its ninth issue during 1861–2, and, on his return from a trip abroad in 1863 he found it impossible to produce a tenth volume. By 1865 he was to receive his last letter from his constant correspondent John Windele from Cork[90] and he was gradually becoming an Oisín-like figure, lamenting the passing of his colleagues of yesteryear, the *Fianna*. He nevertheless persevered as best as he could and in 1888, the year of his eightieth birthday, he accepted the office of president of the Belfast Natural History and Philosophical Society, and was still on the committee of the Linen Hall Library.

In the meantime, business at the Soho Foundry, had declined in the years following the death of his brother James. The workforce dropped to 190 in 1866, with 40 fewer in 1870. Financial difficulties saw the gradual closure of the foundry in 1894, while in the same year he was forced to witness what must have been for him a most demoralising spectacle, the auction of his books. Five years earlier, in 1889, he had undergone a similar ordeal, the break-up his extensive manuscript collection. When the collection was nearing its height around the 1850s, Oscar Wilde's father, Sir William, made the

---

87 On the career of Clare-born Eugene O'Curry (1792–1862), author of lectures on the *Manuscript materials of ancient Irish history* (1861) and many other seminal works on early Irish literary history and manuscripts,, see de Hóir (1961) and Welch (1996: 416–17).   88 Moody & Beckett (1959: 170) note that Edinburgh-born Charles MacDouall (1813–83), the first professor of Latin at Queen's 1849–50, said of O'Donovan: 'we are all proud of his connection with us [i.e. Queen's College Belfast]', and described his work on the Irish language and Irish archaeology as 'celebrated all over Europe'. One may note that this claim of an outsanding international profile is certainly borne out by the showering of the many accolades upon O'Donovan such as his call to the Bar in London (1847) and his being made a Member of the Royal Irish Academy in the same year (with the Cunningham Gold Medal from the RIA following a year later). There was also the award of the honorary degree of LLD, conferred by Trinity College Dublin in 1850, and the extremely prestiguous membership of the Royal Prussian Academy in 1856 – see Boyne (1987: 106).   89 Gregory (1914: 41).   90 On Windele see Welch (1996: 604).

following comments on the medical portion of the MacAdam holdings: 'Robert Mac Adam of Belfast possesses the largest private collection of Irish medical MSS in the country'.[91] As the century drew to a close, however, some 50 of his manuscripts, so painstakingly amassed over a sixty-year period, were bought by Church of Ireland bishop and historian Revd Dr William Reeves,[92] while others were bestowed upon the Belfast Natural History and Philosophical Society.[93]

By the end of his life, MacAdam was an isolated, solitary, almost pitiable figure. Following his death at his home in College Square East on 3 January 1895, the *Belfast Newsletter* said of him, in its obituary column, six days later:

> Of late years he was seen little in public. He had outlived all his intimate friends and most of his contemporaries so that there are now but few remaining who could recall the variety and charm of his conversation and his apparent inexhaustible store of information.

ROBERT MacADAM: HIS LEGACY AND ACHIEVEMENTS

When Robert MacAdam was laid to rest in Knockbreda churchyard,[94] Belfast lost one of the great Irish-language and antiquarian figures of the nineteenth century. Born into a developing and bustling town of the early nineteenth century (where commercial and cultural life was dominated by an enlightened, imaginative and liberal Presbyterian class, and where level-headed business pursuits and patronage of the arts and music went hand in hand) Robert MacAdam finished his days in a fully industrialized city which had increased its population tenfold, from the time of his birth, and where sectarian divisions had become noticeably more marked.[95] Many factors contributed to this regrettable state of affairs but, whatever the exact causes, the period from the 1860s onwards appears to mark a turning point. Before this date many Presbyterians would have found it equally fashionable to have been a member of the Ulster Gaelic Society, the Harp Society, the Literary Society, or

---

91 See Sir William Wilde in his *Report of the Census of 1851*. 92 Cork-born scholar William Reeves (1815–92) would also secure the Book of Armagh for Trinity College Dublin. 93 For full details of MacAdam's collection see Appendix D in Ó Buachalla (1968: 284–7). 94 His tombstone inscription (cited by de Paor 1990: 20) reads: 'In memoriam Robert Shipboy MacAdam, born 1808, died 3rd January 1895. Editor of the Ulster Journal of Archaeology, 1853–1862'. 95 Bardon (1982: 112) draws attention to the sectarian strife which erupted in August 1864 in Belfast which included the burning of an effigy of Daniel O'Connell by Orangemen and a rampage by several hundred 'Catholic navvies' through Belfast only to be confronted by 'Protestant workers from the neighbouring Soho Foundry' who, as Bardon reports, 'surged out to repel the invaders, as a verse from a satirical Orange ballad recalled: ... "But Och! We were chased by the boys of Soho"'.

the Belfast Natural History and Philosophical Society. From this time onwards, however, Irish-language and related activities began to be regarded with circumspection. In 1875, for example, Samuel Ferguson complained that he was being thwarted in his attempts to have a chair of Celtic restored at Queen's (having lain empty since O'Donovan's time some 15 years earlier):

> We have done our endeavour to found such a chair here but all things Celtic are regarded by our educated classes as of questionable *ton* and an idea exists that it is inexpedient to encourage anything tending to foster Irish sentiment.[96]

The careers and pursuits of Robert MacAdam and Samuel Ferguson merit a comparison. Born in Belfast two years after MacAdam, Samuel Ferguson was also educated at the Belfast Academical Institution (and the Belfast Academy) before progressing to Trinity College Dublin. While Robert MacAdam, and his brother James, were establishing their successful business at the Soho Foundry, Samuel Ferguson was embarking upon a highly distinguished legal career, being called to the Bar in 1839, made Queen's Counsel in 1859, and Doctor of Laws in 1864. Like so many Belfast Academical Institution old boys of their day, both MacAdam and Ferguson demonstrated a keen interest in Irish language, history and antiquities. MacAdam, as we have seen, not merely amassed manuscripts and took an interest in Irish archaeology but was also a cosmopolitan and widely-travelled man. In similar vein, one can note how, in the mid 1840s, Ferguson likewise travelled in Europe sketching many cathedrals and churches dedicated to Irish saints.[97] Reminiscent of MacAdam's situation in Belfast, Ferguson's home in Dublin was very much a meeting place for those interested in Irish literature, indeed Sir Samuel's book *Lays of the Western Gael* (1865) and his epic poem *Congal* (1872) were works which did a great deal to pre-empt and inspire much of the flavour of the later Anglo-Irish revival of Yeats' time. While it could be argued that Sir Samuel Ferguson rose to become a more central figure in Irish life than Robert MacAdam, becoming Deputy Keeper of the Public Records in Ireland (1867) and later President of the Royal Irish Academy,[98] their interests and tastes were quite similar. The similarity in tastes and interests between MacAdam and Ferguson is to be expected, especially when one considers their well-rounded schooling at the Belfast Academical Institution, and the fact that they both emerged from such a liberal and enlightened Presbyterian background

---

96 Ó Casaide (1930: 49).   97 Many of Ferguson's sketches from this period are housed in the Linen Hall Library, Belfast.   98 On Sir Samuel Ferguson see Lady Ferguson (1896). For his brief flirtation with the Young Irelanders and his co-founding of the Protestant Repeal Association in 1848, before reverting to Unionism following the collapse of Young Ireland, see Campbell (1991: 226–8), and Welch (1996: 346).

in early nineteenth-century Belfast. Furthermore, it should come as no great
surprise to learn that both men were personal friends, considering their proximity in age. Indeed, they often discussed matters of language and antiquities together as may be seen from the following passage from a letter written
by MacAdam to John Windele, in Cork in 1854:

> I have two Manuscript Genealogies of the MacDonnells [of Co.
> Antrim], one dated 1618, the other 1744. I send you a translation
> comprising both ... I think I shall not be able to procure you any-
> thing more about Colla Ciotach,[99] but I saw Mr Samuel Ferguson,
> the barrister, yesterday and he said he would send you something.[1]

The final years of both MacAdam (d.1895) and Ferguson (d.1896) overlapped,
albeit slightly, with the emergence of the Gaelic League in the late nineteenth
century but there was no sizeable northern Protestant participation in this organization comparable with that within the Ulster Gaelic Society of the 1830s. The
Dublin-based Gaelic League was set up in 1893 by Douglas Hyde (1860–1949),
the son of a Co. Roscommon Church of Ireland clergyman.[2] Although its constitution made it an apolitical and non-sectarian organization, the adoption by
the Gaelic League at its annual congress in 1915 of a motion, proposed by
Piaras Béaslaí, supporting a Gaelic and free Ireland was to precipitate Hyde's
resignation. In addition to this, many Gaelic League figures would also become
associated with Irish nationalist movements, among them Eoin Mac Néill[3] and
Patrick Pearse,[4] leading figures behind the Easter Rising of 1916.

   The first branch of the Gaelic League to be established in Belfast was in
1895, the year of Robert MacAdam's death, but the organization's membership contrasted rather markedly to that of the Ulster Gaelic Society two generations earlier. Cathal O'Byrne has highlighted the tensions experienced by
the arrival of the Gaelic League in Belfast:

> With the advent of the Gaelic League ... the language in Belfast
> came, at least partly, into its own.[5] But the League was never con-

99 Colla Ciotach was a figure in Gaelic genealology (one of the three Collas) from whom the
MacDonnells claimed their ancestry.   1 Letter cited in Ó Buachalla (1968: 241).   2 On Hyde,
see Dunleavy & Dunleavy (1991).   3 Eoin Mac Néill, or John MacNeill (1867–1945) was born
in Glenarm, Co. Antrim, and educated at St Malachy's College, Belfast, before going on to
Dublin where he co-founded the Gaelic League, edited its newspaper, the *Gaelic Journal*, and
played a central role in Dublin life at the turn of the century. A future professor of Early Irish
History at University College Dublin, he was also involved with the Irish Volunteers in 1916
and went on to be minister of Education, 1922–5. See Martin & Byrne (1973).   4 On Patrick
Pearse (1879–1916), author, educationalist and leader of the 1916 Rising, declared President of
the Provisional Republican Government; see Edwards (1979).   5 One feels that Byrne's statement here has not perhaps taken full account of the efforts of earlier bodies such as the Ulster

sidered quite 'respectable' – that awful Belfast word ... To be a Gaelic Leaguer was to be suspected always. The League might shout at its loudest and longest that it was non-political and non-sectarian. The slogan did not impress Belfast. With the League's membership at ninety-nine percent Catholic what could one expect? 'Scratch a Gaelic Leaguer and you will find a Fenian' was the formula in the old days.[6]

The crucial political developments of late nineteenth- and early twentieth-century Ireland (with an accompanying set of sectarian implications) have tended to overshadow the achievements of the Presbyterian-led Irish language revival of the late eighteenth to mid nineteenth century. Jonathan Bardon quotes from the *Belfast Newsletter*, 12 July 1867, which described Orangemen disembarking at Bangor and walking out towards Newtownards 'without interruption save the *cead mile failthes* of hosts of sympathizers'.[7]

Chris McGimpsey draws attention to the close of the era of substantial Belfast Unionist public involvement and association with Gaelic symbols:

> Equally significant was the depiction of Erin's Harp above the phrase *Erin Go Bragh* [i.e. 'Ireland Forever'] in large letters outside the Ulster Unionist Convention of June 1892. It was this meeting, held in a specially constructed pavilion in the Botanic Park and attended by 11,879 delegates, which saw the birth of modern unionism. As late as the turn of the century unionists were not unhappy with reference to the native tongue.[8]

It seems regrettable, in the extreme, that the activities and cultural legacy of liberal Presbyterian Belfast in the late eighteenth and early nineteenth century should be so diminished and erased from the general consciousness of our own times. By focusing on MacAdam's life and that of his associates some of the major achievements of this era have been highlighted: Dr James MacDonnell and Edward Bunting; the Harp Festival, and the *Ancient Music of Ireland*; the work of the Bryson family in Belfast; the Revd William Neilson in the Belfast Academical Institution; and the work of the Ulster Gaelic Society formed, with MacAdam as co-secretary, in 1830. All in all, then, a lively and impressive scene with Irish language, literature and music lying at its core. MacAdam deserves to be remembered for his monumental accomplishments, not merely as an industrialist and businessman, as an archaeologist and antiquarian, but also as a champion of the cultivation of the Gaelic language and its broader culture, old and modern. In many ways it would be appropriate to translate what Breandán Ó Buachalla has to say of MacAdam's

Gaelic Society. 6 O'Byrne (1946: 201). 7 Bardon (1992: 335). 8 McGimpsey (1994: 11).

legacy, as it is Ó Buachalla above all other modern scholars who has been responsible for unearthing the story of the life of this remarkable, modest and most honourable of men:

> It was MacAdam who first had the idea of collecting folklore from the mouths of the common folk, although it is an honour still to be accorded to him; it was he who first had the idea of 'reviving the language' although he has yet to receive credit for this – he truly was 'the First Gaelic Leaguer'. He was a hero and a giant of a man – but a hero and giant who has been forgotten and lost in oblivion.[9]

Robert MacAdam's philosophy and achievements may best be summed up by proverb number 188 from his *Six Hundred Gaelic Proverbs Collected in Ulster*, and his own interpretation of it: '*Sì an dìas is truime is ìsle chromas a cionn* – the heaviest ear of corn is the one that lowliest bends its head'.

This is a beautiful metaphor, implying that the man who has most knowledge is always the most modest.

---

9 'Is é is túisce a chuimhnimh ar bhéaloideas na ndaoiní a bhailiú, bíodh nár bronnadh an onóir sin air; is é is túisce a chuimhnimh ar "aithbheodhadh na teanga" bíodh nach bhfuil an chreidiúint sin tabhartha dó – eisean dáiríribh, "the First Gaelic Leaguer". Laoch agus fathach fir ab ea an fear seo – laoch agus fathach a ligeadh i ndearmad is i ndíchuimhne ámh'. Ó Buachalla (1968: 267), my translation.

The Fadgies: an 'Irish-speaking colony' in nineteenth-century Belfast

FIONNTÁN DE BRÚN

Cathal O'Byrne's collected articles on Belfast history, *As I Roved Out* (1946), contains the following intriguing piece of information concerning some of the residents of old Smithfield, the original market area in the centre of Belfast:

> Until demolished to make room for the Post Office extension, the lime-washed, slated houses in Charlemont Street were occupied mainly by a group of people who sold fish, oysters, and, occasionally, great golden slabs of honey-comb, carried on a huge dish that was balanced by a sugaun on the vendor's head. These people were all from Omeath, and were Gaelic speakers almost to a man, so that, until recently, there was in the heart of Belfast an Irish-speaking colony, the men of which were referred to as 'The Phadyees' (Paddies). (198)

While such an 'Irish speaking colony' might not be remarkable in a city such as Galway, [1] with its Gaeltacht hinterland, there has been little consideration of any specific linguistic community in Belfast before the urban Gaelic revival. [2]

The evidence of such a 'community' of native Irish speakers in Belfast is intriguing because, if true, it represents a direct link to the present-day Irish language revival and, particularly, to the establishment of an urban 'Gaeltacht', even if it transpires that this link is more symbolic than material.

The vast majority of Catholics living in Belfast in the early part of the nineteenth century were housed in the Smithfield area, specifically around Crooked Lane, now Chapel Lane, site of Belfast's first Catholic church built in 1784. [3] As migration to the city during the nineteenth century swelled Belfast's population at a rate of 3 percent per annum, from roughly 20,000

---

1 Writing about Galway City in 1915, Stephen Gwynn says: 'The Claddagh is to-day what it has always been – an Irish speaking village, lying outside the limits of the city proper, and living its own life apart' (103–4). 2 G.B. Adams (1986:22) briefly mentions the Fadgies who he says, erroneously in my opinion, settled in Charlemont Street early in the nineteenth century where they worked as basket-makers. He also adds that, later in the same century, the name 'Fadgies' was transferred to Italian immigrants 'who succeeded them in the same stand and occupation before accumulating enough money to set themselves up in ice-cream parlours.' 3 See Heatley (1983).

in 1800 to 349,000 in 1901 (Clarkson: 153), Catholics continued to settle mainly around the Smithfield/ Hercules Street[4] area. From the mid nineteenth century onwards this centre of Catholic population began to spread increasingly to the Pound, Lower Falls, Millfield and Carrickhill districts as well as to other outlying areas such as the Markets and Short Strand (Heatley: 137–42). It is not surprising, in a city where the vast majority of its population were 'strangers',[5] that the social, cultural and linguistic background of the city's new residents would have been wide and various. There is no doubt that the Irish language was an important feature of the linguistic and cultural mix of Belfast's expanding population, particularly, although not exclusively,[6] in the areas where the city's Catholics lived.

Nineteenth-century accounts of life in Smithfield give a vivid impression of an area which, besides sheltering a chaotic mass of people, was a notorious centre of inner-city poverty and disease: 'a sort of tumour, a morbid ganglion in the heart of the city', in the words of the Revd William M. O'Hanlon, a Congregationalist minister, whose *Walks among the Poor of Belfast* (1853) provides much detail on conditions in Smithfield. O'Hanlon records the obvious social ills such as the disproportionate number of drinking establishments, the wholesale traffic of stolen goods, and the dire absence of proper sanitation, particularly in the Marquis Street area; he also gives an account of the overwhelming mix of people and goods which characterized the market area:

> No inhabitant of Belfast needs any description of the general aspect of Smithfield. It seems a storehouse, or rather salehouse, for all the nondescript wares which can be collected from whatever quarter. How such heterogeneous articles contrived to come together into one and the same place, and set themselves down there side by side, in truce and amity, is a problem which it perplexes the mind to solve … It might seem as if there had been a design to surprise the passer-by, by the strangeness of the contrasts and combinations, such as we might see in a huge kaleidoscope – only substituting ugliness for beauty. (40–1)

Smithfield did not desire for colour and variety in other ways, for besides the trials that faced most inner-city dwellers of the time in Ireland and Britain, residents of Smithfield had the added prospect of sectarian rioting which, even then, was fairly well-established.[7]

---

4 Now a section of Royal Avenue.   5 Thomas Gaffikin, in a lecture given in 1875, remarks that: 'The people of Belfast in the present generation are principally strangers' (42). In 1901 only one-fifth of householders were born in Belfast (Clarkson: 153).   6 In the absence of a full statistical analysis of census material there are no available figures of Protestant Irish speakers in Belfast at this time. Nevertheless, it is clear from even a general survey of census returns that there was a significant number of Protestants who declared a knowledge of Irish.   7 See

It seems that this precarious environment became the home and workplace of some fish and fruit salesmen from the Omeath area of Co. Louth from at least 1856 onwards where the name of Stephen Marley appears on the list of residents of Charlemont Street followed by Michael McEntaggart in 1859–1860.[8] Charlemont Street ran parallel to Hercules Street (now Royal Avenue) from Berry Street to Garfield Street and is first mentioned in Smyth's map of 1790,[9] it has since been subsumed by the Castlecourt shopping complex. The Belfast Street Directory list for Charlemont Street in the following two decades, 1860s and 1870s, records a growing number of people who are described as being mainly fishdealers, and occasionally grocers, and whose surnames, such as Daly, Donnelly, McGivern, McKeown, McManus, McShane, O'Hagan, O'Hanlon and Trainor, are also found in Griffith's Householders Index for Carlingford Parish, Co. Louth.[10] This trend of settlement in Charlemont Street continued through the 1880s: in 1890 nine of the sixteen heads of households were fishdealers, dealers, or grocers, with surnames also found in Carlingford parish, and indeed some of the other residents may well have had connections to the area. Other streets close to Charlemont Street, such as Torren's Market, Torrens Row, and in particular Black's Lane, appear from street directories and parish records to have been mainly populated by Louth fishdealers. According to the Belfast Street Directory of 1877, the residents of Black's Lane included eleven householders whose surnames occur on the list of Carlingford surnames, all of these being fishdealers, dealers or, in one case, butcher, where an occupation is given.[11]

The predominance of the name 'Patrick', especially among the Charlemont Street dealers, offers the most likely explanation of the nickname 'Phadyees' or 'Fadgies', since the name Paddy is aspirated in Irish when addressing its bearer: 'a Pháidí'.[12] While these dealers would have been bilingual, it seems certain that their proximity to one and other in Charlemont Street and Black's Lane would have meant that the language they used would have been Irish. Unfortunately, Charlemont Street's Irish speaking community, or 'colony' as O'Byrne describes it, met the same fate as so many other communities since in the constantly 'redeveloping' city when the houses gave way to an extended General Post Office in the early 1890s.[13] Black's Lane and its immediate envi-

Boyd (1969). 8 Both Marley and McEntaggart/McTaggart are described as fruit dealers who lived in numbers seven and nine respectively. See Belfast and Ulster Directory; Griffith's Valuation, Counties Antrim and Down, Parish of Shankill (1860: 115). 9 See Gillespie and Royle (2003) and also Patton (1993). 10 Householders' Index, Co. Louth, Dundalk Lower Barony, Carlingford Parish, 1854: 42. 11 P. McShane, fishdealer; Arthur Rice, butcher; T. McNamee, fishdealer; Patrick Kane, fishdealer; Lawrence Boyle, fishdealer; Mary Limna; Mary Kennedy; Robert McNamee; Stephen Taggart, dealer; Peter McDermott, fishdealer; James Larkin, fishdealer. 12 It has also been suggested to me that the term 'Fadgie' may be a patronymic (a name derived from one's father or a paternal ancestor by the addition of an affix) such as Eoghan Pháidí (Paddy's Eoghan). 13 Street Directories of the time mention the erec-

rons had been rased two decades before as part of the widening of Hercules Street. Nevertheless, while the demise of these streets led to the dispersal of the specific families that O'Byrne mentions, their work as dealers kept them within the same area and indeed there is ample evidence that many other families from Omeath continued to settle in Smithfield and in other parts of Belfast through the initial decades of the twentieth century. Writing in 1982 (52–3), Liam Mac Carráin adds to O'Byrne's account explaining that the 'Fadgies' lived in the Marquis Street area in the 1880s and progressed from there to the Falls Road where they owned various fish and fruit shops. Nan O'Hara of Meleady's fruit shop on the Falls Road is possibly the last direct descendant of these.[14]

There are three main sources of information on the Omeath Irish speakers in Belfast. Firstly, folk memory, the most elusive and least durable historical source concerning the Fadgies, is scant and difficult to separate from written sources – when asked, people often relate information that they have read somewhere without acknowledging the source. The term 'fadgie' is still recognized by some very elderly Belfast people as slang for a countryman. Secondly, a great deal of information on Smithfield residents, and, in particular, their knowledge of Irish, has been preserved in the returns for the 1901 and 1911 census, their nineteenth-century equivalents having long since been destroyed. We owe, however, the most complete and detailed account of the life of the Fadgies to Seán Mac Maoláin (1884–1973) the Belfast Gaelic Leaguer and writer, who wrote in Irish on the subject in a 1940 article in *An tUltach*[15] and again in his autobiography, *Gleann Airbh go Glas Naíon* (Glenarriff to Glasnevin).[16]

It is worth mentioning that Mac Maoláin was a remarkably perceptive observer of social and linguistic habits. His description of the lives of working-class communities of the Falls Road area in the early part of the twentieth century in *I mBéal Feirsde Domh* (1942) is extraordinary for the time and his mastery of the Irish language led him to become respected even by that most exclusivist of Gaeltacht writers, Séamus Ó Grianna (Máire).[17] As Mac Maoláin explains in *Gleann Airbh go Glas Naíon*, his first encounter with the Irish speakers of Omeath was when, as a youth, he travelled every weekend to the area to perfect his Irish. It was there that the young Mac Maoláin introduced himself to the renowned singer and storyteller, Neilí Ní Anluain who was, for many, the embodiment of the exceptionally rich Gaelic tradition that set Omeath apart.

tion of Workshops for the Blind.   14 Mac Carráin mentions fruit shops owned by Rice (Ó Maolchraoibhe) on Falls Road; Fearon (Eoghan Ó Fearáin) on Falls Road and McNamee (Peadar Mac Con Midhe) in Castle Street. Of these three, Rice is listed in the Belfast Street Directory until 1980 and MacNamee is listed until the 1970s.   15 A monthly publication of the Gaelic League in Ulster.   16 Mac Maoláin's family were originally from Glenarriff, Co. Antrim, and moved to Belfast when Seán Mac Máoláin was a schoolboy (1969: 19).   17 See Uí Laighléis

To properly explain the importance of Omeath in the Ulster Gaelic tradition, one must first of all place the area in its historic setting within the old Gaelic territory of Oriel, which is described by Pádraigín Ní Uallacháin as 'now an undefined territory stretching from north Meath to south Louth and south Down, west to Cavan, Monaghan and south Armagh' (19).[18] Ní Uallacháin's extensive study of the Oriel tradition represents the first full appreciation of the area's cultural history, which is presented here in summary. Besides its central position in the Cú Chulainn story, *Táin Bó Cuailgne*, Oriel is chiefly associated with the life and work of the Ulster poets of the seventeenth and eighteenth centuries: Séamus Dall Mac Cuarta (1647?–1733), Cathal Buí Mac Giolla Ghunna (1680–1756)[19] Art Mac Cumhaigh (1738–73) Peadar Ó Doirnín (1704–69) and Pádraig Mac Giolla Fhiondáin (1666–1733). The work of these poets, and the body of folklore which it generated, became the focus for the Ulster scribes and antiquarians of the nineteenth century, of which Art Bennett and Robert MacAdam, respectively, are probably the best known. Not surprisingly, the Gaelic revival of the late nineteenth century ensured a renewed interest among scholars and enthusiasts in the tradition of poetry, song and story in Oriel among them Seosamh Laoide (Joseph Lloyd), Eoin Mac Néill, Douglas Hyde, Róis Ní Ógáin (Rose Young), Enrí Ó Muireasa and Fr Lorcán Ó Muireadhaigh. It was in Omeath that Ó Muireadhaigh first founded his Irish College before relocating it to Rann na Feirste (Rannafast) in Co. Donegal in 1926 and it was his experience of teaching at the Omeath College that inspired the young Donegal writer, Seosamh Mac Grianna, to write his series of essays on the Oriel poets and other stories from the area.[20]

At the time of Seán Mac Maoláin's visits to Omeath, the early 1900s, Neilí Ní Anluain was an old woman in her eighties – she died in 1906. Among the many scholars who collected songs and stories from her was Father Lorcán Ó Muireadhaigh, who wrote that Neilí Ní Anluain was one of two people in Omeath who were the last traditional guardians of the compositions of the older poets such as Séamus Dall Mac Cuarta (Ní Uallacháin 404). Through his acquaintance with Neilí Ní Anluain and other Irish speakers in Omeath, Mac Maoláin discovered that people from that area had for many years been travelling to Belfast during the summer months in order to sell fish, mainly Ardglass herring, from door to door (1969: 56–59).[21] Unlike their counter-

(25). **18** The Oriel area can be identified fairly clearly in maps, showing concentration of Irish speakers in pre-Famine Ireland, which are included in FitzGerald's (2003) study of Irish speaking in the pre-famine period; see particularly Map 2. I am grateful to Ciarán Ó Duibhín for this observation. **19** Although reputedly born in an area of Co. Cavan outside of the Oriel region, Mac Giolla Ghunna is particularly associated with Oriel, especially in its oral tradition (Ó Buachalla: 34). **20** *Pádraig Ó Conaire agus Aistí Eile* (1936). **21** It is interesting to note here that Bríghid Ní Chaslaigh/ Bríghid na gCeoltaí (Mrs Brigid Casserly), a renowned

parts in Donegal and Connacht, Mac Maoláin tells us, there was no tradition in Omeath of seasonal migration to Scotland and England to work on farms or building sites, rather those who left the area to work in other parts tended to travel around selling goods. This practice was known as *páibhíocht* in Irish and, in English, 'pahveeing' or 'cadging', hence the 'cadgers pad' in Omeath, a shortcut over the hills to Dundalk and Faughart favoured by people bringing seafood in carts to be sold at the markets (Ní Uallacháin 62).[22] Indeed, Mac Maoláin provides a reference from the poetry of Cathal Buí Mac Giolla Ghunna to show that the tradition of pahveeing/cadging in Oriel could be traced back almost three centuries.[23] Interestingly, Lorcán Ó Muireadhaigh gives an account of how a travelling pahvee brought back a particular version of the poet Mac Giolla Ghunna's famous 'An Bonnán Buí' from Connacht. The Omeath pahvee was singing 'An Bonnán Buí' at a fair for pennies when she was overhead by a Connacht woman who told her that she had part of the song wrong. Both retired to a nearby alehouse where the Connacht version was promptly passed on (Ó Muireadhaigh: 146).

Seán Mac Maoláin's friends in Omeath encouraged him to seek out Ailí Ní Mhuireagáin (Ellen Morgan), a fruit seller from the area who had gone from selling fruit around the doors in Belfast to owning, along with her son, one of the most prosperous businesses in the city's St George's Market. Despite having moved from Omeath many years previously, Ní Mhuireagáin was said to be as 'homely and Gaelic' as any of the old women who had never left the area. Mac Maoláin's first meeting with Ailí Ní Mhuireagáin was to be the first of many Saturdays spent in her company sitting outside her son's office in St George's Market learning about the songs and lore of Omeath (1940; 1969: 58–9). Ní Mhuireagáin particularly favoured the song 'Patrún Chill Shléibhe' (The Killeavy Pattern) which laments the passing of the traditional festival held in Killeavy celebrating the local saint, Saint Blinne or Moninne.[24] While there are many reasons for the demise of the traditional 'pattern days' in the nineteenth century, Ní Mhuireagáin's explication of the origin of the song, 'Pátrún Chill Shléibhe', focusses on an issue of great relevance to Belfast, sectarian strife. Adding to the evidence of one particular verse which inveighs against a local yeoman who it is claimed destroyed the festival, Ní Mhuireagáin spoke of how Protestants would arrive from Portadown to attack Catholics who attended the festival. As though to reaf-

traditional singer from Omeath, who is pictured on the cover of Ní Uallacháin's study (2003), was baptized in St Patrick's, Donegall Street, Belfast as were some of her siblings. I am again indebted to Ciarán Ó Duibhín for this information. **22** *Páibhíocht* is most often equated with peddling cloth. See Murphy (106) and Evans (156–61). **23** From the poem 'Beatha Chathail Bhuí' (The life of Cathal Buí) where the poet mentions 'is mé ag dul le hearra go Loch gCál' (and I taking goods to Loughgall) see Ó Buachalla (72). **24** See Ní Uallacháin (307–18) for the text, translation and background of this song. See also Ó Dubhda (109–16).

firm the song's continuing relevance, Mac Maoláin noticed that Ní Mhuireagáin's singing in Irish was attracting the disapproval of some of the passers-by in the market. On hearing this Ní Mhuireagáin replied defiantly: 'I'm in no bother about them. I'm not depending on them – I could thatch St George's Market with five-pound notes.'

Ailí Ní Mhuireagáin went on to mention the recent death of a childhood friend who had also lived in Belfast. Before her death, this woman had confided a fear to her friend that she would be unable to make her final confession to the priest, as this would be in English. Ní Mhuireagáin explains that since her friend had come to Belfast when she was 'of a good age', she had virtually no English. This woman, Mac Maoláin explains, was the mother of Stephen Marley, 'one of the wealthiest fishdealers in Belfast'. It is likely that this was the wife of the Stephen Marley who had been resident in Charlemont Street from at least 1856. Street directories show that Marley and Sons had, by 1895, acquired three business premises in Smithfield, Berry Street and York Street as well as being resident in the rather exclusive 204 Falls Road.[25] Until at least 1956, S. Marley and Sons were listed as fishmongers at 74–6 Oxford Street.[26]

It seems that, despite the undoubted commercial success enjoyed by the Morgans and the Marleys, many of the Omeath fish and fruit dealers were less fortunate. Where Seán Mac Maoláin's account of the 'fadgies' in his autobiography mostly concerns his friendship with Ailí Ní Mhuireagáin, his first article on the Omeath Irish speakers gives a more general picture of the small community in Smithfield and particularly of those who had not 'met with any great luck in life'. Mac Maoláin tells us that it was common to see ten or so of these men on a summer's evening, sitting on the cobblestones in Marquis Street, the day's work done, smoking their pipes and conversing in Irish. These men would be in Belfast only for the summer months, according to Mac Maoláin, yet census records, which I will return to, and street directories for the initial years of the twentieth century would appear to show that many Omeath families were permanently resident in Smithfield and elsewhere in Belfast. Many of these families kept lodgers from Omeath which, together with the fact that families may have settled in Belfast in stages, would account for what Mac Maoláin says.

Ever eager and gregarious, Seán Mac Maoláin befriended several of the Omeath Irish speakers and of these, in particular, Brian Ua Ruairc impressed

25 See Belfast Street Directory 1895. 204 Falls Road is directly opposite the Beehive bar (beside St Mary's University College) today. Unfortunately, there is no census return for the Marley residence in 1901 which the street directory for that year lists as 55 King Street. 26 Merrick (1984: 225) gives the full gravestone inscription of the Marley family as well as some background information. Stephen Marley died in 1899, aged 70 years, and was predeceased by his wife Mary who died in 1876. It is possible that the woman mentioned above was Marley's second wife.

him with his wit and intelligence. Ua Ruairc never failed to engage the young
Gaelic Leaguer in conversation save on one occasion when Mac Maoláin was
walking towards Ballmacarret dressed in his Sunday best accompanied by two
young female relations similarly attired. Being shabbily dressed and apparently tipsy, the fish dealer thought it best not to embarrass his young acquaintance and pretended not to see him. Mac Maoláin, however, greeted him
warmly, whereupon the older man, in appreciation of the irony of the situation, regaled them with a verse from the song 'An tUltach Beadaí' (The Proud
Ulsterman) in which a similar encounter is related:

> *Ag dul trí Chill Chainnigh domh 's mo chroí bocht tuirseach,*
> *Mar bhí mé folamh gan éadáil,*
> *Sé an smaoineamh a rinneas go raibh céad fear folamh,*
> *A thiocfadh arís in éifeacht.*
> *Ansin chím iad chugam an dís bhan fearúil*
> *Ag bualadh an bhealaigh in m'éadan,*
> *'Fóill, fóill,' arsa bean acu, 'seo an tUltach beadaí*
> *'S ródheas a chanas sé véarsaí!'*

Going through Kilkenny my poor heart was weary,
For I was penniless and destitute,
Until it struck me that there were a hundred others like me,
Who would yet prosper again.
Twas then I spied the two fine women,
Making their way along the road towards me,
'Wait, wait,' said one, 'here's the proud Ulsterman
and it's he that sings verses right well.'[27]

Another of the Fadgies Mac Maoláin recalls was an especially colourful
character, Eoghan Pheadair Duibh (Owen O'Hanlon), a seaman and brother
of the Neilí Ní Anluain who Mac Maoláin had met on his first visits to
Omeath. It seems certain that this is the same Owen O'Hanlon, seaman, who
is listed among the residents of Charlemont Street during the 1860s and 1870s.
Having spent his life at sea, O'Hanlon found work in his later years as a watch-
man in the docks. Mac Maoláin spent many evenings 'ag áirneáil' (ceilid-
hing/night-visiting) with the old man whose life at sea was the source of innu-
merable stories as may be expected. Ó hAnluain claimed to have heard fluent
Irish spoken in the West Indies by black people with red hair – possibly referring to the people of Montserrat, who are descended from African slaves and
Irish slaves or indentured servants of the seventeenth and eighteenth century.

27 See Ó Muireasa (54–5; 219–20) for the text of this song in Irish, without translation, and a
note, in English, on its origin.

Besides his tales of foreign wonders, Ó hAnluain had a rich repertoire of Fiannaíocht (Stories and lays from the Finn cycle) and had some knowledge of Rúraíocht (the Ulster cycle), a fact which, as Mac Maoláin notes, would have surprised many scholars, since Fiannaíocht had survived at the expense of Rúraíocht in the oral tradition. Yet, Ó hAnluain reserved special affection for the eighteenth-century Ulster *aisling* (vision) poem 'Úr-Chill an Chreagáin', where the Oriel poet Art Mac Cumhaigh agonizes over whether to leave his native place and go off with the fairy maiden who has come to lure him away to 'a land of honey where foreigners have not been granted rule.'[28] Ó hAnluain, who longed to return to Omeath, expressed particular sympathy with the poet Mac Cumhaigh's final wish, that he should be buried in the churchyard of Creggan.

Seán Mac Maoláin's invaluable memoir of the Fadgics is complemented to a large extent by the information stored in contemporary census returns. Regrettably, no census returns survive from the nineteenth century and the earliest available returns after that, those of the 1901 census, show a Charlemont Street bereft of residents. Nevertheless, streets surrounding Charlemont Street, such as Chapel Lane, Mill Street, Millfield and Millar's Lane, housed at least ten families where the heads of the households had been born in Louth, spoke Irish and English, and almost invariably worked as fish or fruit sellers.[29] Interestingly, with the exception of O'Hanlon, the surnames of these families – McCann, Fearon and O'Rourke – are not among those recorded in either Charlemont Street or the Black's Lane area. Another notable feature reflected in the census returns is the number of people from Louth who are recorded as lodgers.[30] Indeed, only two of the families mentioned did not keep lodgers, and in the case of Thomas and Bridget O'Hanlon and their ten children, this was, perhaps, understandable. One of the lodgers kept by the O'Rourkes of Millar's Lane, Michael Keenan, a fishmonger born in Louth, was married, a fact which points to the practice noted by Mac Maoláin of Louth dealers spending summers in Belfast.[31] The prevalence of lodgers is a phenomenon which has been observed before by Clarkson (156) who notes that in 1901 nearly a quarter of all Belfast households contained related kin other than children. This pattern is well manifested amongst the

28 For a translation and discussion of this poem see Hughes (2001: 526–8) and Ní Uallacháin (250–8).   29 An example of a household in Millar's Lane is Elizabeth O'Hanlon, laundress, born in Louth, spoke Irish and English; lived with her daughter Christina, born in Belfast, worked as a smoother (no entry in the language column of the census return). An example of a household in Campbell's Row is Stephen Teggart, dealer, born in Louth, spoke Irish and English; lived with his Monaghan-born wife, Mary, and their Belfast-born son Stephen, neither of whom have any entry under the language column. There are no census entries for fish and fruit dealers P. O'Rourke and Owen Morgan of Mill Street as their addresses are listed as shops.   30 Nan O'Hara has told me that many people from Omeath stayed at Mick McKeown's lodging house at Carrickhill.   31 The census was taken for the last day of March.

Louth families in Smithfield and elsewhere and gives us the impression of a distinct network of families from Louth who lived and worked together in Belfast. A study of census returns available for Smithfield shows that these families were concentrated in the area around the market area. In all cases their houses were no more than adequate, generally being described as 'second class' with two windows to the front and with no more than four rooms.

Two families at least, however, the Morgans and Marleys, discussed by Mac Maoláin, enjoyed considerably more material success than their peers. While there does not appear to be any return for Stephen Marley and family in the 1901 census, the census return for the family of Ailí Ní Mhuireagáin has survived. Mac Maoláin's assessment of the family's wealth was well founded, for their address at the time of the 1901 census, 7 Annesley Street, off Carlisle Circus, was in an area reserved for the expanding middle-class. Neighbours of the Morgans were Russian Jews, presumably part of the large numbers of Jewish people who had fled religious persecution in Russia and Lithuania. Indeed, the largest immigrant group in Belfast at that time was Russian, despite the relatively large number of Italian immigrants.[32] In the census return for the Morgan household we find that John Morgan, aged 43, was a 'fish salesman' who was born in Louth, as was his wife, Ellen, aged 40, who also worked in fish sales and was mother to six children ranging in age from three to nineteen, all of whom had been born in Belfast. This would indicate that the Morgans had lived in Belfast from at least the early 1880s. The Morgans had two lodgers both born in Louth, Henry Woods, 'fruit buyer', brother-in-law of John Morgan, and Micheal O'Hagan, servant.

Perhaps the most interesting detail concerning the Morgans is their answer to the question on their ability to speak Irish. Everyone in the household, including the Belfast-born children, is recorded as speaking Irish and English – further evidence of Ailí Ní Mhuireagáin's robust defence of the language. This appears to be an exception to the general pattern evidenced in the census returns for the Louth fish and fruit sellers which is that while the parents in the household tended to answer 'Irish and English', in answer to the language question, they recorded their children as speaking English only. Conversely, many householders in the Smithfield Electoral Division who had been born in Belfast described themselves and their children as speaking both Irish and English. In one case, James Sharp of Cape Street completed his census form in Irish giving his name as Séamas Mac Fhaobhair, *Casóir iarrainn* (iron turner) and stating that his wife and seven children knew Irish and English. Sharp was born in Co. Cavan and it is possible that he was a

---

32 See Hyman (209). Annesley Street was chosen as the location for a new synagogue in 1904; the Morgans had by then moved to nearby Lonsdale Street where, besides several Jewish residents, their neighbours included the photographer Robert Welch.

native speaker of Irish rather than an enthusiast who had been encouraged by the Gaelic League's campaign for the use of Irish in census forms. Yet there are many other examples of manual workers who had been born in Belfast but claimed a knowledge of Irish in their census returns. Indeed, this is a trend that has been also noted in the census returns for Derry.[33]

It is tempting to see the enthusiasm of non-native speakers of Irish, who claimed the Irish language for their children, against the apparent indifference of native speakers about their children's knowledge of Irish, as a reflection of the birth of the urban revival and the simultaneous decline of the Gaeltacht. This might, of course, be a more viable conclusion if more detailed statistics were available but, at present, our reading of the census returns can only be on a surface level in the absence of statistics that give place of birth alongside ability to speak Irish. Nevertheless, if the census returns are an accurate indication of the attitudes of the 'Fadgies' towards the perpetuation of the Irish language, then it seems that the notion of a traditionally rural language surviving in the city was more likely to have been promoted by those, like Seán Mac Maoláin, who were raised in the city. Certainly, the only monoglot Irish speaking children in Belfast recorded in the 1911 census (the only monoglot Irish speakers in Ulster outside of Donegal) were not the children of native speakers. The parents of these four children, Seaghán and Caitlín Ó Catháin (O'Keane), were Gaelic Leaguers from Co. Limerick and Co. Cork respectively. Seaghán Ó Catháin, a customs and excise officer, had learned his Irish at the League's classes in London and after being transferred to Belfast, became *príomhoide* (headteacher) of Coláiste Chomhghaill, the Gaelic League's Irish College in Bank Street.[34]

In his autobiography, Mac Maoláin makes the point that native speakers of Irish tended to undervalue the language and he is quite bitter about the wanton decline of Irish in the Omeath area. Nevertheless, the success of the Gaelic League in Belfast was in no small measure the result of an effective collaboration between native speakers who were keen to pass the language on and enthusiasts who had learned Irish as a second language. Indeed, the Belfast Branch of the Gaelic League was founded in the home of P.T. Mac Fhionnlaoich, a native speaker from Donegal who played a pioneering role in the League's activities in the city (Mac Giolla Domhnaigh: 7). This new

---

33 See Mac Suibhne and Dickson (54).   34 See Breathnach agus Ní Mhurchú (1986: 55–6) and Mac Giolla Domhnaigh (198; 200). The census return for the Ó Catháins (completed in Irish) tells us that they lived at Glenburn Park (2 Ashgrove Villas) off the Cavehill Road with their four sons, Pádraig (aged 7), Seaghán (5), Fionnbarr (3) and Caoimhghin (1), along with their maid, Máire Stacach (16) from Co. Kerry who spoke Irish and English. Seaghán Ó Catháin and his wife are returned as speaking Irish and English while the four children are returned as speaking Irish only. The family left Belfast in 1922 when Seaghán Ó Catháin was transferred to another post (Breathnach agus Ní Mhurchú 1986: 56).

alliance of native Irish speakers and revivalists often owed itself to the type
of chance encounters that are possible in cities: in one instance a Gaelic
Leaguer who also worked for the Post Office noticed that surnames associated with the Donegal Gaeltacht were marked on letters addressed to houses
in the affluent Malone area. He made it his business to wait outside of the
houses in question until the addressees emerged – all of them Donegal women
in service – and successfully invited them to teach classes for the Gaelic
League.[35] This symbiosis of Gaelic League and Gaeltacht was further invig-
orated in the period leading up to the 1960s where exchanges between
Gaeltacht and Belfast Irish language groups became increasingly frequent and
were complemented by a cohort of native speakers resident in Belfast who
voluntarily taught Irish night classes in the city, the most celebrated of these
teachers being Domhnall Ó Grianna, one of the famous family of
writers/poets/storytellers from Donegal.[36]

One of the ironies of the Charlemont Street Irish speakers was that their
dispersal should occur just as the first branch of the Gaelic League was
formed in Belfast in 1895. It is a matter of speculation, given the strict class
divisions of the time, as to whether or not the mainly middle-class aficiona-
dos that constituted that Belfast Gaelic League branch would have cultivated
links with some lowly fish and fruit sellers, however, these same middle-class
enthusiasts seem to have had no hesitation in adopting often the poorest residents of Omeath as their teachers. What is in no doubt is the extent to which
we are indebted to Seán Mac Maoláin whose initiative and energy secured a
permanent record of the Fadgies, and this record is in itself testament to the
positive social dynamic that the Gaelic revival engendered.

The importance of the existence of a community of native Irish speakers
in Belfast has been hinted at earlier in this essay. The comparison with the
present-day Shaw's Road urban Gaeltacht seems the most obvious. Yet, alongside the fact that these communities are not historically contemporaneous, the
many differences between the two – the one a community of native speakers
whose existence is founded on an economic imperative, the other a community of initially second-language learners whose existence is founded on a cultural political imperative – makes for a rather uneven comparison.
Nevertheless, the link between the two communities is unquestionable, since
Seán Mac Maoláin, who was an inspirational figure in the Belfast revival,
learned much of his Irish in Belfast, from native Irish speakers from Omeath.
Also, it seems that some of those related to Stephen Marley, the first Omeath
dealer to settle in Charlemont Street, were involved with the Gaelic League

35 I am grateful to Bairbre de Brún MEP for this anecdote which concerns her uncle Peter
Marley.   36 Domhnall Ó Grianna (1894–1962), see Breathnach agus Ní Mhurchú (1994: 123–4)
for biographical information.

even in its very earliest years.[37] Indeed the legacy of both the Fadgies and Gaelic Leaguers such as Mac Maoláin is inescapable today in the very area where the Fadgies lived and worked – more than anywhere else in Belfast, the pubs in the area around Marquis Street[38] and Chapel Lane are patronized by Irish speakers, mainly due to the traditional music which is played there. The Irish mass is said in St Mary's Chapel Lane on Sundays, the local community having been replaced by a linguistic community drawn from various parts of Belfast.

Despite the important sense of continuity which the Fadgies add to the present Irish language community in Belfast, the Omeath Irish speakers are of great significance to a wider social and historical context. Indeed, Cathal O'Byrne's use of the word colony is, perhaps inadvertently, a signpost to this broader issue. If by the use of the word colony, in his description of the Fadgies, O'Byrne implies that this was a somewhat incongruous settlement of newcomers set apart from the 'native' community, then it is necessary to take issue with him. Belfast, it can be argued, became the city that we recognize today by dint of the huge population growth of the nineteenth century and the attendant economic and social circumstances, including the phenomenon of sectarian violence, which brought about the city's transformation. It is this period, more than any other, that defined the city within and without its boundaries. The Omeath fruit and fish sellers who settled in Belfast in the nineteenth century are, therefore, among the earliest inhabitants of the new city and as such an essential part of its story.

37 Peadar Ó Mearthaile (Peter Marley), a Post Office inspector who had relatives in Omeath, was Liam Mac Carráin's source about the Fadgies (Mac Carráin: 53). This is the same Peter Marley, mentioned above, who recruited Donegal women to teach classes for the Gaelic League. Another Marley, Seán Ó Mearthaile, an employee at the General Post Office in Belfast, was one of the earlier members of the Belfast Gaelic League (Mac Giolla Domhnaigh: 22).   38 An Irish language club was based in Marquis Street in the 1930s and, according to Mac Carráin (1982: 4–5), was mainly frequented by native speakers.

Irish in Belfast, 1892–1960: from the Gaelic League to Cumann Chluain Ard

AODÁN MAC PÓILIN

Belfast was the crucible of the Irish language revival movement in Ulster, whether we date that movement from 1895, when a branch of the Gaelic League was established in the city, or go back to the Ulster Gaelic Society of 1830. It was also where the main battle for the survival of the language in Northern Ireland was fought out in the 1920s and early 1930s. The new state, fiercely opposed to Irish, set up its headquarters in Belfast City Hall before moving to Stormont Buildings in 1932. Opposing the state was a group of amateur language enthusiasts whose only institutional support came from the Catholic church, which proved to be both an indispensable and an erratic ally. Belfast was also the locus of some important experiments; Cumann Chluain Ard, the first 'English-free zone' in Ireland, and, slightly outside our time-frame, the Shaw's Road community, the most significant urban Gaeltacht in Ireland, which in its turn sowed the seeds for the Irish-medium education movement in Northern Ireland.

As early as 1892, a year before the Gaelic League was founded, the Belfast Naturalists' Field Club, nearly thirty years old, set up an Irish class in the premises of the Belfast Natural History and Philosophical Society in College Square North. Its teacher was P.S. Ó Sé, a native speaker of Irish from Kerry who had been posted to Belfast by the Customs and Mail Service.[1] The field club movement combined a strong self-improvement ethos with what was, for its time, a remarkably advanced sense of social inclusion – while essentially middle-class, working-class members were made welcome, as were women. By the end of the century, these clubs had become a magnet for the bright young things of the period, and although Ó Sé described it as 'a sombre body', it probably offered the nearest thing to an intellectual bohemian lifestyle that Belfast could offer. It is not entirely surprising that such a gathering, pre-dominantly led by young, middle-class Protestants, should take up Irish.

From the Field Club class emerged the Belfast branch of the Gaelic League in 1895. Another Customs and Mail officer, P.T. McGinley, hosted the first meeting of the new branch in his house on the Beersbridge Road. McGinley had caused some consternation among learners of Irish, accustomed as they were to the melodious Irish of Munster, with his Donegal accent, which they found somewhat harsh.[2] In the excitement of setting up the

---

1 Breathnach & Ní Mhurchú, *Beathaisnéis a hAon* 1986, 105.   2 Alice Milligan, in *An*

branch, no one thought to inform the Belfast Natural History and Philosophical Society that the class had turned itself into a branch of the Gaelic League, and when they returned to College Square North they were shown the door. The first Gaelic League class in Belfast, it is reported, was held in the doorway of Robinson & Cleavers.[3] They eventually found premises in the Belfast Art Society Rooms, 49 Queen Street.[4]

The original makeup of the Belfast Branch was, like that of the Field Club, remarkably inclusive. Its founders certainly went out of their way to present a broad front. Patrons included the Catholic bishop of Down and Connor and the Church of Ireland bishop of Down, Connor and Dromore, the moderator of the Presbyterian Church in Ireland, and a galaxy of clergy of all denominations, including the redoubtable Revd R.R. Kane, Grand Master of the Belfast Orange Lodge, organizer of the Anti-Home Rule Convention and a man noted for his fiery denunciations of Popery. The patrons were led by a liberal unionist, Dr John St Clair Boyd, and included Francis Joseph Bigger, Protestant nationalist romantic, bibliophile, indefatigable committee-man, dabbler in literature, history, folklore, traditional music, kilts and nonsense. Ó Sé and McGinley were perhaps untypical in being Catholics from Irish speaking districts. The *Gaelic Journal* noted the range of membership the following May, claiming that the language could 'unite in honest and thoroughgoing sympathy on thoroughly National grounds, Irishmen whose religious and political principles are sundered as the poles.'[5] At its AGM in September 1896, reporting on a growth of membership from 22 to 120 in the first year, St Clair Boyd repeated this theme: 'it is pleasant to state that the society includes members of all creeds and classes, being strictly non-political and non-sectarian.'[6]

The religious and political make-up of the early membership in Belfast has not been analysed in depth,[7] but the active members appear to represent a colourfully wide range of backgrounds. Among those who attended classes in the early days was Mary Hutton, wife of a Unitarian minister, and a formidable scholar who worked on the original texts of several Old Irish versions of the *Táin*. Rather than editing them, Hutton recreated a unified version of the story in verse, an unfortunate judgment, as the verse was not very good. Rose Maud Young of Galgorm Castle near Ballymena was involved at an early stage and later published a three-volume anthology of Irish Gaelic

Claidheamh Soluis, 1 and 8 Oct. 1904.   3 Foreword, *Leabhar na Feise*, Feis Uladh, 11–12 Dec. 1902; *Irish Peasant*, 30 Dec. 1905.   4 'Feis Uladh', *Irisleabhar na Gaedhilge – the Gaelic Journal*, Jan. 1901, p. 25.   5 'The movement in Belfast', *Irisleabhar na Gaedhilge*, May 1896, p. 1.   6 *Irisleabhar na Gaedhilge*, Oct. 1896, p. 96.   7 For an interesting study of the make-up of the membership of the Gaelic League see T.G. McMahon,: '*All creeds and classes?* Just who made up the Gaelic League?' In *Éire-Ireland* 37:3–4 (2002), 118–68.

poetry. An aunt of Lady Brookborough, her brother was to organize the Larne Gun-Running. Other members included Éamonn Ó Tuathail, later Professor of Irish in TCD, who published Gaelic folktales from Tyrone and Cavan and Hugh McMillen who, under the name of Aoidhmín Mac Gréagóir, collected the folklore and the word-horde of Rathlin and the Glens of Antrim. The sculptor Rosamund Praeger was involved. Among the more politically radical were the Catholics Ailbhe Ó Monacháin, an artist who later took part in the 1916 Rising, and Cathal Ó Seanáin, active in the labour movement and the Irish Republican Brotherhood, and the Protestants Alice Milligan, poet, playwright, feminist, socialist and political activist, Bulmer Hobson, Quaker and IRB organizer.

Early language enthusiasts, unless they were native speakers, usually acquired Irish in night classes, but a number adopted more unorthodox ways. Séamus Ó Ceallaigh learned the language in the Sperrins during summer holidays with his grandparents. Cathal O'Boyle, father of the music collector Seán O'Boyle, used to accompany an Irish speaking RIC constable from Kerry on his night-beat through the streets of Belfast. Seán Mac Maoláin took day-trips to the Omeath Gaeltacht every Saturday, quizzed his father, who turned out to have been a native speaker, and finally married a native speaker from Donegal. The League organized trips to the Glens of Antrim, the Sperrins, Omeath and Donegal. Some members on Field Club trips sought out and found native speakers in the Mournes.

However, many of those involved in the early days of the Gaelic League in Belfast had little or no knowledge of the language. Of the patrons, Monsignor O'Laverty certainly had a scholarly understanding of Irish, and probably spoke it, the Revd Canon Crozier, then the Church of Ireland vicar of Down, had won a prize in Irish in TCD, St Clair Boyd did his best to acquire Irish, and Bigger never got around to learning it. We know little about the rest. R.R. Kane had ensured that the Ulster Unionist Convention of 1891 had a banner declaring, 'Erin go bragh' – Ireland for ever, but there is no evidence that he spoke the language. It is possible that there is truth in the oft-told story that he used the Irish version of his name when signing the minutes of his lodge meetings, but this has yet to be authenticated.

The list of active members above includes one, Alice Milligan, who never succeeded in learning Irish, and another, Praeger, for whom we have little information, but most of the rest had acquired the language to a very high degree. However, this cohort may not have been typical. A description of the annual general meeting of the Belfast Gaelic League at the turn of the century survives. Its author, Osborn Bergin, was already demonstrating that tetchiness that was to make him a legend even within the notably cantankerous confederation of Celtic scholarship. His main complaint, besides the difficulty of getting a cup of tea in Belfast, was that even P.S. Ó Sé was speaking

English. He had a point. A rule ensuring that business of the Gaelic League in Belfast was conducted through the medium of Irish was not implemented until 1933.[8]

The language movement scored some successes in mainstreaming the language in the education system in the early years. Irish was introduced to the curriculum of the Catholic teacher training college for women in 1902, and the education authorities recognized and funded two colleges in Belfast to provide in-service training in the language to working teachers. What looks on first sight as an unnecessary doubling of effort hinged partly on disagreements in the city on methodology, but mostly on the issue of whether to use Ulster or Munster Irish. In 1906, a young Protestant medical student at Queen's College Belfast established the university Gaelic Society whose aim was to restore Irish as the common language of Ireland. William MacArthur was supported by the flamboyant Professor R.M. Henry, brother of the painter Paul Henry, and a political nationalist, who was prepared to support any movement that would annoy his more staid colleagues. MacArthur was not so much apolitical as anti-political where the language was concerned; he included a rule in the constitution of the Gaelic Society that is now probably illegal: 'Any member introducing a religious or political subject at any time shall cease to be a member ...'[9] He went on to become a pillar of the establishment. By the time he wrote an introduction – in limpid Irish – to a pamphlet celebrating the half-centenary of the Gaelic Society, he was Lt.-Gen. Sir William MacArthur, D.S.O.; O.B.E.; K.C.B.; B.B., B.Ch.; B.A.O.; D.P.H. Oxon.; M.D. Belf., D.T.M.&H. Cantab.; HON. D.Sc/Oxon.; M.R.C.P.I.; F.R.C.P.I.; F.R.C.P. The early Gaelic Society, like the early Gaelic League, transcended sectarianism. Over fifty people attended its inaugural meeting in 1906, more than double the number of Catholics attending Queen's at that time. The society continued to involve Protestants and unionists until the outbreak of the First World War, but an account of its history written in 1956 returns repeatedly to its subsequent failure to break the sectarian mould that was established between the end of the war and the early 1920s.[10]

Irish had not been taught at Queen's since the death of the great scholar John O'Donovan in 1861. Henry and MacArthur succeeded in having the subject restored in 1908–9. According to the official history of Queen's: 'the inclusion of Celtic as a subject for the faculty of Arts aroused no controversy, partly, perhaps, because the appointment of a Church of Ireland clergyman (F.B. O'Connell) as the first lecturer made it impossible for Protestant opinion to take alarm on sectarian grounds.'[11] Controversy followed the appoint-

8 'An saoghal Gaedhlach i mBéal-Feirsde', *An tUltach* (Nollaig, 1934), 6.   9 Roger Blaney, *Presbyterians and the Irish Language* (Belfast 1996), p. 186.   10 Seán Mac Airt, 'An Cumann Gaelach, 1906–1956', *Fearsaid, Irish Iubhaile an Chumainn Ghaelaigh* (1956), 9–19.   11 Moody

ment, however. Another Protestant clergyman attacked the new lecturer in print for his interest in Irish; the usual intimidation followed and he had to be put under police protection. O'Connell was a native speaker of Connemara Irish, and a first rate linguist, speaking at least ten languages, including Hebrew, Aramaic, Hindustani and Russian. He published a grammar of Old Irish and a book on the poetry of the Koran (which he apparently knew by heart), edited a version of *The Midnight Court*, an astronomical tract, and *Selections from Keatings Three Shafts of Death*.

He was also highly eccentric. As an undergraduate in TCD he and two other divinity students had established a 'Druidical Society' in which members were forbidden to speak English, drink ginger beer, or mention politics, religion or dialects; they could be expelled for talking sensibly. The society's short-lived magazine, *An tEorpach* (The European), accepted any language but English, and O'Connell edited contributions in Spanish, Dutch, Japanese and Irish. His undergraduate high spirits seem to have followed him into adulthood – he wrote a story in Irish in 1921 called 'The rejuvenation of Ivan Smithovitch'. As a lecturer he was a disaster. He had neither the organizational or political skills to make a success of the post, and loathed giving lectures, marking exams, setting papers and attending faculty meetings. Henry, who had in abundance the skills he lacked, spent most of O'Connell's final decade in Belfast protecting him. At one stage Henry chased him to the railway station to recover that day's examination papers, which O'Connell, the archetypal forgetful scholar, was bringing to Dublin in his pocket. In 1925 his incompetence finally caught up with him and he was sacked.

In Dublin he finally found a job he could do when he was appointed deputy head of the new radio station. Four years later, on his way to lunch with de Valera, he absent-mindedly stepped out in front of a bus and was killed. In death he ran into more trouble – the train that carried his body back to Connemara was met in Clifden by a large crowd of Catholics in what the local press described as 'a state of tense excitement'. The reason for the excitement was that O'Connell was rumoured to have converted to Catholicism – his second wife was Catholic – and the local parish priest had decided he should be buried in a properly consecrated, Catholic graveyard, whether his family wanted this or not. The family eventually succeeded in burying him with his parents, but had to guard his remains overnight.[12]

O'Connell added colour and learning to the life of Irish speaking Belfast. Given his loathing of teaching, he is unlikely to have added much to the sum of the city's speakers. That was left to others. No fewer than three language

& Beckett, *Queen's University Belfast 1845–1949*, 1959, cited in Breathnach & Ní Mhurchú, *Beathaisnéis a Dó* (1990), pp 81–2.   12 Breathnach & Ní Mhurchú, *Beathaisnéis a Dó*, pp 81–3. Seán Mac Airt, *Fearsaid*, pp 13–15. Séamus Ó Searcaigh, 'Is Cumhan Liom', *Fearsaid*, pp 22–4.

courses were written in Belfast in the first twenty years of the century. McGinley based his 1903 course – in Donegal Irish – on the Gouin method. The Belfast Gaelic League had identified the Gouin method, which involved short verb-based action narratives, as early as 1895, and had adapted it to Irish.

Another Customs and Mail officer, Seán Ó Catháin,[13] having learned Munster Irish in London, arrived in Belfast in 1905 and set up a training school following his own version of the Berlitz method, later identified as the 'direct method'. By 1909 Ó Catháin had designed a grammar-based conversational course that was once held in such high regard that it ran through eight editions. More than ninety teachers, two thirds of whom were National School teachers seeking a college certificate in Irish, attended the second course, which was held in the League's new headquarters, 'the walls of which are decorated with all sorts of language charts, and also strange-looking phonetic diagrams, charts and pictures'. The article describing the training school adds a sentence in Irish which notes that 'you would think that it was a doctor's surgery'.[14] Another description says that 'Pictures, charts, diagrams, etc., cover the walls on all sides, so thickly indeed as almost to shock the aesthetic sense.'[15] Among the material decorating the wall was a six feet by eight chart showing the various groups of consonants in columns, and vowel diagrams showing frontal and side views of the lips, tongue and teeth. The college was more than a grind-school for teachers, it provided classes in Classical and Old Irish, Scottish Gaelic, Celtic philology, history and literature as well as modern Irish, and ran a series of public lectures by prominent writers and academics.

The third course, based on the phrase method, was published in 1919. By an odd coincidence, its author's father and brother worked for the Customs and Mail. Fr Dónall Ó Tuathail had learned Irish from old people in the Glens of Antrim when serving there as a priest from 1909 to 1912, and became one of the most revered teachers in the north. A description survives of one of his classes some time between 1916 and his early death in 1922:

> In a large school in Donegall Street I found many classes studying the Gaelic idiom of Tír Chonaill [Donegal]. The largest and most elementary, composed mainly of undernurtured mill workers, was in charge of a small, delicate, keen-eyed priest whose dress was stippled over with chalk and classroom dust.[16]

Both the courses and the teachers were needed to keep up with the demand for classes among all economic groups. In 1902, there were 20 branches of

13 Breathnach & Ní Mhurchú, *Beathaisnéis a hAon*, p. 55. This is the Seaghán [Seán] Ó Catháin who is discussed in the previous essay. 14 *An Claidheamh Soluis*, 24 Nov. 1906. 15 *An Claidheamh Soluis*, 13 April 1906. 16 Séamus Ó Fiannachta, 'A weekend by the Lagan', *Catholic Bulletin*, Jan. 1923, cited in Breathnach & Ní Mhurchú, *Beathaisnéis a Ceathair*, 1994, p. 163.

the League in Belfast alone, and the west Belfast branch was reported to have had 500 members of whom 440 attended classes regularly. A snapshot of the League in this year may be useful. The Belfast District Committee had established premises in Lombard Street, founded a Gaelic choir, staged a couple of plays (one written by the ubiquitous McGinley), and successfully campaigned to have Irish taught in St Mary's Catholic teacher training college on the Falls Road – the first 'professor' of Irish appointed was Fr Gearóid Ó Nualláin, a speaker of Munster Irish and an uncle of Brian O'Nolan/Flann O'Brien/Myles na Gopaleen. What was known as the Irish-Ireland movement was in full swing. Carmichael's Hat Factory in North Street advertized the Irishness of their headgear, and monumental sculptors in Divis Street let it be known that inscriptions in Irish were a speciality. Twelve Belfast branches of the League had established hurling clubs – attending classes in the Irish language and history was compulsory. Irish was also being taught in a number of Catholic primary schools in the city as an optional or extra subject. Significantly, except for the original branch and another one operating from middle-class Mount Merrion, most of the new classes at this time were held in Catholic primary schools and the branches were organized on the basis of Catholic parishes.[17]

Four years later, the movement had taken over an entire building in Murray's Terrace. The new premises, renamed Craobh Ruadh, are described at length:

> The League has secured possession of the entire premises, containing over a dozen rooms. In a few of these one hundred or one hundred and twenty can be comfortably seated, and one (that occupied by the Irish Training School) provides accommodation for about one hundred and sixty persons ... Craobh Ruadh forms probably the largest and best equipped headquarters of the Gaelic League anywhere.[18]

In a comparatively short time, the movement had undergone both an extraordinary expansion and a significant change in its makeup. Since the early 1900s, language activists in Belfast have been overwhelmingly Catholic, a pattern which dominated the movement for the next century. Seán Mac Maoláin became involved as a teenager in the 1890s, and was active in the movement in the city until 1930. From the evidence of his 1969 book, *Gleann Airbh go Glas Naíon*, the circles he moved in appear to have been exclusively Catholic. This may have been a class issue, the Protestants tended to be middle-class and Mac Maoláin and his associates, barring the inevitable scattering of priests,

17 Gearóid Mac Giolla Domhnaigh, *Conradh na Gaeilge Chúige Uladh ag tús an 20ú Chéid*, 1995, pp 108, 127, 139, 142–5, 155, 157.   18 *An Claidheamh Soluis*, 1 Dec. 1906.

schoolteachers and Customs and Mail officers, were working-class. The sole reference to a Protestant Irish speaker in the book relates to a visit to Belfast by Douglas Hyde around 1912, by which time there were few unionists still active in the movement, and the IRB was poised to take it over. Hyde's speech was held in St Mary's hall in Bank Street, and when he argued passionately that language enthusiasts should be motivated by love of Ireland rather than hatred of England, P.T. McGinley responded ('with a twinkle in his eye'): 'I agree with the Craoibhín (Hyde), but, in the absence of that pure love of Ireland, hatred of our English rulers is not at all a bad working substitute.'[19]

McGinley, it should be remembered, hosted the inaugural meeting of the Belfast branch of the League in 1895. By contrast, a 1913 article he wrote for the first and only issue of *Craobh Ruadh,* issued by the Belfast district committee, leaves little room within the movement for unionists. Entitled 'Cá bhFuil ár dTriall?' (Where are we going?) the article analyzes various motivations for learning the language:

> Why do people learn Irish? It is a great deal of trouble for many of us to learn or teach Irish, with perhaps little to show for it at the end. Is it as a pastime or is it to sharpen our intellects so that we can learn some other academic subject better: or do we want to read and discuss Irish literature in the Irish language? It may be worth learning for any of these reasons, but I do not believe that any of the above-mentioned motives is the fundamental or most weighty reason for cultivating Irish. Ordinary people are not interested in these things. We want a more restful pastime than being immersed in books and wrestling with idioms and phonics and the accent of a strange tongue. There are those who would pursue scholarship for its own sake and would learn a language to enable them to acquaint themselves with its literature; but ordinary people would not do anything like that. It is because of nationalism alone, and dignity and racial pride, that ordinary people will take the trouble to learn a new language. It is because of the spirit of nationalism that so many of the people of Ireland learning Irish and having their children learn Irish. And they have that right.[20]

The association of Irish with nationalism, and after 1915 with republicanism, fuelled unionist hostility to the language. This hostility should not be underestimated. In 1920, the unionist leadership, waiting in the wings for

---

19 Mac Maoláin 1969, 78. 20 Cú Uladh (P.T. McGinley) 'Cá bhFuil ár dTriall?' *Craobh Ruadh: Irisleabhar Chonnartha na Gaedhilge ghá chur amach ag muinntir na hArd-Sgoile Ultaighe Béal Feirsde,* May 1913, 9.

the state of Northern Ireland to be established, drew up a blueprint for the survival of the new state. Its message was blunt, and somewhat chilling: 'The essential point to remember is that the Unionists hold that no rebel who wishes to set up a Republic can be regarded as merely a 'political opponent', but must be repressed.'[21] For these leaders of unionism, the word 'rebel' encompassed both constitutional and physical force nationalists, as both wings of the nationalist movement wished to incorporate Northern Ireland into the southern state. The same suspicion applied to Irish language enthusiasts. This crude summary requires some qualification; more sophisticated unionists were aware that the language movement had another tendency which reflected its early principle of political and religious inclusivity, and the movement, even as a nationalist activity, was sometimes seen by pragmatic unionists as being relatively harmless. Mac Maoláin notes with some surprise that the League's headquarters were never raided.

There were two more elements in the unionist mind-set which must be taken into account. Ulster unionism by this point was in the final stage of a redefinition from an Irish unionism – culturally Irish and politically British – to a British unionism which rejected on principle all forms of Irish identity beyond the purely geographical. As there is no more unequivocal manifestation of an Irish cultural identity than the Irish language, interest in the language was itself seen as subversive to the state. As late as 1945, when a nationalist MP, Eddie McAteer, spoke Irish in Stormont, he was interrupted by the minister of Education and the prime minister calling out 'No foreign language here'.[22] Woven through these political and cultural threads was, inescapably, a deeply embedded and ugly sectarianism. Institutional unionist sectarianism found its most dramatic formulation when Northern Ireland's first prime minister defined it as 'a Protestant state for a Protestant people'.

The language movement had expended much of its energies on educational issues, and Irish in the education system became one of the first targets of the new government. Lord Londonderry, the minister of Education, tried but failed to ban the teaching of what he dismissed as 'the so-called Irish language' in St Mary's teacher training college, but had other successes. By 1923 he had abolished the government-funded Organizer for Irish Instruction, limited the amount of time which could be devoted to the language in primary schools as an optional subject, and withdrawn recognition and funding from the two independent Irish language colleges in Belfast. It is possible that even more restrictions may have been put on the teaching of Irish, but at this stage

21 Liam Andrews, '*The very dogs in Belfast will bark in Irish*: The Unionist government and the Irish language 1921–43', in Aodán Mac Póilin (ed.), *The Irish Language in Northern Ireland*, 1997, p. 49. 22 Mac Póilin (ed)., *The Irish language in Northern Ireland*, p. 184.

the language lobby had some leverage. Up to a third of primary schools under Catholic management had refused to recognize the new ministry of Education, and were being funded by the southern government. The campaign lasted from February to December 1922, and according to the Belfastman John Duffin, its chief organizer, the minister's opposition to concessions on the teaching of Irish was the last stumbling block in the negotiations.[23]

However, in 1924 a new set of regulations restricted the teaching of Irish as an optional subject to the upper classes of the primary system. It was then marginalized to the outer edges of a crowded curriculum. Of the optional subjects, at least two had to be chosen from the A-List of subjects, history, science, nature study or horticulture; only then could Irish be chosen from a list which included French, Latin, algebra or geometry. As a result, the numbers of primary schools teaching Irish as an optional subject was halved – to 78 – between 1924 and 1927. In response to the squeeze on Irish as an optional subject, teachers and pupils had begun to switch to the only alternative within the curriculum, the teaching of Irish as an extra subject for fees, and increasing numbers took up Irish as a fee-paying subject (from third standard up). In 1926 the ministry of Education banned the teaching of Irish in the third and fourth standards, resulting, within a year, in a drop of 70 percent in the numbers studying the subject. Between 1923 and 1926 the numbers studying Irish as an extra subject in Northern Ireland fell from 5,531 to 1,290, and in 1934 the subsidy towards Irish as an extra subject was finally withdrawn.

Given the polarization of attitudes to the language and the unchallenged power of the Unionist Party in Northern Ireland, it is perhaps surprising that Irish survived within the education system at all. Its survival may have been partly due to a decision taken by pragmatic unionists not to ban Irish outright from the education system, but to marginalize it, and to make whatever teaching was undertaken as ineffective as possible. Lord Charlemont, Londonderry's successor, provided the most quotable rationale for this policy in 1933, one which demonstrates the centrality of west Belfast to the language movement: 'forbidding [Irish] under pressure will stimulate it to such an extent that the very dogs in Belfast – at any rate the Falls Road dogs – will bark in Irish.'[24] Charlemont may have been the most liberal of the ministers of Education during the period; in an internal memorandum to the prime minister he did make a case for the academic study of Irish as the ancient language of Ireland, but any public statement aimed at a unionist audience, while avoiding the gratuitous abuse of other ministers, was uncompromising:

> There is no doubt that the fact that some recognition is given Irish by the Ministry has greatly disarmed criticism on the part of anti-

23 Andrews 1997, 63–4.　24 Ibid., 81.

British elements in the population, while the actual results in spreading a knowledge of the language are insignificant.[25]

In the early years of the state, there was little resistance to the under-
mining of Irish in the education system. The instability and violence which
accompanied partition had left the Gaelic League demoralized and in disar-
ray in the north. Liam Andrews, an authority on the history of the language
movement in Northern Ireland, could find records of only one branch, in
Belfast, which was still functioning in 1923.[26] Mac Maoláin gives an account
of his efforts to keep the language revival work going during this troubled
period, sometimes travelling through sniper fire to maintain his classes.[27]

Early in 1926, Fr Lorcán Ó Muireadhaigh made the eminently sensible
suggestion that, as the condition of the language in the two jurisdictions was
significantly different, the Gaelic League should be organized separately within
the six counties of Northern Ireland. He was immediately accused of parti-
tionism, a serious charge in Irish language circles at the time, and particularly galling for a priest with an impressive republican record.[28] Ó
Muireadhaigh was a fine scholar and a superb organizer with a short fuse and
a domineering personality. He was also a dialect bigot and, as we shall see, a
Catholic triumphalist. His response to the accusation was to form a new organization, Comhaltas Uladh (The Ulster fellowship), for the ten counties of
Ulster (Louth was annexed to Ulster on dialect grounds, but it may be no
coincidence that Ó Muireadhaigh was himself a Louthman).

It is a testament to the force of Ó Muireadhaigh's personality that, with
Seán Mac Maoláin's help, he succeeded in establishing Comhaltas Uladh
before the end of the year. He also used the Catholic church effectively: of
the twenty members of its first executive committee, twelve were priests.[29]
Comhaltas Uladh remained technically within the Gaelic League but it was,
and still is, effectively independent, guarding that independence with a jeal-
ously approaching paranoia. The achievements of Comhaltas Uladh, particularly in its first three or four decades, were in the circumstances remarkable.
In 1926 there were only a handful of branches of the Gaelic League in the
north. This rose to 78 by 1940, peaked at 182 in 1946, and averaged 155 per
annum over the next nine years.[30] Its involvement in the Gaeltacht summer
colleges provided exposure to the language in a natural setting to tens of thousands of learners, and, where the teaching was effective, a high standard of
tuition. The continuing importance of these colleges in stimulating interest

25 Ibid., 80. 26 Liam Andrews, 'Unionism and nationalism and the Irish language, 1893–1933',
PhD thesis, Queen's University Belfast, 2000, p. 143. 27 Seán Mac Maoláin, *Ó Ghleann Airbh
go Glas Naíon* (1969), pp 135–7. 28 Proinsias Mac Aonghusa, *Ar Son na Gaeilge, Conradh na
Gaeilge, 1893–1993* (1993), p. 221. 29 Andrews 2000, 205. 30 Liam Andrews, 'The Irish

in Irish and establishing social networks among young speakers and learners of Irish cannot be overestimated.

The greatest achievement of Comhaltas Uladh may have been in ensuring that Irish maintained a presence in the education system in Northern Ireland. The organization made its first approach to government in February 1927, when a deputation, which included Ó Muireadhaigh, five other Catholic clergy and a nationalist MP, met the minister of Education, and argued that Irish should be restored to the status it had in 1922. They were unsuccessful, endured the minister telling them that Irish was dead or dying and that French would be much more useful, but did get one concession, the restoration of Irish as an optional subject in standards three and four – as an alternative to history. This was actually the revival of an earlier strategy; as far back as 1922 the ministry had considered linking Irish and history as alternative options, on the principle that the kind of Irish history which would be taught in Catholic schools would be even more subversive than the language.

This tiny concession, finally formulated in a ministry circular in March 1928, was the subject of a unionist backlash in June from the extremist Loyalty League, whose membership was 'confined solely to men and women of British race and blood.' The League reproached the Ministry with a charge that still has resonance; some things never change:

> As loyal subjects of his Majesty the King, we strongly resent this pandering to a cunning foe, for although presented in the form of an optional subject, it can soon be arranged that each school will require a Gaelic teacher, even in Protestant districts, and each teacher will be as a rule a secret fomenter of strife.[31]

If unionist opinion on the language question could range from the patriarchal condescension of Charlemont to the knuckle-trailing intensity of the Loyalty League, those who supported the language were by no means monolithic. By the time Comhaltas Uladh was founded, the transition from an inclusive language movement that genuinely hoped to sidestep sectarianism and politics, to one more or less dominated by a Catholic/nationalist ethos, was complete. However, even within that narrowing of its terms of reference, there was still a wide ideological range within the movement.

The principle of inclusivity remained, as it were, on the statute-books. Sometimes the non-sectarian non political mantra was trotted out, cynically, to a world that, in as far the world took notice, was deeply sceptical of the

language in the education system of Northern Ireland: some political and cultural perspectives', in R.M.O. Prichard (ed.), *Motivating the majority: modern languages in Northern Ireland*, 1991, pp 97–8. 31 Andrews, 1997, 74

claim. Sometimes the non-sectarian principle was used to disguise the intention to use culture to convert unionists to nationalism. The movement did, however, involve a number of people who clung to the old ideal; this it must be said, was by no means a majority activity, but it remained remarkably durable. During the *dáil mhór* [AGM] of Comhaltas Uladh in 1931, for example, a number of delegates proposed, without success, that the organization drop the references in its constitution to a free and Gaelic Ireland that had been inserted in 1915 by a clique led by the IRB. Their hope, admirably unrealistic in the context of its time and place, was that this might encourage Orangemen to join.[32] We will be examining later another attempt in the 1940s to side-step the reductive political and religious structures of Belfast.

Irish nationalism consisted of a number of overlapping ideological strands, two of the most important of which were a secular republicanism which had its roots in the enlightenment principles of the eighteenth-century United Irishmen, and an instinctive Catholic nationalism with its roots in the religious wars of the sixteenth and seventeenth centuries. That these very different ideologies could be blurred in everyday discourse does not negate the profound differences between them. The latter half of the nineteenth century had also seen the growth of ultramontanism – a rigidly centralized and reactionary Catholicism with theocratic tendencies – in the institutional church. Unionists, with their exaggerated attachment to the British crown and empire, were hostile to secular republicanism, but the triumphalist tendencies within contemporary Irish Catholicism, as demonstrated south of the border, scared them witless.

For a long time, Catholic nationalism was in the ascendant among the nationalist community in Northern Ireland, and was itself reinforced by social forces. One of the hallmarks of Catholicism, both in doctrine and practice, is a highly developed sense of social cohesion. After partition, institutionalized discrimination by successive unionist governments in Northern Ireland towards its Catholic minority forced the community to develop this to an exaggerated level, a phenomenon described by observers in recent times as 'Catholic communalism', and experienced by many of its dissidents as Catholic coercion. But it worked. In an extremely effective form of passive resistance, cultural, social and sporting activities among the Catholic community in Northern Ireland were organized as an alternative society within the state, usually on a the basis of parishes. Catholic communalism was itself reinforced on an institutional basis by segregated education and on a social basis by the fact that much of Belfast is divided into exclusively Catholic and Protestant areas. It could be argued that, whatever harm it has done in other ways, the ghettoization of Belfast actually worked to the advantage of the language movement.

32 Andrews 2000, 264.

Irish in Belfast became integrated into this matrix of resistance. For both unionists and nationalists it was a highly emblematic cultural expression of resistance to the state. To the nationalist community it was a source of communal and personal dignity, even for those who could not speak it. Comhaltas Uladh could not have ignored the only institution that had the power to deliver the survival of the language in the education system, and given the times that were in it and the nature of the organization's founder, it is unlikely that they wished to do so. As a result, the organization was dominated by what Liam Andrews describes as its clerical faction; ten of its sixteen presidents between 1926 and 1970 were Catholic clergy,[33] and every public event swarmed with Catholic churchmen, supplemented by a sprinkling of Catholic teachers and an occasional constitutional nationalist politician.

While one is left with a sense of an organization whose ethos was overwhelmingly Catholic, the Irish language movement was not entirely monolithic, and other factions also existed quietly within and on the edges of Comhaltas Uladh. A police report of one public meeting held in a Catholic parish hall in Belfast in October 1927 noted the presence in the hall (but not on the platform) of 'local suspects and a large number of past and present members of the IRA.' Inevitably, the majority of these would have been from a Catholic background, although the republican movement always had a thread of anti-clericalism running through it, and a tiny number of Protestant members. The public face was, however, clerical and constitutional. At this particular meeting the speakers included Bishop (later Cardinal) MacRory, seven priests, including Ó Muireadhaigh, and Lord Ashbourne, an eccentric, bekilted, Catholic peer of the realm who regularly addressed the House of Lords in Irish. Joe Devlin, the leader of the constitutional nationalist party, sent his apologies, and the event was closed by a song from the Christian Brothers' choir.

The range of opinions from the platform is instructive. MacRory's address was couched in an inclusive language which was subverted by the reality of the platform party, but was doubtless sincerely meant:

> You do not ask a man or woman when they come to you whether they are orange or green – whether they are republicans or unionists. Every man and woman, every boy and girl who wants to learn the Irish language … is welcome. Anywhere in the world, and especially in the city of Belfast that has been torn by dissension, any movement … that brings the people together is doing a public service deserving of support.

Ó Muireadhaigh, always combative, took a significantly different tack. He severely criticized the Catholic Truth Society for not using Irish, although

33 *An tUltach*, March 1972, 6 (cited in: Gordon McCoy, 'Protestants and the Irish language', PhD thesis, Queen's University Belfast, 1997, p. 85).

the language movement was, he said, doing the work of God in fighting a battle against English civilization, whose values were represented in the cinema, the newspapers, the dance halls and the jazz dresses in shop windows (this was the era of the flapper, whose short dresses outraged puritans throughout the western world).

Andrews comments that Ó Muireadhaigh's language activism was permeated 'by his desire to protect the values of rural patriarchal Irish Catholic society from Anglicization and modernism'.[34] Indeed, his agenda was capable of going even further than his obsession with short dresses, jazz and the debilitating moral effects of the mass media. Andrews records a speech given by Ó Muireadhaigh, again in Belfast, in September 1932:

> The Gaelic League is fighting to keep the old civilisation of our country alive. It is a fight between the civilisation which Patrick started at Tara, Saul and Armagh, and the civilisation begun by Martin Luther and has carried on since, the fruits of which we see today ... We want to make Ireland what she was, a great Catholic and Gaelic nation that had her own pride and glory and that brought the Faith and civilisation to the rest of the world.[35]

Ó Muireadhaigh was not the first member of the clerical faction to take such an extreme position. In 1929, another member of the Comhaltas Uladh executive, Fr Clenaghan, had described the Irish language as 'a rampart of defence against the principles of the Reformation', and as 'a sacred tongue interwoven with the spirit of faith', while English was 'the language of the foreigner impressed by the blighting cold of Protestantism.'[36] Without the overt sectarianism of remarks such as these, similar sentiments can be detected underlying statements from other leading members of Comhaltas Uladh – the word 'pagan' was often used to describe England and Anglicization, and came to include the Americanization of popular culture through film and music, but may have been a code word for anything Ó Muireadhaigh and his friends disapproved of.

While these ideological battles were being waged, some people got on with the job of reviving the language. Mac Maoláin describes his last major project in Belfast, the building of the *ardscoil*, the League's headquarters, in 1928. This had involved the delicate task of bringing together constitutional nationalists and republicans, and had one major gimmick, an invitation to Éamon de Valera to open the key fund-raising event. The RUC warned Mac Maoláin not to proceed with the invitation. De Valera indicated that he was not particularly keen to challenge the northern authorities without good reason, but

34 Andrews 2000, 218–20.   35 Ibid., 265–6.   36 Ibid., 253.

[NO. I.]

Bolg an Tsolair:

OR,

GÆLIC MAGAZINE.

CONTAINING

Laoi na Sealga:

OR, THE FAMOUS FENIAN POEM, CALLED

THE CHASE;

WITH A COLLECTION OF CHOICE

IRISH SONGS,

TRANSLATED BY MISS BROOKE.

TO WHICH IS PREFIXED, AN ABRIDGMENT OF

IRISH GRAMMAR;

WITH

A VOCABULARY, AND FAMILIAR DIALOGUES.

BELFAST:

PRINTED AT THE NORTHERN STAR-OFFICE.

1795.

1 Title page of *Bolg an tSolair or Gaelic Magazine* (1795); courtesy
Belfast Central Library.

2 Dr William Neilson.   3 Dr James MacDonnell.

4 The Ulster Unionist Convention of 1892 with its Erin-go-Bragh slogan.

5 Crooked Lane, later Chapel Lane, Belfast; courtesy PRONI.

6 Fishdealer, Belfast, *c*.1905; courtesy PRONI.

7 Coláiste Chomhghaill's certificate in teaching Irish awarded to Seán Beckett, signed by Seaghán Ó Catháin, 1909; courtesy Anna Beckett.

8 An Ardscoil Ultach, headquarters of the Belfast Gaelic League in Queen's Sreet, 1913; courtesy Cormac Ó hAdhmaill.

9 Modh Díreach charts used in Ardscoil classes; courtesy Anna Beckett.

10 Advertisement in *Craobh Ruadh*, a Gaelic League publication, 1913.

11 Advertisement in *Craobh Ruadh* for Eudhmonn Mac Aonghusa, tobacconist, the first Belfast shopkeeper to display his name in Irish above his shop (1901).

12 Irish volunteers marching in Smithfield, *c.*1914; courtesy PRONI.

13 Belfast Gaelic League group at Coláiste Bhríde, Omeath, in 1916 with Fr Dónall Ó Tuathail (seated, right); courtesy Anna Beckett.

14 P.T. McGinley
(Peadar Toner Mac Fhionnlaoich).

15 Seán Mac Maoláin.

16 Opening night of Cumann Chluain Ard's new premises in Hawthorn Street, 1944, with Séamus Mac Fearáin as 'fear an tí' and Alf Ó Muireadhaigh (Lurgan) as guest speaker (both men were later to become presidents of the GAA); courtesy Méabha Uí Chriagáin.

17 Thomas Davis centenary march, Oakman Street, Falls Road, Belfast, 1945; courtesy Marcas Ó Murchú.

18 *Scoraíocht* (social evening) for young people attending the Ardoyne branch of Gaelic League in 1950.

19 Aisteoirí Naomh Bríd actors rehearsing in 1950 (left to right) Eibhlín Vaughan, Méabha Uí Chriagáin, Seosamh Mistéil, Bob Crombie (director).

20

21

22

20 Committee of Cumann Chluain Ard, 1962 (left to right) Liam Ó Duibhir,
Seán Mac Aindreasa, Alf Ó Murchú (chair), Bríd Nic an tSionnaigh,
Tomás Ó Monacháin (secretary); Séamus de Brún (treasurer); courtesy *An tUltach*.

21 Bríd Nic Gaoithín of An Ceann Garbh, Co. Donegal, teaching in Cumann Chluain
Ard 1962; courtesy *An tUltach*.

22 Staff and pupils of the first Meánscoil in 1978 (left to right) Máire Mhic Sheáin, Áine
Mhic Aindreasa, Bríd Mhic Sheáin, Colm Mac Aindreasa, Conall Ó Coisneacháin, Adam
Mac Giolla Chatháin, Eilis Ní Bhruadair, Nuala Nic Sheáin; courtesy Séamus Mac Seáin.

23 Orange Order banner of the 1303 lodge, Ireland's Heritage.

24 Loyalist mural, Ballybeen estate.

25 Slogan in Irish on wall of former Andersonstown RUC barracks in 2005 from
Seosamh Mac Grianna's Irish translation of the song
'The Bold Fenian Men'; courtesy *Lá*.

26 New houses completed at Shaws Road, 2006, with one of the first residents, Séamus Mag Aoidh.

27 Nan O'Hara of Meleady's fruit shop, Falls Road, whose grandparents were 'Fadgies' from Omeath; courtesy Brendan Murphy, *Irish News*.

that he would follow the advice of the organizing committee. The committee decided to cancel the invitation, and Mac Maoláin telegrammed de Valera to inform him of the decision. On leaving the post office, he was met by a priest who was outraged by the committee's decision, had brought the chairman (another priest) around to his point of view, and rescinded the decision. This behaviour was extraordinary, but is a fair indication of the power of the Catholic clergy within their community at the time, and their uncontested dominance of the language movement in the north. The unfortunate Mac Maoláin had to send a second telegram, de Valera took a northbound train, was arrested in Newry and tried in Belfast. After addressing the judge in (Munster) Irish, he was held to be in contempt of court and sent to prison for a month. It was a month well spent; such was the outrage that money poured in. The *ardscoil* was built in Divis Street and remained the headquarters of the League in the city until it was accidentally burnt down in 1985.

A split developed immediately within the Belfast Gaelic League. Some republican members were indignant that the Devlinite nationalists had been given too much credit during the fund-raising drive, feared that they could take over the movement in Belfast, and began one of those destructive power struggles which plague minority language movements. This turn of events disgusted Mac Maoláin so much that he resigned from the League in 1929 and the following year he left Belfast for Dublin, where he spent the rest of his life.

By the mid-1930s the Irish language lobby and the government had reached a kind of uneasy equilibrium on the issue of Irish in the education system. Comhaltas Uladh then turned its attention to the radio. Broadcasting was controlled by London, which was comparatively relaxed about broadcasting minority languages, indeed, the BBC had broadcast programmes in Scottish Gaelic and Welsh since the 1920s. As it turned out, Irish was barely heard or seen on BBC Northern Ireland until 1981. Comhaltas Uladh made representations in 1936 for programmes in Irish, especially lessons in the language. This request was considered by the local regional director, George Marshall, a morose and gloomy Scot who had been startled to earn the social acceptance of the unionist ministers he met in the Reform Club. He turned the request down: 'The number of Gaelic speakers in Northern Ireland is negligible, and, as far as schools are concerned, the proportion of those where the Irish language is taught is quite small and is practically confined to secondary schools.'[37] However, the representations did have some effect; the request to help learners of the language was ignored, but for a couple of years a live broadcast of the Derry *feis* included a number of songs in Irish.

37 Rex Cathcart, *The most contrary region: the BBC in Northern Ireland, 1924–1984* (1984), p. 85.

In the early 1940s, at a time when the war was going badly, the British government considered initiating a charm offensive on southern Ireland, which was then still a member of the Commonwealth. With this in mind, the Dominions Office in 1940 proposed to the BBC that a 'Gaelic period' be broadcast 'ostensibly for the benefit of Gaelic speaking people in Northern Ireland and among the Irish population of English and Scottish cities.' In the best traditions of BBC independence, Marshall consulted Andrews, the prime minister of Northern Ireland, for whom Irish was 'a language expressive of separatism',[38] received a predictable reaction, and responded frostily to the proposal:

> I do not quite understand what the Dominions Office mean by the introduction of a Gaelic period into the programmes broadcast from the Belfast station ... you might point out that there are no Gaelic speakers in Northern Ireland, by which I assume is meant Erse or Irish ... it would be most unwise to introduce the Irish language into programmes from the transmitter in Northern Ireland, as this would certainly bring a great deal of criticism from listeners in this Region.[39]

Marshall had bought so completely into the unionist Ulsterization programme that he was pursuing a bizarre censorship of Irish culture in the BBC. The results of Gaelic sports fixtures, played mainly by non-Sabbatarian Catholics on Sunday, were not broadcast until Monday, by which time, in Rex Cathcart's words, 'they were history, not news', and Marshall carpeted the distinguished broadcaster Sam Hanna Bell for giving air time to the Belfast Gaelic Choir.[40] In 1943 he even managed to block a proposal from BBC Scotland to broadcast a golden jubilee celebration of the Gaelic League in Glasgow.[41]

About the same time that these battles were being lost, the seeds of a new development in the language movement were sown when the O'Neill Crowley GAA club set up a branch of the Gaelic League in the Clonard district of west Belfast in 1936. None of the original members could speak Irish fluently. Two years later, in 1938, with one fluent learner and two native speakers,[42] the branch acquired new premises, renamed itself 'Cumann Chluain Ard' and began to expand. This development was not halted by the internment of some of its members during the Second World War. Cumann Chluain Ard was rather more radical than other branches of Comhaltas Uladh at the time; its membership was mostly working-class, republican and left-leaning. Because the club had no links with the church, it attracted the militant, the disaffected and the mildly disreputable – artists, actors, Protestant nationalists, Esperanto

---

38 Cathcart 1984, 199.   39 Cathcart 1984, 111.   40 Cathcart 1984, 142.   41 Cathcart 1984, 127.   42 *Glór Uladh 1893–1943: Féile Leith-chéad an Chonnartha*, 1943, 108; *Leabhar Túirisge Chumann Chluain Árd*, Membership list, 16 Oct. 1938.

enthusiasts, free-thinkers and communists as well as republicans and a sprinkling of ordinary decent citizens. Early on, the club introduced an important
innovation, when Tuesdays became Irish-only nights.

Cumann Chluain Ard moved to new, much larger premises in 1944 and
for the next nine years the club worked on a broad front with a distinct
nationalist and socialist agenda. Two consciousness-raising pageants 'Ireland
Live On' and 'One Easter Morn' were staged between 1950 and 1952. A pamphlet produced about this time gives some flavour of the group's ideology:
'the language and its natural corollary, Irish nationalism, will take its place in
the public life of Belfast.' The pamphlet attempted to grapple with economic
realities: 'a Gaelic Speaking Ireland was not something mystical or abstract,
but a definite cultural and economic objective', and called for the language
to be aligned with the social and economic consciousness of the Irish worker
'who should be made to understand that the revival of the language is not of
only academic interest but an essential part of the age-long struggle in Ireland
for freedom.'[43]

In 1953 the club became involved in a campaign organized by a radical
group of language activists in the Republic to have a proper support structure
for the Irish speaking districts of the west of Ireland. They persuaded the normally staid Belfast district committee to back the campaign, called *Sábháil an
Ghaeltacht* [Save the Gaeltacht], and made a couple of serious tactical mis-
takes, refusing, for example, to speak English to reporters, and being run out
of Dundalk for their over-vigorous criticism of local politicians. This activity
proved to be a turning point, changing the group from a broad-front Irish-
Ireland cultural organization with an interest in the language, to one deeply
implicated in linguistic politics. The same year, the club became an 'English-
free zone', initiating what became known among its critics as 'The great purge
of '53.' From that point, Cumann Chluain Ard was to have a fraught relationship with Comhaltas Uladh, establishing a pattern of noisily leaving the
organization at irregular intervals and then storming back vengefully.

In 1953 the club also underwent a significant ideological transition. Its
radical stance on the language issue had caused a significant number of its
members to question the relationship between the language movement and
politics, both in the sense of political parties and political ideologies. They
believed that where the interests of a political ideology and those of the language clashed, the political ideology tended to prevail. They argued that political parties, as soon as they got into power, temporized and wriggled but
always betrayed the language. The Gaeltacht campaign had been partially suc-

---

43 Mag Aonghusa, n. date (*c*.1950–3?), quoted in: Camille C. O'Reilly, 'Teanga Dúchais: the
Irish Language and Ethnic Identity in west Belfast', MA thesis, Queen's University Belfast,
1992, pp 48–9. I am indebted to my colleague Gordon McCoy for drawing my attention to this
source.

cessful, resulting in the establishment of a Ministry for the Gaeltacht, but, uniquely among Irish-language groups in the north, Cumann Chluain Ard subjected the new ministry in the Republic to heavy criticism, even before the new minister had time to make a pig's ear of drawing the Gaeltacht boundaries. The Catholic Church at this period was entering its long retreat from the language, proving that no church could be trusted either (members picketed the local bishop in the 1970s). Politics and religion were therefore left at the door. In a strange but satisfying completion of the circle, Cumann Chluain Ard had repossessed the ideals of the early Gaelic League.

The club attracted a number of highly idealistic activists who became involved in various experiments, not all of them with the blessing of the organization. One group tried to revitalize the economy of the Gaeltacht by setting up a factory in Gweedore. Another loosely associated group tried to establish an alternative language-based economy in Belfast, setting up a newspaper, shops and services, and a barter system. Both schemes failed through an excess of idealism compounded by insufficient capital or business expertise. A later attempt to set up a bank, on the model of the Credit Union system, was better thought out, but failed to develop. One group became involved in the organization Misneach [Courage], led by the writer Máirtín Ó Cadhain, which was regarded by most of the Irish language establishment as being very extreme.

Comhaltas Uladh had long been stuck in an intellectual rut. As well as its stultifying conservatism, the organization failed to develop a strategic vision, continuing to act as if the priorities of 1926 were the only possible priorities, as if a course of action undertaken in the era of the flapper was not a response to the circumstances and ideology of its time, but true for all time and in all circumstances. The organization failed to embrace new approaches and new thinking on language maintenance or revival. Unconventional approaches were what Cumann Chluain Ard did best, and possibly the most unconventional development of the twentieth-century language movement in Belfast was the founding of the Shaw's Road Gaeltacht in Belfast. This belongs to a period outside the scope of this essay – the first meeting to establish the new community taking place in 1961, but that development can be understood only in the context of its organizational and ideological background.

Cumann Chluain Ard was not the only important development in the period between the 1930s and 1950s. Crises seem to bring the issue of identity to the forefront of people's consciousness, and the war years had seen an increase in language activity, the most interesting of which took place, not on the back-streets of the Falls Road, but in Crumlin Road Jail. The IRA, acting on the principle that England's difficulty was Ireland's opportunity, sided with Germany during the Second World War. As a result, thousands of active IRA-men, with a sprinkling of retired IRA-men, brothers of IRA-men, and people who looked as if they might have been IRA-men were interned during the war.

In the enforced leisure of imprisonment without trial, republicans traditionally learn Irish, and Belfast became one of the most effective centres for language transmission on the island: the other was the Curragh in Kildare.

Tarlach Ó hUid, our main source for the language movement in Crumlin Road Jail, was something of a fantasist, which undermines the value of his testimony. He claimed to have been baptized Terence Samuel Caesar Augustus Walter Hood in Deptford, London in 1917. Only the first and last names are true, and there appears to be no basis for his claim that his parents came from the north of Ireland. At the age of eighteen he joined the Greenshirt Movement for Social Credit, a fringe radical group equally opposed to Fascism and capitalism, but enthusiastic about the street-politics of the time. Ó hUid began to learn Irish in London, swapped his green shirt for a kilt, came to Ireland, converted briefly to Catholicism, joined the IRA and became involved in a border bombing campaign. After a period in Dublin learning bomb-making skills, he was transferred to Belfast on the outbreak of the Second World War.

Ó hUid had strong anti-sectarian principles, filling the pages of *War News* with quotations from the United Irishmen and John Mitchel, and his language enthusiasm found expression in a section entitled 'useful sentences in Irish', with examples such as 'throw the hand-grenade', and 'aim the rifle at him'.[44] The second volume of Ó hUid's autobiography, *Faoi Ghlas* (In Prison) deals with his five years of internment, most of which was spent in Crumlin Road Jail. If he is to be believed, when the internees in Crumlin Road Jail founded a Gaelic Society in 1941 there were fewer than ten reasonably fluent speakers among them; by the following year there were seventy-five who spoke only Irish to each other, and by 1945 fluent speakers were to be counted in their hundreds.[45] Prison was to have an effect on the class profile of (male) Irish speakers in the city:

> The boys of Company F were the poorest, and most unhealthy-looking of any I met in the IRA. They had been born and raised in tiny kitchen houses in the back streets of the Pound Loney on the Falls Road, ill-fed, ill-clothed, barely educated, all of them of below average height, all skinny, pasty-faced ... In prison, nearly all of them did their level best to learn and speak Irish, and some of them became fully fluent.[46]

The Catholic church had worked out a *modus vivendi* with republicans; left-wingers were another story entirely. Since the Russian revolution the church

---

44 Tarlach Ó hUid, *Ar Thóir mo Shealbha*, 1960, 181.　45 Tarlach Ó hUid, *Faoi Ghlas* (1985), 70, 72, 135.　46 Ibid., 51–2.

had been obsessed by 'atheistic communism' and saw socialism as the first dangerous step in that direction. In 1931, at the height of the depression, Pope Pius XI published an encyclical warning his flock that they could not be both Catholics and socialists, and asking those who had drifted into socialism to return to the bosom of the church. Those leftists who were involved in the language movement were inevitably regarded with suspicion by the clerical faction.

The clerical axe fell, however, not on the subversives of Cumann Chluain Ard, who probably were too unimportant to show on the church's radar, but on one of the most prominent figures in Comhaltas Uladh in Belfast. Cathal McCrystal, a fervent if independent-minded Catholic, and a prominent trade unionist, took part in a cultural delegation to Russia in 1955, and incautiously praised the USSR for its treatment of women. He returned to a storm of abuse, and was denounced from numerous altars and in the pages of the nationalist newspaper, the *Irish News*. According to his son, Comhaltas Uladh disassociated itself from him; he was removed as chairman of the Belfast district committee, was sacked as editor of *An tUltach*, the journal he had edited for twenty years, and many of his former friends never spoke to him again in any language. Other versions indicate that he was treated to a relatively short period of quarantine until clerical wrath could find another target. McCrystal, an imperturbable little man with a great flair for the dramatic, used to ostentatiously read a Russian-language missal during Sunday mass in his local church.[47]

McCrystal was among those who were distressed by the exclusivity of the language movement. In 1943 he wrote an introduction in Irish to a handbook celebrating the half-centenary of the League in which he insisted that the celebrations, which, while well earned, were flawed because 'only the Catholics of the Province are involved. We could easily, by ignoring Protestants, create a division between us that is more powerful than the political gulf that separates us. We have to show them that we want their assistance and their company, that this heritage belongs to them too ...'[48]

Tarlach Ó hUid, freshly released from prison, also believed that the language could and should transcend politics and religion. In the late 1940s, he managed to establish a class in the premises of the Young Men's Christian Association in Belfast specifically aimed at Protestants. The group called itself the Gaelic Fellowship, and had two teachers, Seán Pasker and Drew Donaldson. Pasker, a civil servant from Dublin who had left Ireland after the 1916 Rebellion and learned his Irish in London, spoke Munster Irish; Donaldson spoke a Donegal dialect and each had a hearty contempt for the

---

47 Cal McCrystal, *Reflections on a Quiet Rebel* (1997) (London, 1998), pp 110–15. 48 Cathal Mac Criostáil, *Glór Uladh 1893–1943: Féile Leith-chéad an Chonnartha* (1943), pp 7–8.

dialect of the other. Some of the group were nationalists, and mixed easily with Catholic Irish speakers when Pasker arranged visits to Irish language events run by Comhaltas Uladh, but others found it more difficult to do so. This left a deficit in the opportunities to practise the language, and in 1955 the teachers approached the secretary of the YMCA to suggest that fluent Catholics should be invited into the classes to help. Donaldson reported indignantly to a friend that the response was less than full-hearted, and that it looked as if there was a question mark over whether or not Catholics could be recognized as Christians. The idea was not pursued by the teachers, but at a later date, one of the class members invited a young Catholic woman to come along. Finding this situation rather daunting, she brought two Catholic friends with her. Within a short time a number of 'big Catholic lads' had joined the group, and Pasker became alarmed, as this was breaking the conditions under which he had rented the premises. In early 1961 he drafted a letter to the class, to inform them that all members of the Gaelic Fellowship would be required to register as associate members of the YMCA. As none of the Catholics would be eligible to join the YMCA, they would obviously have to leave the class.

There was no way in which this situation could have turned out well, but in the event it turned out as badly as it could have. One of the members pre-empted the letter by disclosing its contents to the Catholics. Her own sister immediately resigned, followed by Donaldson and another member, complaining that if Harold Meek, a Jew, could attend, fellow Christians should not be excluded. The three who resigned were all nationalists. The class continued until 1966, although often without an effective teacher; Seán Pasker suffered a series of strokes and died in 1965.[49]

This period begins and ends with two attempts to maintain the Irish language without the endemic sectarianism and reductive politics that blight Belfast. Both failed. Against the odds, however, the language has survived and sometimes thrived. Against the odds it may still be possible in the future to grow and sustain a language community that genuinely embraces the entire population.

---

49 I am indebted to my colleague Gordon McCoy for use of his unpublished account of these events.

The Shaw's Road urban Gaeltacht: role and impact

GABRIELLE NIG UIDHIR

The decline, resilience, survival and changing fortunes of the Irish language have been documented from many historical perspectives. Most historical frameworks include some reference to the impact of colonization and the subsequent language shift and emergence of bilingualism which has survived into modern Ireland. Social, economic and political forces impact upon the nature of the competitive relationship between the indigenous language and the national and international currency of the more dominant English language. Joshua Fishman discusses the difficulty of saving threatened languages within the context of America-dominated globalization (2001: 6–9). The Irish language is also under intense pressure to hold its own as a living, spoken language with a cultural, educational and economic value in the twenty-first century. The Shaw's Road initiative will be identified by future historians as an important strategic step in light of the social, political and economic environment of its time.

Shaw's Road Gaeltacht has shaped the functional development of the language by giving it a more significant urban relevance and by sharpening and strengthening its function within education. The growth of Irish-medium education during the years since that first *bunscoil* (primary school) was opened in 1971, has catapulted the language onto a new economic and social platform. Today's population of Irish speaking pupils and past pupils requires third-level educational facilities through the medium of Irish. They expect to find employment choices which include opportunities for Irish speakers. They also expect their educational, economic and social experiences to be enhanced by their bilingual competence. When the Shaw's Road parents founded a *bunscoil* for nine young children, over three decades ago, they created a challenge for that younger generation and for subsequent generations to meet those expectations. High targets were set to influence the reversal of a language shift which had already eliminated the Irish language through most of the country. How could one small group of people achieve so much? Hopefully, in this chapter, the reader will gain some insights into key factors influencing the emergence of this community and also into some of the ways in which it has inspired, moulded, shaped and guided a much more extensive language development.

The emergence of a Gaeltacht settlement on the periphery of west Belfast in the late 1960s represented a key link in a chain of projects and developments. Even the smallest and most fleeting of these other language-related initiatives played a role in leading Irish speakers towards a clear and determined conclusion: that there was a need for a cohesive community nucleus where Irish speaking families could interact together through Irish, raising their children in a supportive linguistic environment and providing education in the children's first language. In the mid 1960s, the pattern of Irish speaking in the city was characterized by activities supporting second language learning and by a cluster of families who attempted to raise their children through Irish while living in English speaking neighbourhoods. One newspaper article in 1965 refers to the existence of thirty-six Irish speaking families in Belfast at that time (*Irish Press*, 14 November 1965).

Founding members of the Shaw's Road Community refer to their growing awareness of the difficulties and challenges experienced by these earlier families during the 1950s and 1960s. As young adults, although still engaged in learning the language themselves, they had some opportunities to interact with this slightly older generation of Irish speakers at Irish language clubs, societies and through other social activities. On the one hand, the fact that some families, living in various parts of the city, managed to raise their children with Irish was inspiring for the Shaw's Road generation. On the other, it was apparent that these families had to plan and organize opportunities for their children to meet Irish speaking peers. Contact with the traditional Gaeltacht areas, particularly in Donegal, was highly valued by these families as one way to support their use of Irish. Some of these families managed to raise the first child through Irish, but younger children were raised through English. The experience of being different was not perceived as a positive one by all the children. Some children rejected the language for periods of years. Others responded positively and even went on to become active promoters of the language in adulthood. In various families, some of the siblings have raised their own children bilingually. This choice is not uniform and some siblings decided not to use Irish in their own families. One of these explained that he did not want to 'impose' the language on his own children (Maguire, 1991: 68). In a bilingual situation, language can be added to the list of values, such as religious, moral, educational, which parents espouse and try to inculcate in their children. It is natural for young people to question these values before making their own decisions. Sometimes, this process involves fluctuations, periods of indecision and even 'testing' adults' reactions to their choices. Clearly, no single pattern of language behaviour emerges when one listens to family members from that pre-Shaw's Road generation recounting their responses to being raised bilingually in Belfast, during the 1950s and 1960s. In relation to the founding of an Irish speaking community at Shaw's Road, however, the experience of these families offered a valuable lesson about the importance of social and linguistic community cohesion. It also instilled the confidence that active, functional bilingualism could be achieved outside the Gaeltacht.

The socio-political and economic conditions within west Belfast, during the late 1960s, helped shape the mindset of the founders of the Shaw's Road Community. In another historical era, this initiative would not have been conceived of as viable or even as 'worth a go'. The original members had grown up in a city where political and social injustices and unrest existed as an undercurrent to everyday life. Divisions, ghettoization, discrimination and waves of sectarian violence had come to characterize many parts of the city. The civil rights movement had emerged during the 1960s, as a reaction to social injustice. During this period of conflict and tension, a sense of cohesiveness within communities was strong and created conditions that can sometimes foster community initiative and enterprise.

By the time the aspiration to build an urban Gaeltacht community moved through the planning phase, five young families remained at its core. This initiative then gathered a momentum of its own. The core members brought with them practical skills and trades that enabled them to construct the houses. They were also helped by the professional expertise of other members of the broader Irish speaking community, in particular, those in the legal and architectural fields. The insight and personal strengths of the individuals involved in planning and implementing this project played a key role in its success. These men and women stand as role models for all who know about their work, including the thousands of people who would later benefit from their achievements. The early members of Shaw's Road shared a common goal and a common vision. That vision is understood and still in place today. Indeed, during the 1960s and 1970s, the Shaw's Road families were members of Teaghlaigh (Families) which had been set up to provide a network of support for Irish speaking families. Today, the organization Comhluadar[1] which has over five hundred families on its register, is also very aware of the important links between the use of Irish in the home and the prosperity of the language on a more extensive scale, 'The decision of parents to speak Irish to their children is central to the future of the Irish language as a home language and as a community language' (*Comhluadar*, 2005:3).

Both of these organizations demonstrate the value of using the language to reach out to others, a concept that was central to the Shaw's Road vision. Jacqueline Ní Fhearghusa, chairperson of Comhluadar explained that view:

> I hope that we will see an increase in the numbers of people speaking Irish at home because it is in the home, I believe, that the future of any language lies. If Irish is not being spoken as a family language,

---

1 Literally (social) company.

then we cannot honestly claim that it is a living language.'
(*Comhluadar*, 2001, 4)

Even during the early design and planning phase, when Shaw's Road founder members were still working towards the realization of their dream, there is ample evidence of this open-minded approach towards working alongside others, being aware of the efforts of others and the value of other people's role in the broader picture. One of a prolific range of information booklets published or printed by language groups and individuals (many of which have been since lost) was *Gaeltacht 1965: Treoraí na Gaeltachta* (1965). This little guidebook was published in Belfast and contains a comprehensive guide to Irish language organizations, competitions and events, broadcasting and publications. *Gaeltacht 1965* includes reference details on two of the co-operative organizations, with contacts, that were fundraising for the Shaw's Road initiative at that time, Comhar Creidmheasa Ghaeilgeoirí Bhéal Feirste (Bríd Bean Mhic Sheáin) and Comharchumann Cholmcille (Séamas de Brún).[2] Interestingly, its author presents statistics on Irish-medium schools in the south of Ireland and on the teaching of Gaelic in Scotland. Other data relevant to Irish or Scottish Gaelic cover such an extensive geographical range that it highlights the significance of links with the rural Gaeltacht communities and other communities throughout Ireland and Scotland and their relevance to the lives of Irish speakers in Belfast.

The drive which motivated the Shaw's Road Community, was to regenerate the language by enabling people to use Irish in their everyday lives, creating links across interested groups and communities, and introducing strategic projects aimed at opening up access to the language. There is a sad irony in the fact that Northern Ireland was not yet ready for all-embracing inclusiveness in any project, at that time and the Irish language was often perceived in purely political terms. An article entitled, 'Some Northern Ireland Views', published in the *Irish Times* (2 April 1975), gives some insights into Unionist views on the language, during those early years of the Shaw's Road development. Brian Faulkner, who had been Prime Minister of Northern Ireland prior to the suspension of Stormont in 1972, described a two week period during his education in Dublin, while awaiting his exemption certificate, 'and much against my will I had to learn elementary Irish with the rest.' Lord Brookeborough of the Northern Ireland Unionist Party referred to the Irish language as 'divisive and antagonistic'. The journalist, Andrew Boyd, stated that many Loyalists viewed the Irish language as a threat to the constitutional position of Northern Ireland. He asked, 'Why don't the state schools themselves make a contribution to better understanding by encouraging the study

2 Belfast Irish-speakers' Credit Union and the Colmcille Co-operative.

of Irish?' An incongruously placed view by Pádraig Ó Maolchraoibhe, offered a personal view from Belfast (translated here from Irish), 'And what about the next generation, those who will be about my age in the year 2000? Well, my son attends an Irish language primary school in Belfast.' In his reference to Irish-medium education as the hope for future generations, Ó Maoilchraoibhe referred, of course, to the Irish-medium primary school that had been opened by the Shaw's Road Community in 1971 and would propel the Irish language onto a dynamic and exciting course and would contribute to a language shift in Ireland during the remainder of that millennium.

The story of that primary school, Bunscoil Phobal Feirste, is a narrative with many players, enhanced by a colourful reserve of revealing anecdotes and sub-plots, each of which cast light on social, cultural, linguistic and educational developments of the 1970s and 1980s, in particular. The first of the Shaw's Road families had taken up residence only two years before the school was founded by parents. Indeed, the first of the Shaw's Road children had already commenced primary education in a local English-medium school before the school building was erected and a suitable teacher was appointed. It was therefore with a certain sense of urgency that parents travelled to Gaeltacht areas and to Dublin before finding a qualified teacher who would come to Belfast and teach in the first Irish-medium primary school in the city. Over the next thirteen years, much of the energy and efforts of Shaw's Road parents would be channelled into fundraising to pay for teachers' salaries and into negotiating with the education authorities for voluntary maintained status and funding for the school. This was a frustrating process. However, the experience gained by the Community during those years would prove useful in guiding other primary and secondary schools through that same process during subsequent years. That instinct to share experience and resources which had been so characteristic of the Shaw's Road Community from its planning stage, continued to be a prominent feature of the Community's response to the surge of interest in Irish-medium education. Bunscoil Phobal Feirste proved to be a success in terms of pupils' general academic progress, their cultural and linguistic awareness and with regard to the status of the school in the wider local community. This fact influenced other communities to take the same step. Irish-medium schools began to appear in other urban centres and later in rural locations where parents followed the example of Bunscoil Phobal Feirste parents. The increase in pupil intake into the first *bunscoil* is explained by the decision to offer Irish-medium pre-school education to children from outside the Shaw's Road neighbourhood and to facilitate access to the *bunscoil* for non-Irish speaking families living outside the Shaw's Road. When the children of Shaw's Road approached the age for secondary education, parents showed the same tenacity and creativity in their response to the children's need. Even while they were still intensely involved in the effort to secure recognition and funding for the *bunscoil*, they were also facing the challenge of providing secondary schooling through Irish to their eldest children. It was impossible to fund both projects simultaneously. The secondary provision was based on the commitment made on a voluntary basis by secondary teachers, some of whom were employed in other schools. This system lasted two years before it was withdrawn in favour of other options. Children from two families attended an Irish-medium boarding school in Dublin where they completed their secondary education. That choice was not open to everyone and other children attended local English-medium secondary schools. This was a traumatic choice for the first children from the Community to transfer to the English-medium system. Later, it became more common. The next attempt at introducing Irish-medium education by Shaw's Road members, would harness the experience and insights gained during that earlier attempt at secondary provision, from 1978 to 1980. Eleven years later, Meánscoil Feirste (Belfast Secondary School) opened in Cultúrlann Mac Adam Ó Fiaich with eight pupils. Two teachers were appointed who could deliver a range of subjects in the arts and in science and the process of negotiating with the education authorities for funding began again. In the same year,1991, Gaeloiliúint was founded to support and direct developments in Irish-medium education. One of the achievements of that organization was to contribute to the introduction of Irish-medium initial teacher education at St Mary's College, Belfast, 1996. Two members of the Shaw's Road Community became principals in two of the Belfast *bunscoileanna*. Another member was very active in the provision of teaching materials and in translating texts into Irish for the schools. Other members have been active in areas of the arts – drama, music, broadcasting in the Irish language. Each one of the families at Shaw's Road contributes to the promulgation of the language via a range of projects and initiatives both within and outside their own Gaeltacht community.

In recent years, the Community has been able to build more houses for Irish speaking families on the Shaw's Road site. Indeed, the construction of six houses was completed in Occtober 2005 and five of the new families to take up residence were themselves raised in the Shaw's Road Community. This final phase of construction brings the number of houses in the Shaw's Road Community to twenty-two. The neighbouring area has also drawn a number of Irish speaking families whose children attend the local Bunscoil Phobal Feirste. However, the creation of an Irish speaking residential unit did not develop into a network of other such communities in the city or beyond. The momentum has been driven by the vigorous pace of growth in Irish-medium educational provision and in related areas such as the production of resources, curriculum and assessment developments, Initial Teacher Education, translation services, strategic planning and advisory bodies. All of these developments create employment opportunities for Irish speakers across a range of professional specialist areas.

Further and higher education and employment opportunities for Irish-medium pupils have also been enhanced by the success of the Shaw's Road initiative and by the leadership and participation of key members of the Community in a variety of well-planned projects. The most recent of these initiatives is the innovative plan for a Gaeltacht Quarter which involves partnership with many other Irish language community groups and enterprises, Forbairt Feirste (Belfast Development) and St Mary's University College. This vision should contribute to urban regeneration in the city in an inclusive and dynamic way. The potential of the Irish language as a powerful economic tool has been identified in these negotiations between these partners (*Daily Ireland*, 15 February 2005).

The impact of the Shaw's Road Community on the fortunes of the language on a much larger scale has been realized is two ways: (a) the leadership and supportive role played by members of the Shaw's Road Community in a range of significant social and educational developments and (b) the generation of a growing strategic network of Irish-medium schools and relevant services and infrastructure that have been established indirectly or directly as an outcome of the pioneering work of the Shaw's Road Community in those areas.

A third area where the influence of the Shaw's Road Community is evident concerns the increasing number of bilingual families who have been encouraged by the Shaw's Road Community but who do not live in an Irish speaking neighbourhood. In this context, certain questions arise, e.g. What has been learned about trans-generational trends in language use? Have the values espoused by Shaw's Road parents concerning language choices survived in the busy world of younger generations where inherited values can be vigorously challenged? These questions can be applied to the subsequent generations of Shaw's Road families and also to the expanding number of families passing through the Irish-medium system. A detailed insight into these questions would require a research initiative. However, even a cursory exploration of the issues involved raises interesting observations about patterns of language use.

When Shaw's Road founder members planned their future as a Gaeltacht community, influenced by the experiences and efforts of an earlier generation of bilingual families, they were guided by a simple set of criteria that would support their language choice. Today, the spectrum of bilingual profiles among Irish speakers has broadened to embrace a diverse range of possibilities. This phenomenon has also emerged in Irish-medium schools. Between 1971 and 1978 the pupils at Bunscoil Phobal Feirste came from a background where Irish was their mother tongue and was used as the first language in the home and in the neighbourhood. As the school attracted pupils from non-Irish speaking backgrounds and parents engaged in language learning activities, the linguistic profile of families changed. Most children attending Bunscoil Phobal

Feirste during the early 1980s came from homes where parents' competence in the language and the use of the language at home both increased after the eldest child commenced the Irish-medium *naíscoil* (pre-school) (Maguire, 1991, 107–32). When some of these children became parents themselves, patterns of language use in the home tended to include more families where at least one parent was a competent Irish speaker. This changing profile of linguistic backgrounds creates stimulating challenges for Irish-medium teachers, particularly in the early years.

Outside the classroom, the spectrum of language has also diversified considerably from the more homogeneous base provided by the Shaw's Road Community. Bilingual families in Belfast, at the start of the second millennium, include (a) families where both parents are competent Irish speakers and have an extended family who also speak Irish. Among these families are adults who were themselves raised with Irish in Belfast, (b) families where one parent is a competent Irish speaker. The other parent may have some Irish from classes or from the home. The bilingual spectrum also includes hundreds of family units where one or both parents are second language learners, whether beginners or more advanced learners. This profile in Belfast is typical of the changing patterns in the process of bilingualization that is found in other places, particularly within the catchment areas of Irish-medium schools. This broader development merits a concentrated study to identify common experiences, trends, difficulties and to identify language planning issues. However, for the purpose of this chapter which traces the impact of a language initiative in Belfast, a small pilot study was carried out to identify some of the factors which influence language use in the home and to provide some possible directions to be considered in a more comprehensive study. Eight parents from outside the Shaw's Road Community were interviewed about the language use in their families. In four cases, one parent was proficient in Irish and in the other four cases, both parents were proficient in Irish. The eldest of the children was fifteen years old. Most of the children were of primary school age. Three factors seemed to be significant in determining how successfully parents felt they managed to encourage the use of Irish among their families:

- Whether one or two parents were proficient in Irish;
- Whether the children attended an Irish-medium primary and /or secondary school;
- Whether or not the families' social activities included participation in Irish-language social or cultural events.

Among the eight families, all of the Irish speakers used Irish in the work domain, whether in journalism, administration, education or business. (It is interesting that every one of these individuals had directly benefited, in their professional roles, by the pioneering work of the Shaw's Road Community in education and in other community initiatives. In most cases, parents had also been guided and supported in various professional endeavours by the expertise and experience of members of that community.)

Some general observations relating to families where both parents were Irish speakers: In three of these families, at least one of the parents had also been raised bilingually. These four families also tended to be active in other Irish language social and cultural activities such as community festival events or regular drama or musical activities organized in venues like Cumann Chluain Ard. Two of the families made particular references to their children's enjoyment of these activities and to their own awareness of support gained by involving the whole family in the social events organized by the broader Irish speaking community. Where both parents spoke Irish, a degree of confidence was conveyed about the amount of Irish in their children's social and home environment. Occasions where Irish was not used tended to be related to child-care arrangements and other situations where neither parent was present. The choice of schooling was perceived to affect the use of Irish at home. One of the two families with older children had chosen the Irish-medium secondary school and the other family had chosen the local English-medium secondary school. In the latter case, a reduction in the amount of Irish spoken at home was seen to result from that choice of schooling.

General observations relating to families where one parent was an Irish speaker: The Irish speaking parent in these families expressed a much greater sense of 'hard work' involved in sustaining the effort to raise the children bilingually. In one case, the father kept a language diary for one week to give a record of the language profile in the children's lives. This record highlighted that a considerable amount of Irish was used by and with the children during a typical week. The children enjoyed Irish language programmes on television and also watched favourite videos that were in Irish. Other occasions where Irish was used outside school involved their father's presence, e.g., at play, driving in the car, visiting Irish speaking friends.

Parents in this category emphasized the conscious effort and planning that was required to encourage their children to use Irish. Two of these families chose Irish-medium nursery and primary education for the eldest children and opted for a local English-medium primary school for the youngest. Three of them chose the post-primary English-medium system for/with their children. These decisions were often complex. Two of the latter expressed an awareness of the disadvantages resulting from this option. Views differed as to how these balanced out with the perceived advantages. In all cases, the use of Irish among the children was more difficult to sustain and had significantly decreased since they left their Irish-medium primary schools. Three of these parents observed that their eldest child responded more favourably to attempts to encourage the use of Irish than younger children. In one case, the parent traced this observation back to when the children were very young. This parent used mostly Irish with his first child. The language environment of the second baby included much more English which became the language favoured between the siblings. All of the parents made some reference to the children's sense of loyalty to Irish. Even though the use of Irish had declined and efforts to check that process were sometimes rejected by the children, on occasions they still communicated a sense of pride in their own bilingualism and a love for the language. Three parents in these families also described the language-switching required when they used Irish at home as unnatural and difficult. In families with older children, television also tended to influence language patterns at home. Although certain programmes in Irish had gained the children's attention, generally, this was not the case.

It was interesting to listen to observations about language behaviour associated with play. A parent whose partner also spoke Irish commented upon the tendency of the children to use English only when playing the *play-station* and computer games. English was also the language of play in the street, although some of the children's friends were beginning to show an interest in Irish. Several parents commented upon the children's tendency to speak English when at play with friends, even when the friends were also Irish speakers. In all of the eight families, there was clearly an awareness of the need to plan and create opportunities for the use of Irish with and among the children. Families where two parents had Irish seemed to achieve this with greater ease and, in most cases, with more success. The choice of Irish-medium secondary schooling also impacted upon the balance of Irish and English in the families' lives.

When the founder members of Shaw's Road planned their Gaeltacht community, they also took decisive action to create an environment where their children could use Irish in a meaningful and functional way. The diversity among bilingual families in Belfast today is vibrant, colourful and inspires optimism. Even families who feel that challenge to be at times complex and daunting, also communicated a degree of commitment and determination to sustain it. The families residing in the Shaw's Road Gaeltacht continue to play an important role, proving that bilingualism in Belfast can be the most natural choice for families and that the effort required to achieve it is worthwhile. Shaw's Road was the springboard for the emergence of bilingualism. Although this chapter focuses on Belfast, it must be noted that the influence of the Shaw's Road Community extends beyond one city.

Finally, while the Shaw's Road Community will inspire creativity and courage in other individuals and groups who seek to achieve something great, it would be remiss not to acknowledge the remarkable stature of the individuals who contributed to that initiative. Any historical record of developments in the Irish language over the past forty years – in community initiatives, primary, secondary and tertiary education, legislation, journalism and other areas, would mention the name of Séamus Mac Seáin in each of these sections or chapters. After Séamus Mac Seáin resigned from the board of governors of Meánscoil Feirste, having founded the school and steered it through the many challenges in its early development, pupils planted an oak tree in his honour. That symbolic gesture reflected the strength and steadfastness of the individual as well as communicating some idea of the scale of his achievements. This metaphor could be applied to all the men and women who helped found and build and who joined the Shaw's Road Community. The little acorn has certainly flourished and is now well-established and deserving of continued care.

Protestants and the Irish language in Belfast

GORDON McCOY

In the first part of this article I will examine the attitudes of Belfast Protestants towards the Irish language over the last hundred years, and in the second part I will recount the experiences of some who decided to learn the language. I will explain these views in the light of Protestant beliefs, the political dynamics which inform them, and examples of minority language debates elsewhere. It will be seen that many views are shared by Protestants across long periods of time, but that opinions diverge, often reflecting class differences, with working- and middle-class Protestants expressing radically divergent views.

The usual response of Belfast Protestants to the Irish language since the beginning of the twentieth century has been one of hostility, although the nature of this hostility has changed over time, partly reflecting developments within the language movement. In 1904 an article in the unionist *Belfast News Letter*, 'The Gaelic League: its aims and methods', described the language as worthless, referring to first-hand accounts of the decline of the Gaeltacht, but conceded the right of Irishmen (perhaps including Irish unionists) to learn their language, given the unionist principle of individual liberty:

> Unionists have no objection to the Irish language, and they recognize the fact that Irishmen – and, for the matter of that, Englishmen and Scotchmen, too – have a perfect right to learn their language, and have their children taught to read and speak it, if they will. While they hold that from a business point of view the Irish language is altogether unnecessary, and that it is worse than useless when it occupies time that could be more profitably devoted to other subjects, still they are willing that where the parents desire it their children should have every facility for learning the language ... [unionists] have no desire to force their convictions on those who differ from them, and, consequently, they are prepared to concede perfect freedom of opinion and action.

Nevertheless, the article condemned the League for what the author saw as its totalitarian outlook:

> But freedom is the last thing the Gaelic League desires ... If the founders intended the organization to be non-political and non-sectarian, then the local branches have travelled very far from the original design, for at present the great majority of the local branches are

hotbeds of political and religious agitation. Their meetings are usually held after mass, or on Sunday evening, and generally the local
curate is in the chair. The chief business is usually an address from
the chairman, an address bristling with hatred of England and everything English, with exhortations to his hearers to hold fast to the religion and language of their fathers. They are told to look to the future,
to that happy day when the English language shall die out in Ireland;
for, deny it as they will, the real aim of the Gaelic League is to create an Ireland peopled solely by Irishmen of the Gaelic League stamp,
and cut off by impenetrable walls from all intercourse with the
heretics without. (*Belfast News Letter*, 28 May 1904)

This text can be seen as an example of modernist ideology, a distinctive feature of unionism, which posits an opposition between malign 'traditions' and
a benign process of 'progress', manifested in increased industrialization, widespread literacy, market economies and democratization. Minority languages
are regarded as handicaps that impair individual mobility (Williams 1992).
Motives attributed to the Gaelic League included a mixture of anti-English
racism, Catholic supremacism, cultural and social isolationism, and nationalist and/or republican politics. The preoccupation with all things Irish seemed
narrow-minded and insular to unionists, who looked outwards to Britain for
social and cultural enrichment (Todd 1988: 11). An attempt to create an Irish
speaking Ireland also smacked of compulsion and cultural autocracy, which
offended the Protestant devotion to freedom and individual choice (cf. Nelson
1984: 17). The habit of organizing events and meetings on Sunday was offensive to Protestant sabbatarians who set Sunday aside exclusively for religious
observance. A further deterrent was the prominent role of the Catholic clergy
in the language movement, a phenomenon which lasted for many years.[1]

More than seventy years later, during one of the worst years of the troubles, a feature article in the *Irish Times* recorded interviews with three unionists on the Irish language issue (*Irish Times*, 2 April 1975). Their replies were
surprisingly mild, indicating that Irish was not considered to be an element
of the Northern conflict. Brian Faulkner remembered being forced to learn
Irish at the College of St Columba in Dublin, and recalled a little song 'Is
truagh gan peata'n mhaoir agam'. John Laird noted that while staying with a
Tyrone relative some housekeepers used Irish in his presence, 'safe inside the
total security of the language barrier.' He remarked that Irish was 'a cancer

---

1 Ulster Irish speakers formed their own branch of the Gaelic League, Comhaltas Uladh, in
1926. The organization was dominated by the Catholic clergy, from which ten out of the organization's sixteen presidents of Comhaltas between 1926 and 1970 were drawn (*An tUltach*,
Márta 1972, p. 6).

eating away at the Republic of Ireland' and concluded rather ironically, 'However, from my point of view, I say, long may the corpse of Gaelic receive the kiss of life – long may it be spared to divide.'[2] Lord Brookeborough was of the opinion that the language was 'divisive and its promotion in Ireland has been antagonistic.' He had no interest in learning Irish, and complained that he had enough trouble with his English as he tried to write speeches for the House of Lords. Nevertheless, he enjoyed visits to the western Gaeltacht and approved of the academic study of the language. A former reader of the *United Irishman*, he recalled a rather militaristic tone to its Irish lessons:

> I remember it had a series of phrases in Irish described as useful in everyday life and the one phrase which sticks in my mind was [translated] 'Don't throw the hand-grenade yet.'

While these unionists obviously did not identify with Irish, and objected to the revival of the language in the Republic, their musings reveal little of the unionist hostility of later years, probably because republicans shared their lack of interest in the language at this time. The predominant images of Irish seem to have been as a symbol of old-style republicanism and authoritarian public policy in the Republic, and, in Northern Ireland, a language of Catholic chauvinism, used to exclude Protestants from conversation. Albert Fry, president of Cumann Chluain Ard, told me that few Protestants in Belfast knew the Irish language even existed before the troubles:

> Ní chualaidh siad í – ní rabh a fhios acu go rabh a leithéid ann. Ní rabh, mar shampla, caint ar bith ar Ghaeilg ar na páipéirí, ní rabh iomrá ar bith ar an Ghaeilg. Déarfainn nach mbeadh a fhios acu oiread le cuid de na *Irish Americans* – shílfeadh siad go bhfuil tú ag caint i nGaeilg dá mba rud é gur dhúirt tú 'bedad'.

> [They did not hear it – they did not know that such a thing existed. For example, there was no mention of Irish in the papers, Irish was unheard of. I'd say they would be as unaware as the Irish Americans – they would think you were talking Irish if you said 'bedad'].

During the first decade of the troubles the republican movement took little interest in Irish language issues, and the compliment was often returned by Irish speakers. In 1980 an editorial in the west Belfast newspaper, the *Andersonstown News*, accused all politicians, including republicans, of ignoring the language (*Andersonstown News*, 15 March 1980). Bernadette McAliskey

2 At a conference in 2005 John Laird (now Lord Laird) said he had met many Irish speakers and was now more favourable to the language than he had been in former years.

(nee Devlin), the prominent civil rights activist, accused members of the Gaelic Society at the Celtic Department of Queen's University of being too Gaeltacht-oriented, ignoring the Northern Ireland issue (*Scáthán*, Summer 1980: 5–6). However, loyalist paramilitaries seemed to take a malevolent interest in Irish speakers. In the 1970s three attacks (two of which included bombs) were made on Queen's Celtic Department. The third attack was so serious that in 1973 the Department scattered its staff throughout the Faculty of Arts, so that loyalists would not have a single target to attack. This diaspora lasted until 1976, yet to this day the Celtic Department does not have a name plaque on the outside of the building in which it is housed.

Sinn Féin's decision to contest elections in the 1980s brought the Irish language issue into the chamber of Belfast City Council, where republican councillors recommended the implementation of bilingual policies, including the erection of public signs in Irish, the provision of translation facilities and the use of bilingual stationery. Sinn Féin's promotion of the language was strenuously resisted by unionist politicians, who accused republicans of 'hijacking' the language from 'genuine' language enthusiasts. In council chambers Sinn Féin and unionist parties often quoted each others' more vitriolic statements. Sinn Féin often referred to a DUP councillor's memorable description of the Irish language as a 'leprechaun language'[3] (Ó Muilleoir 1999: 121), while unionists quoted a Sinn Féin member who described every phrase in Irish as 'a bullet in the freedom struggle' (Sinn Féin 1984: 4). Unionist hostility to the language reinforced Sinn Féin's representation of Irish as a symbol of collective pride and victimization.

In an attempt to limit the political and cultural impact of the Irish language revival, unionist councillors often stated that there were more fluent speakers of Cantonese than of Irish in Northern Ireland. In 1994 the unionist-dominated Belfast City Council passed a motion condemning the amount of money spent on the Irish language and calling for a pluralist society which cherished the diverse languages of the city, including those of the Indian subcontinent. The use of multicultural approaches in this way is viewed by some minority language enthusiasts as mischievous, as they re-categorize national minorities as ethnic minorities, and encourage minority groups to fragment, as they compete with one another for limited resources (May 2001: 290).[4] In the late 1990s and early years of the new century Irish language issues gradually became less contentious in Belfast City Council. This is due to many

3 This statement was made by the DUP's press officer, Sammy Wilson, the self-styled *bête noire* of the Irish language movement. He explained his term 'leprechaun language' thus: '... it would be easier to find a leprechaun in modern-day Ireland than an Irish speaker' (Ó Muilleoir 1999: 121).   4 The New Zealand government's multicultural policy was interpreted by Maoris as an attempt to undermine their national importance, and exaggerate the status of immigrant groups (May 2001: 290).

factors, including the zeitgeist of the peace process, the low number of Sinn Féin councillors who could speak Irish, the Council's consultation on an Irish language policy, and the new-found enthusiasm of unionists for Ulster Scots, which prevented them from expressing contempt for other minority languages.

Irish became an issue for negotiation in the peace talks of the 1990s, as Sinn Féin argued for an improved status for the language. This led ultimately to improved provision for Irish in the Belfast/Good Friday *Agreement* and the formation of the cross-border implementation body for Irish and Ulster Scots, one of six bodies created in response to nationalist demands for increased cross-border co-operation. The identification of Sinn Féin with the Irish language increased after the *Agreement*; for example, Gerry Adams used Irish in his speeches, although his halting delivery evoked curiosity from many unionists about his level of fluency. During the conflict republican Irish speakers appeared more strident in Irish and more conciliatory in English; they feared drawing the attention of loyalists and wary funders if they spoke in English. These fears waned as the post-ceasefire ethos of inclusivity entails funding republican groups and Belfast loyalists are more concerned with shooting each other than attacking Catholics. As the peace process took hold Irish speakers felt less danger in expressing republican views in English, which in turn seemed to validate unionist suspicions of them.

When a senior negotiator for Sinn Féin, Martin McGuinness, became Minister of Education in 1998, unionists were appalled. Some schoolchildren in working-class Protestant secondary schools staged protest marches, claiming, among other protestations, that he would make the Irish language a compulsory subject of study. The protests fizzled out after a few days when headmasters announced that in future marchers would be punished for truancy. Another bone of contention was during the incumbency of Sinn Féin's Bairbre de Brún as minister for the Department of Health, Social Services and Public Safety. Her introduction of a bilingual policy in the Department of Health led to job advertizements appearing in both English and Irish. Unionists claimed that patients were suffering because resources were being diverted from health care. For her part, de Brún insisted that the advertizements were financed from the Department's administrative budget.[5]

Since 1998 the Irish language has acquired a higher profile and official status in Northern Ireland. This has led to some unusual British/Irish hybridities which challenge the Irish nationalist hegemony of Irish and create images of the language that are more agreeable to unionists. For example, the Irish language version of the Northern Ireland Census Form for 2001 carries the

---

5 The official bilingual policy of the Department of Health backfired in November 2004, when it launched a 'No room for racism' beer mat campaign. Most racist attacks occurred in loyalist areas, yet bars in these areas refused to accept the beer mats because they carried the title of the department in Irish as well as English.

royal coat of arms (www.nisra.gov.uk/Census/pdf/Irish.pdf: accessed 18 November 2004). The British Council, which is responsible for promoting British culture worldwide, has become interested in the regional cultures of the United Kingdom, including the Irish language. The Council helped to organize a conference on language and law at the Stormont Assembly in February 2003; many of the talks involved the status of the Irish language. Yet high-level 'British' images of Irish have little effect at the communal level, where Irish is a *de facto* nationalist language, both at the levels of participation and ideology.

Protestant hostility to Irish has focused on the language as a bureaucratic 'waste of money' as a result of the increased amount of official bilingualism in recent years. This is a version of the old image of Irish as a dead and irrelevant language. Another emergent image was of Irish as a growing menace or plague – nationalists were seen to be extending their influence and territory through use of the language. Occasionally these images merged, as in Sammy Wilson's description of Irish as 'a dead language promoted by terrorists and Sinn Féin' (Ó Muilleoir 1999: 120–1). Unionists who believed that nationalists gained at the expense of unionists maintained that state support for Irish language projects represents an ill-advised attempt to placate republicanism which would fail.

Unionist reaction to the growing 'plague' of Irish has had some comical results. In 1996 Castlereagh Borough Council complained to Ulsterbus about the introduction of Irish language signs on the company's vehicles. The council was forced to apologize when the firm indicated that the signs were actually in French; they were part of a tourist initiative. It transpired that a ratepayer had contacted the council about the 'Irish' signs, but the council had not checked the story before lodging an official complaint (*South Belfast Herald and Post*, August 29 1996). In east Belfast loyalists ripped down a bilingual sign which read 'Tullyard Way' and *'Heichbrae Airt'* as they mistook the Ulster Scots on the sign for Irish (*Irish News*, 18 October 1999).

INTERVIEWS WITH PROTESTANTS

The following text consists of a series of excerpts taken from a 1994 study involving interviews with 21 Protestants, who were mostly working-class, on their attitudes to the Irish language (Kudos: n.d.).[6] Here are the responses of some Belfast participants, obtained during a visit by the author to a community centre:

6 The study is an unpublished draft copy, which has no page numbers.

John [51-year-old ex-shipyard worker]:
It's Provo talk. You hear them on the TV and they start their speeches with that stuff. Maybe it's just so they can understand it because we can't ... I mean it is a Catholic thing to me ... It is a political statement made by those who speak it. Every time they talk it they are saying up yours, we are what we are: Irish and not British ... It seems that the Catholics are getting everything these days and we're getting "nothing". The schools around here are falling apart and in need of serious money to refurbish them ... [on Irish language television programmes] All you see is Irish football and singing on as well. It's all part of the problem of trying to force us to watch and enjoy these things ... [on Irish speakers] I suppose there are some genuine ones but as far as I can gather most of them are the Provo type. They seem to use the language as part of their campaign to make us all Irish.

Tracy [17-year-old trainee]:
It's more for the Taigs (Catholics) than us.
[*on question on the right to learn Irish*]
I really don't care, it's up to them.

Robert [39-year-old unemployed youth worker]:
Most of the young people, and the adults around here are worried about enough things in life like unemployment, paying the bills, under-aged drinking or taking drugs without worrying about a language. The Irish language thing is not a major problem because it doesn't come into the reckoning. To me it would be like fly-fishing or opera, only some people would be into it ... I feel that given the present situation we should be looking for things to bring us together not keep us apart. I think that there may be a problem pushing the Irish thing too much ... [on unionists learning Irish] I don't know too much about it but if it is being learned on the Shankill Road that's something to build on ... It all seems a bit foreign to me, if you know what I mean ...
[*When asked about Irish being part of the school curriculum of his children*]
The parents would go spare around here. This is a fairly staunch Loyalist area and it would be as bad as Gerry Adams leading the Twelfth[7] saying they would be putting it in the schools.

---

7 Gerry Adams is the president of Sinn Féin, and as such is a unionist *bête noire*. The Orange Order is a Protestant organization dating from the late eighteenth century. The organization takes its name from William III (William of Orange), whose victory over James II in 1690 ensured Protestant succession to the English throne. The Order organizes many demonstrations to celebrate this victory, the most important of which are held annually on the Twelfth of July.

Sam [48 years old, registered disabled]:
I think that the Irish language crowd are just part of the whole republican thing and they would be more interested in the unification of Ireland more so than speaking another language. See I don't think it is just about a language but it's more to do with a way of life. The Irish crowd over on the Falls Road and elsewhere are determined to remove the British from Ireland and because me and my family are British it's about getting us out too ... Most of the groups who push for the Irish language are just fronts for Sinn Féin ... It seems to me that they just gurn [complain] away all the time just to let everyone think they are hard done by ... It's their choice whether they want to speak a different language or not ... They're all wrapped up together in one big family, the bands, the Irish speakers, the Sinn Féin/IRA, the footballers and all the rest of them: they're all the same to me. Look at the wall paintings they have sure half of them are done in Irish and all their election posters are done in Irish. They're even trying to change the names of the streets.
[*When asked about Irish as part of the school curriculum of his children*]
There would be a full-scale riot and I would be in the middle of it ... Before you would know what was happening we would all be expected to go to mass and learn Latin too.

John [22 years old, Armagh student staying in Belfast, on visit to community centre]:
I have a few Catholic friends at Queen's and they're dead sound just the same as me ... We even went to an Irish music night one night. I thought all the songs sounded the same but I enjoyed it ... Don't pick me up wrong there are some really great people about here but there are some moonmen too. They would burn the place to the ground if they thought that there was anything that remotely sounded of being Irish. I played a U2 tape once and one of them said they were a republican band ... If you live all your life in isolation from the other side and are given a diet of stories and headlines then it is only to be expected that they would learn to hate the unknown ... Perhaps it's one of the ways that those pushing the Irish language could make it more popular if young Protestants were to meet those speaking it ... you have to start somewhere, don't you?

Mark [19 years old, unemployed]:
[*When asked if unionists will ever speak Irish*]
No way, its for the Taigs and not us.
[Note: Interview duration: 11 minutes; it was abandoned after the interviewer received vitriolic abuse from the respondent]

Anita [36-year-old civil servant]:
I think it is an irrelevant language which has no place in the modern world. How would it have any practical use?

These interviews reveal a strong perceived association between the Irish language and republicanism. This is because many Protestants only experience the language when it is used by republicans in a symbolic political fashion, such as in the broadcast media, on election posters, and on wall murals. Motives attributed to Irish speakers include: a spurious manipulation of the language to achieve a united Ireland; a wish to annoy unionists; or on the contrary, a wish to convert unionists into nationalists. John's comment on the attempt to 'force' Irish is a familiar one; unionists often perceive exposure to the language as a form of compulsion.

Robert thinks that Irish is divisive in the light of the peace process, reflecting the unionist belief that the language drives a wedge between Protestants and Catholics, thwarting efforts to bring the two communities together. John, the ex-shipyard worker, hints that there are genuine Irish speakers apart from republicans; this illustrates the widespread belief that republican Irish speakers have 'hijacked' the language movement and are cynically manipulating the language for political purposes, whereas non-republicans who speak Irish are regarded more favourably, perceived as having 'real' motives to learn the language. Irish can arouse sectarianism and strong negative emotions among Protestants, as evinced by Mark's abuse of the researcher and Sam's promise to riot if Irish were introduced into Protestant schools. Robert expresses some ambivalence about the language, which appears 'foreign' to him, but thinks it could be taught to unionists all the same.

The Protestant student seems more favourable to Irish speakers, given his 'dead sound' Catholic friends, yet understands the hostility of loyalists, owing to stereotyping arising from media reports and the lack of contact across the community divide. His views illustrate a more liberal middle-class outlook, which is often more favourable to the language. But even the working-class Protestants do not object to Catholics speaking Irish among themselves, as demonstrated by Carol and the otherwise vociferous Sam; there is no mention of banning Irish, which is a recognition of *realpolitik* or an expression of 'British' liberal values (cf. Todd 1988: 13).

One significant difference between these interviews and the 1904 *Belfast News Letter* article is the lack of references to the participation of Catholic clerics in the language movement. Republicans had long replaced clerics as the main promoters of Irish in Belfast. However, Sam hints at an attempt to convert Protestants to Catholicism, unless Protestant vigilance is maintained. This suggests Irish speakers and the Catholic Church work together, reflecting Protestant working-class conspiracy theories of collaboration between different Catholic groups (including actual opponents of each other, such as the IRA and the Catholic Church). Sam's and John's references to Catholic gains and 'gurning' reflects the widespread belief that Catholic community groups (including Irish speaking ones) receive the lion's share of public funding, despite Catholic complaints of discrimination. Many of the speakers view Irish as irrelevant to Protestants as it is a Catholic language, or one that has no place in the modern world – for Protestants or Catholics.

These views demonstrate an identification of the Irish language with another (often unpalatable) ethno-political group, and a belief that the Irish language is dying or dead. The student is left to condemn 'moonmen' for their dismissal of Irish, although he contextualizes their dismissal, and hopes that by meeting Irish speakers Protestants will change their views. Irish speakers are presented as using the language to annoy unionists – it is an *anti-language*, used to maintain a boundary with others, rather than express positive in-group values (see Cohen 1994: 120). Unionist opposition to the Irish language now concentrates on Northern republicans, rather than the Southern state's gaelicization policy; Sinn Féin has become a more dangerous enemy to unionists than the 'irredentist' Republic. Furthermore, many unionists, particularly working-class ones, are totally unaware of the existence of the Gaeltacht, and so assume that everyone who speaks Irish is a native English speaker who uses Irish for political reasons.

While talking to Protestant community groups in Belfast I encountered many misconceptions about the Irish language movement: that parents are 'advised' by Sinn Féin workers to send their children to Irish-medium schools; that these schools subsequently brainwash children with republicanism; that Irish language groups give half their money to the IRA; that all government documents are translated into Irish at great expense; that all Irish speakers are republican; that Irish classes are recruitment grounds for the IRA; and that 'in ten year's time you'll need Irish to get a job'.[8] Other opinions stress the burden of the language for those who speak it, especially children who are raised through Irish. A policeman told me a child died after a road accident in west Belfast, as the street sign was only in Irish, and the ambulance driver had difficulty locating the scene of the accident. Other stories tell of children taken into emergency units in hospital and being unable to discuss

8 The *Andersonstown News* published secret minutes of One Island – Two Nations, a shadowy loyalist group which bemoaned the consequences of a bilingual Northern Ireland, 'If this were to happen then Protestants would find it impossible to get employment. Street, road, bus and destination signs would be in Irish ... we would be strangers in our own country' (*Andersonstown News* 14 Feb. 1998). Curiously, the statement was happy to report, 'We are still getting very valuable information about the Irish cultural movement from Protestants who take part in Irish language classes and Irish dancing.' This stretches the boundaries of credulity; I have never met a Protestant who learned Irish in order to uncover a nationalist cultural masterplan.

their conditions in English with nurses. In these apocryphal tales, the Irish language is at best a handicap, at worst literally lethal. These stories are typical examples of modernist discourse; the failure of minority language speakers to improve their lot is blamed on their lack of knowledge of the majority language (Williams 1992: 30).

The response of some loyalists to the Irish language revival has been of mimesis rather than mockery. For example, one convicted loyalist shouted the republican slogan 'Tiocfaidh ár lá' ('Our day will come') as he was taken to the cells of Belfast Crown Court (*Belfast Telegraph* September 10 2002). The linguistic inquiries of the Ulster Volunteer Force (UVF) and a smaller aligned group the Red Hand Commandos (RHC) have had some surprising results. Prominent UVF members learned the Irish language while in jail and the RHC adopted the Irish motto 'Lamh Derg Abu' ('Lámh Dearg Abú, 'Red Hand for Ever') on its flag; in 2003 the motto also appeared on RHC murals, which appeared on the Shankill Road (in west Belfast) and Ballybeen estate (in east Belfast). This symbolic use of Irish has not led to a significant loyalist demand to learn the language.

The current interest of unionists in Ulster Scots is due in part to the strong association between the Irish language and political identity established by Northern nationalism. The Ulster Scots revival also represents the abandonment of modernism by some unionists for an alternative self-minoritizing approach.[9] Institutionalized multiculturalism in Northern Ireland has led to positive benefits being associated with minority status, leading to a proliferation of cultural claims which are difficult to arbitrate. Competing claims of victimhood seek to negate each other in a depressing scenario in which each side presents itself as the victim of the other; 'there is no succour for the former or redemption of the latter' (Finlay 2004: 153).

The Department of Culture, Arts and Leisure commissioned a report on views of the Irish language in 2001. The report found little antipathy in the Protestant community to Irish-medium education, which reflected less Protestant hostility to Irish language projects based within the Catholic community. There was often 'general mystification' among Protestants about people who voluntarily agree to have their children taught subjects such as maths and history through the medium of Irish (Dunn et al. 2001: 42). Some Protestants were strongly opposed to their own children being forced to learn Irish.

Between 47 and 48 percent of Protestants were in favour of a number of Government services in Irish, such as census forms, birth certificates, and voting cards, being made available on request. However, the report found con-

9 For example, on the BBC Radio Ulster programme 'Seven Days' (broadcast on 18 Semptember 2005), the Orange historian Clifford Smith suggested that Protestant alienation from the peace process could be alleviated by establishing a quota for Ulster Scots recruits to the PSNI.

siderable Protestant hostility to the use of public signage in Irish.[10] Forty-three percent of Protestants believed that Irish language signs should never be provided in any circumstances, although 38 percent believed that signage in Irish should be provided in circumstances where the majority of people coming into contact of it would be in favour (Ibid: 52). It appears that signage in Irish signifies nationalist or republican control of an area to unionists.

As a consequence of the community divisions on the Irish language, visitors to Belfast will hear or see little Irish in the city centre, and can be forgiven if they do not know it exists. However, in situations where Irish appears with many other languages, it seems innocuous. The multilingual sign for the bus station information centre reads 'eolas' ('information'), a visitor arriving at the Belfast tourist centre or at the main train station will read 'Fáilte' ('Welcome') alongside many other languages, and the person arriving by ferry will see FÁILTE GO TUAISCEART NA HÉIREANN ('Welcome to the North of Ireland', but translated as the more unionist-friendly 'Welcome to Northern Ireland'). The fact that the signs recognize Irish indicates a greater public acceptance of the language, as there was no signage in Irish in the city centre whatsoever in the 1980s. Irish seems acceptable to unionists on multilingual tourist notices where it appears alongside many other languages,[11] but a binary English/Irish framework meets with more resistance.

The peace process has not led to significant interaction between Catholic Irish speakers and Protestants in the city. There are many reasons for this, the most salient being that the two communities learned to live apart during the troubles; Belfast is one of the most residentially-polarized areas of Northern Ireland. Moreover, Catholic Irish speakers could have less contact with Protestants than other Catholics. If they work in the Irish language movement they will be employed in all-Catholic environments, while other Catholics who are employed in larger workplaces are more likely to meet Protestants. The interest of Catholics in Irish concentrates their social activities within the Catholic community, whereas other activities, some sports for example, are far more likely to encourage greater Protestant and Catholic interaction. Most Catholic Irish speakers have a lack of experience of Protestants which will make interaction with them perhaps awkward and certainly novel. The converse is also true; most Protestants have never met an Irish speaker.

Although there are many cross-community schemes in the city, there are few concerning the Irish language; the language is not a focus of reconciliation

10 The 1999 *Northern Ireland life and times survey* found that eighty percent of Protestants were opposed to the Stormont Assembly introducing bilingual road signs (http://www.ark.ac.uk/nilt/1999/Political_Attitudes/ASSMBDO4.html#religion: accessed 18 Jan. 2005). 11 In 2004 a poster even appeared outside an Ormeau Road Presbyterian Church welcoming potential worshippers in many languages including the Irish 'Fáilte'.

efforts. Some Irish speakers suggest that the authorities should educate Protestants about the Irish language, but this represents a misunderstanding of the problem on their part. Much Protestant suspicion of the Irish language focuses on its speakers, and only by meeting these speakers will Protestant views be confirmed or invalidated. Such meetings would have to be arranged in an environment in which both groups feel comfortable, which is easier said than done, given the numerous spatial, cultural and political tensions in the city.

In an era of so-called 'benign apartheid', stereotypes multiply as the two communities perceive each other as monolithic and having fixed, inflexible attitudes (Lennon 2004: 122, 137). Catholics can be surprised to meet Protestants who have liberal views on Irish and Protestants can be surprised when they meet Irish speakers who are not republican, as these speakers often keep a low public profile. The seminal study of Irish speakers in Belfast (O'Reilly 1999) confirms this more complex profile, with many hidden voices and non-republican interpretations of Irish which do not appear in the media.

Although there is little contact between ordinary Catholics and Protestants in Belfast, there has been more communication between community groups. In particular, women, who are not perceived to be combatants, find it easier to move between the communities. Catholic and Protestant women's centres also arrange exchange visits and often discover commonalities which overcome the sectarian divide. This precedent helped Irish learners in the Shankill Women's Centre to arrange visits to Irish language projects on the Falls Road. I learned something of these inter-community dynamics during a presentation I gave on the Irish language in the loyalist estate of Mount Vernon in October 2004. Two of the female workers told me they had enjoyed a lunch in the *Cultúrlann*[12] (cultural centre) in predominantly Catholic west Belfast; I assumed that as community activists their work would have brought them across boundaries they might otherwise not have crossed. The workers also remarked that Irish was spoken in the Kennedy Centre, a shopping mall in west Belfast. Many working-class Protestants, particularly women, visit the bargain stores of west Belfast, thereby increasing their chances of hearing the Irish language.

PROTESTANT IRISH LEARNERS

There has been a long tradition of Protestant Irish speakers in Belfast. Furthermore, there have also been more opportunities for Protestants to learn

---

12 Cultúrlann MacAdam–Ó Fiaich is the main Irish language cultural centre in Belfast. The centre was founded in 1991 and currently includes a café, bookshop, theatre, art gallery and offices. An Chultúrlann is named after Robert MacAdam and Cardinal Tomás Ó Fiaich, both celebrated Irish scholars and representative of the two main religious traditions.

the language since the 1990s, with the development of classes in Belfast city centre and various self-instruction courses.[13] Protestant learners of Irish can be viewed as intercultural speakers, who learn about their own culture and that of others in a mutually reinforcing relationship, noticing what other speakers of a language take for granted (see Roberts et al. 2001: 30–1).

For most of the twentieth century, Protestants who wanted to learn Irish had to travel into west Belfast to learn Irish in the Ardscoil or Cumann Chluain Ard. Tomás Ó Monacháin, who was secretary of Cumann Chluain Ard before the troubles, remembered a local priest becoming concerned about the number of Protestants attending the Irish classes in the mid-1940s. The priest warned the club to remove the Protestants or he would denounce Cumann Chluain Ard from the altar. The committee refused, and the matter was dropped.[14] The incident was, according to Ó Monacháin, an example of how the Irish language movement was ecumenical before it became fashionable to be so, although there were difficulties:

> Ní rabh sé furast i gcónaí an polasaí sin a leanstan, an dtuigeann tú, ins an áit a rabh Cumann Chluain Árd suite – i gceartlár gheiteo na gCaitliceach i mBéal Feirste, ach san am chéanna, thuig daoine gur cineál Halla na Saoirse a bhí ann. Duine ar bith a raibh suim aige sa Ghaeilg ba chuma cérbh é féin, ba chuma cé acu bhí sé acfuinneach nó bocht, nó dubh, nó bán, nó buí, ba chuma. Thuig daoine go raibh fáilte rompu i gCumann Chluain Árd agus lean Cumann Chluain Árd den pholasaí neamhsheicteach sin nuair a bhí eagraíochtaí cosúil le CLG, ba chuma leo cad é an blas Caitliceach a bheadh ar a gcuid imeachtaí ... Bhí seort eagla ar Chaitlicigh roimhe Phrotastúnaigh agus ar Phrotastúnaigh roimhe Chaitlicigh – níor thuig siad a chéile i gceart ... Caithfidh mé a aidmheáil go rabh Caitlicigh ann agus shíl siad gur leofasan an Ghaeilg agus i gcónaí bhí eagla ormsa roimhe na daoine sin – go dtabharfadh siad achmhusán do na Protastúnaigh, b'fhéidir de thaisme nó d'aonturas fríd chomhrá – go n-abróchadh siad rud éigin aingiallta nó amaideach a ghortachadh iad.

> [It was not easy to follow that policy, you know, where Cumann Chluain Ard was located – right in the heart of the Catholic ghetto in Belfast, but at the same time, people understood that it was a sort of Freedom Hall. Anyone who was interested in Irish, it did not mat-

---

13 For more information on Protestant learners of Irish , see McCoy (1997) and McCoy and Ní Bhaoill (2004).   14 Another version of the dispute attributes the priest's hostility to the strong socialist element in Cumann Chluain Ard. Whatever the reason for the dispute, it was clear that the club rejected the influence of the Catholic Church, thus creating a niche for Protestants to learn the Irish language.

ter where he was from, it did not matter if he was well-to-do, or poor, or black, or white, or yellow, it did not matter. People understood they were welcome in Cumann Chluain Ard and Cumann Chluain Ard followed that non-sectarian policy when organizations such as the GAA did not care if their events had a Catholic tinge to them ... Catholics were sort of afraid of Protestants and Protestants were afraid of Catholics – they didn't understand each other well ... I must admit that there were Catholics who thought Irish belonged to them and I was always fearful that they would insult the Protestants, perhaps by accident or on purpose through conversation – that they would say something irrational or stupid that would hurt them.]

Cumann Chluain Ard acquired the reputation of being non-sectarian and non-political.[15] The troubles brought to an end to Protestant involvement in the club for a long time, much to the regret of its stalwarts. In the early 1970s, barricades presented a physical impediment to travelling into the area. Albert Fry told me that a blow to the cross-community ethos of the club came when the IRA killed a Protestant, Sam Llewellyn, in August 1975; he was a Belfast Corporation worker who was delivering repair materials after an explosion in the Clonard district. A few Protestants resumed going to Cumann Chluain Ard in the late 1980s, as the city settled somewhat, and they felt much more comfortable going into west Belfast after the ceasefires of 1994.

Since the 1980s a number of classes have sprung up in 'neutral' central and south Belfast; the classes are run by important educational organizations such as Queen's University, the University of Ulster, the Belfast Institute of Further and Higher Education (BIFHE), the Ulster People's College, and the Linenhall Library. One problem is that BIFHE classes in the centre and south of the city can be undersubscribed, so they may have to close, and Protestant learners are deprived of classes where they would feel safe. Another problem is that classes for advanced learners tend to be concentrated in the west of the city, and Protestant learners are reluctant to venture there. Belfast-based Protestants who wish to become fluent often have only two options – go to west Belfast or the Gaeltacht.

15 Cumann Chluain Ard is nationalist in ethos, like the rest of the Irish language movement (O'Reilly 1999: 75), although language issues predominate, which creates space for learners of different political backgrounds. The club has been wary of republican control, and the organization's constitution still forbids committee membership to anyone active in a political party. As such, Cumann Chluain Ard is perceived by many Irish speakers to be non-aligned in terms of nationalist politics and consequently 'non-political'; in the early years of the Gaelic League 'non-political' implied 'opposing physical force', and 'political' suggested 'inclining towards physical force' (Dunleavy and Dunleavy 1991: 314). Nationalist views were taken for granted as 'natural', and therefore 'non-political'.

Irish has made small inroads into schools attended by Protestants. The presence of Irish in integrated education has aroused some Protestant interest. In Lagan Integrated College in south Belfast, Irish is a compulsory subject of study for the first three years. Gael Linn, an Irish language educational organization, provides short language courses in non-Catholic grammar schools. The pupils volunteer for the classes, which are held during their free periods. Belfast Royal Academy has been among the schools availing of the service, although at the time of writing no Belfast-based schools are currently participating in the project. Therefore, there are few opportunities for Belfast Protestants to encounter the Irish language at school, much to the regret of those who learn the language later on in life.

One significant development since the peace process began has been the founding of Cumann Cultúrtha Mhic Reachtain (McCracken Cultural Society), an Irish language organization based in North Belfast. This was initially based in the former Duncairn Presbyterian Church on the Antrim Road, which lost its congregation as the religious demographics of the area changed, and the district became predominantly Catholic. Cumann Cultúrtha Mhic Reachtain has now moved nearby, but still uses the church building for events. The society is sensitive to Protestants interested in Irish, given its location and the active involvement of the Revd Bill Shaw in the 174 Trust. Furthermore, the society holds many events for Irish learners, which attract a number of interested Protestants.

The McCracken Society has links with the University of Ulster part-time diploma and degree programme based in the university building at York Street. This programme has recruited many Protestants interested in Irish, for a variety of reasons. It is based in the neutral centre of Belfast and provides an opportunity for Protestants who come to the language too late to study for a full-time degree. In more recent years more Protestants have also studied Irish at degree level at Queen's University, including Ian Malcolm, a unionist columnist with the Irish language newspaper *Lá*. Formerly, Protestants wishing to study Irish at degree level tended to go to the University of Ulster at Coleraine.

Many Protestant Irish speakers only meet each other on a regular basis at An Tor ar Lasadh ('The Burning Bush'), which organizes services on the third Sunday of every month in Fitzroy Presbyterian Church, near Queen's University. This group comprises Catholics and Protestants of all denominations, and is in fact the only regular social event where Protestant Irish speakers meet one another. *An Tor* has a core group of around twenty members who attend the monthly meetings, with over seventy on its mailing list; many people attend the larger Christmas and Easter services and special attempts are made to attract guest preachers and choirs to these occasions. The group is a model of cross-community co-operation, as many Irish speaking Catholics are supportive and attend the services.

MOTIVATIONS TO LEARN IRISH

Protestants give various reasons for wanting to learn Irish: interest in family history, Irish history, or place-names; nationalist aspirations; traditional music; work-related activities (such as publishing); hearing the language in the Republic; an interest in languages; an interest in the arts, including literature; a desire to reach out to Catholics; and having friends who speak Irish.

Protestants, including unionists, accentuate their Irish identities when abroad. British people are often equated with the English, who have a bad reputation in some areas, whereas the Irish tend to have a positive image almost everywhere. Furthermore, many unionists will say they come from 'Ireland', not 'Northern Ireland', as they are not interested in explaining the border to people who know little about Ireland. Therefore, Protestants who would otherwise identify themselves as British do not mind 'becoming' Irish while abroad (Zwickl 2002: 86). Some of these Protestants recount the disappointment of foreigners when they cannot speak Irish, as Irish people are often expected to have a language of their own. This leads to reflections upon this 'new' Irish identity when they return home, stimulating a desire to learn the Irish language. In the following interview, a Protestant with a strong Ulster identity describes how he became interested in Irish while talking to a taxi driver in Romania:

> He was saying to me, 'Where are you from?' and I was saying 'Ireland' and when I had worked it out geographically so that he knew where Ireland was, he said to me, 'What's the Irish for that?', pointing at a horse, you know, and I had to say, 'I don't know,' and then I thought, 'Wait a minute, you don't even know your own language. That's ridiculous.' So I came home thinking, 'Stuff it, I'm going to learn it. I'm going to learn my language. Why should they take my language? I have as much right to it as they do.'

Irish classes were held in the Shankill Women's Centre between 1993 and 1998. One learner discussed her interest in the language with me:

> I'd been to Donegal quite a few times myself, with my family and I hadn't a baldy what it was – 'cos to read it is very hard for me – and I was keeping looking at the signs and I hadn't a clue what they were about, and I thought if I had a basic knowledge when I came up here again, maybe I could practise, put it into practice a bit. So I suppose that was the main interest in it, through Heather [the teacher] speaking it, and it sounded great and travelling as well ... And I think it's a way of breaking down barriers – I see it as that – where there's lots

of people who see it as a Catholic or nationalist ... I often think Catholics in general have so much more knowledge of their history. I see it as a way of being able to talk to Catholics as well.

The learner noted that 'more Protestants are learning Irish'. I asked why?

Probably because there is such an interest in the Catholic, within the Catholic community, they think to themselves, 'Well, if they're going to do it, why can't we?' But I would say that ten years ago you were very limited in access within the Protestant communities [to Irish].

INSTRUMENTAL MOTIVATIONS TO LEARN IRISH

Sociolinguists often divide motivations to learn languages into affiliative categories (attempts to identify with the speakers of the language) and instrumental categories (practical reasons to learn a language which do not entail a shift in identity) (Baker 1992: 32). Members of the security services have learned Irish for many work-related reasons. Some prison officers learned Irish to understand what republican prisoners were saying in the 'Jailtacht'. Members of RUC Special Branch have learned Irish to study republican documents.[16]

Jack Hermon, a former chief constable of the RUC, told me he had an interest in Irish since he had heard it while posted as a constable in Tyrone. Later, while stationed in Belfast during the 1960s, he walked into an Irish class in the Ardscoil dressed in full uniform, asking to join, but noted that the learners 'looked at me as if I had come from Mars'. When Hermon became chief constable he instigated a series of Irish classes for the RUC, especially officers stationed in areas with high concentrations of Irish speakers, although he also hoped the classes would help officers discover respect for the 'two traditions'. The plans were shelved in 1985, after the Anglo-Irish Agreement, when many RUC officers were attacked in their home districts by angry loyalists who accused them of being complicit in the British government's 'sell-out'. According to Hermon, a civil servant wrote in the file concerned 'This is not the time'. Hermon insisted the classes should be established, and they have continued since.

The Irish teacher for the police told me that few Irish speakers were aware that she taught Irish to the RUC and its replacement, the PSNI. Republicans were hostile to police officers learning Irish, as they believed they were using

---

16 The RUC (Royal Ulster Constabulary) policed Northern Ireland during the troubles. The force was predominantly Protestant and was replaced by the PSNI (Police Service of Northern Ireland) in 2001.

Irish to spy on them, or wanted to use learning the language as part of a 'charm offensive' to make the police force acceptable in nationalist areas. The teacher was greeted with suspicion when she first arrived in an RUC centre to teach Irish, although matters have improved greatly, especially since the PSNI was established. She recounted meeting many enthusiastic pupils over the years, some of whom received an 'A' grade in the GCSE Irish examination. The officers also went to the Donegal Gaeltacht to improve their Irish, although they were careful to conceal their occupation from the locals.[17]

The enthusiasm of some of the police officers suggests that the binary opposition of affiliative and instrumental motivations to learn languages may be erroneous (see Baker 1992: 34–5). It appears that rather than learn Irish simply as a counter-insurgency or community relations strategy, some police officers came to identify with the language, which in turn increased their motivation to learn more.

'I'M MORE AFRAID OF MY OWN': PROTESTANT LEARNERS' FEARS OF THEIR OWN COMMUNITY

Protestant learners of Irish can fear the attitudes of their own community to the language. Working-class people tend to live in communities that are built up over several generations, and in which relationships of kin, neighbourhood, occupation and friendship overlap. The density of these relationships results in their operating as norm-enforcement mechanisms, producing a homogeneity of values. Thus we have 'urban villages' in Belfast (Burton 1978). Protestants living in working-class areas could be threatened by loyalists for learning Irish, unless they are loyalists themselves, and thus have proven their unionism beyond doubt. The above learner who was inspired by a visit to Romania had many fears of his own community. He lived in the Protestant Suffolk estate in west Belfast and listened to Irish language tapes at home with the volume down and the windows closed. He did not listen to them when walking around the estate in case the earphone came out and the Irish was heard, or a local stopped him to ask what was on the tape. Another learner recounted to me how he was expelled from his flat on a loyalist estate after a neighbour spotted his Irish language books. Classes in the Shankill Women's Centre ended in 1998 when other users felt they were giving the centre a 'bad name' and they feared loyalist attacks.

17 Since the PSNI was established, the number of Irish speakers in the force has risen with the number of Catholic recruits, especially those from the Republic who all have at least a basic knowledge of the language. The police teacher told me that one Southern recruit attended her class to familiarise herself with the Northern dialect, although she was already a fluent speaker of Connemara Irish.

Middle-class people place greater emphasis on their personal friendships, have greater social mobility and live in districts characterized by relative anonymity. They have more opportunity to separate the worlds of kinship, residence, work, and recreation. Less moral pressure is exerted on middle-class people in their residential districts by their neighbours. Furthermore, for the most part they have escaped the ravages of the troubles, and can be more open-minded as a result. In more middle-class circles, there is no fear of threat from fellow Protestants, but the Irish language is certainly not a genteel topic of conversation. In the following quotation, an artist relates the reaction of his work colleagues to his interest in Irish:

> It makes them step back. I think it's bewilderment more than anything else. And some of them don't want to ask any more after that. If they overhear somebody saying, 'How's your Irish class going?' It's like, well, as if they don't want to go into it any more, or something … When you say 'I'm learning Irish', it sort of stops there, and you can see all the meanings that go along with that coming down in front of them right away, and you see that's sort of symbolic, 'Irish must mean this, must mean that, and must mean nationalism at least, and republicanism'. They don't really talk about it, and whether or not they feel, 'What's his motive behind it and do we want to go into all that'. And you know, people don't like talking politics. And if a language is associated with politics then they might not want to be led through that back door into a political discussion.

In other circumstances middle-class Protestants like to appear favourable to the Irish language, in order to demonstrate how tolerant and cultured they are, in contrast to 'bigoted' loyalists. Protestant learners will often reveal their interest in Irish to their close friends and family, although they will have acquaintances, such as work colleagues and neighbours, who they assume would be hostile if they knew. One learner was told she was being 'very fashionable' when she told her friends she was learning Irish. Another teenage learner said her friends were encouraging because they were 'arty', 'laid-back', and had gone to a grammar school where they mixed with Catholics.[18] She said she was able to change her family's view of Irish:

> Dad was a bit iffy but Mum said 'it's not a foreign language.' Dad was worried what other people in the community would think – peo-

---

18 State grammar schools are ostensibly Protestant in terms of staff and pupil numbers, but in Belfast those with a very high reputation for educational success attract large numbers of Catholic pupils.

ple have a very blinkered view of it all. My dad has, I think, lightened up now. My brother was a wee bit funny as well, but when I started describing phrases to them and why people say such-and-such a thing, like whiskey is 'water of life', it is translated from Irish, and funny things like that, I've turned things around.

THE BRITISH AND IRISH IDENTITIES OF PROTESTANT LEARNERS

Catholic Irish speakers have a range of motivations for attracting Protestants to learn Irish. One reason is that nationalists often wish to convert unionists to their cause, and believe that Irish is a useful method to achieve this goal. For example, Gerry Adams noted the reason for loyalist hostility to the Irish language was 'obvious enough: for the Protestant people to embrace the Irish language today would be for them to reject loyalism'(Adams 1995: 139). Catholic Irish speakers subscribe to a folk version of the Sapir/Whorf hypothesis, which argues that language shapes our thought processes, rather than just reflecting them (O'Reilly 1995). According to proponents of this linguistic determinism, learning Irish will lead to the adoption of an Irish outlook which is assumed to be nationalist. Language enthusiasts often assume that the identity of 'Irish speaker' will become a master identity which subsumes all others. Similar trains of thought assume that greater education or socialising with nationalists will lead unionists to shed their political beliefs and embrace Irish nationalism.[19] As two Protestant nationalists put it:

> [Irish] brings you closer to the Catholic people of this island. It brings you closer to them in a certain way and it encourages you to think in a more sort of Irish way.

> ... if they [unionists] show an interest in Irish, it's something like, a wee bit like the thin end of the wedge. In a way they'll come to conclude, 'Well, Irish isn't too bad at all and the Irish aren't too bad.' People who learn Irish have a leaning towards nationalism.

Nevertheless, there are counterexamples which indicate that unionists may interpret the language in their own ways:

> I would come from the unionist tradition, and I could actually use my knowledge of Irish at the moment to defend the unionist position

19 For example, an American academic commented, '... the cross-cultural efforts of alternative Irish-language activists are of potential benefit to Sinn Féin because they may serve to re-spark Protestant nationalism, thus making Irish-speaking Protestants more receptive to a united Ireland' (Kachuk 1994: 149).

an awful lot better than most of the unionists ... the absurdity of
Ireland as a sort of Gaelic, Catholic nation and the idea that because
the sea is round it that makes it a nation. The language links us with
Scotland and with Wales and with Cornwall, and actually England
too. England is as Celtic a nation as we are. So I would see the Irish
language as linking us with the other Celtic peoples, and I think it's
a blind spot, this obsession with England as an enemy. The English
are the same people as we are, so it seems to me that Irish language
is something which holds the British Isles together. I mean the very
word 'British' speaks to me of a Celtic language, you know, and not
of English. Old Shakespeare with his England and her sister nations
bound together by the triumph of sea. I see the sea as binding nations
together. The sea has always bound Kintyre and County Antrim, and
for these absurd people to draw a line down there and say, 'This is
Ireland and that is Scotland.' That's rubbish.

Learning a language involves a cultural journey, and a process of 'becoming' rather than 'being' (Agar 2002: 28). Yet while nationalists may reinforce
their sense of Irishness by learning Irish, there is no evidence to support the
theory that by learning Irish a unionist will become a nationalist. The
Sapir/Whorf hypothesis of linguistic determinism has been challenged by
many linguists.[20] Furthermore, an Irish identity is not equivalent to a nationalist identity. Unionists can have hyphenated or situational identities, expressing aspects of Irishness and Britishness at different times (Todd 1987: 16).[21]
As one unionist learner of Irish put it:

> I've no difficulty in saying I'm Irish. I don't have a great deal of dif-
> ficulty with saying I'm British either because many aspects of my life
> would have been very different if it hadn't been for Britishness, like
> straight teeth – things like the National Health and university edu-
> cation which my family would have been far too poor to afford. And
> it's not just gratitude, but I can identify with things like the British
> Labour movement which also moulded me to a degree.

The more doctrinaire of nationalists insist that mixing Britishness and
Irishness cannot be done. One Protestant nationalist comments on Chris
McGimpsey, a unionist councillor with an interest in Irish:

---

20 Some sociolinguists still maintain a 'weak' version of this theory, arguing that languages still
offer insights into the cultural views of their speakers, and that users of languages can distin-
guish experiences in different ways (Kramsch 2000: 13–14 May 2001: 133).   21 It is a common feature of modern political life for people to believe that they belong simultaneously to
two nations (Smith 1986: 166). There is increasing recognition that ethnic and national affilia-
tions are fluid, as people choose social identities strategically, according to the context.

What's the point? If it's not saying something about your identity as an Irish person, I mean if you're learning *Irish*, it's inevitable. I cannot see the point of doing it, other than that. Why would you learn it? Except in a kind of disruptive way, you know, it's fun whenever Sinn Féin stand up in Belfast City Council to be able to speak more Irish than them and score a point that way. But I mean for me you want to learn a language because of something positive to say about yourself, and Irish culture, and a sense of place, and there's absolutely no point in being into it to score a point against republicans or nationalists.

Thus unionists who learn Irish are represented as having negative, 'political' objectives and nationalists are portrayed as having positive 'cultural' motives. This view is an inversion of the usual unionist claim that republicans are 'politicising' Irish.

PROTESTANTS AND THE IRISH LANGUAGE SCENE IN BELFAST

The ideology of Belfast Irish speakers contains inherent contradictions which allow for different approaches to Protestant learners of the language. The inclusivity of nationalist ideology and Catholic friendliness vies with Catholic communalism and hostility to unionists, who are perceived as irredeemable bigots. Nationalist Protestants have few problems with the Irish language scene, as their religious beliefs and background arouse Catholic curiosity rather than resentment. However, nationalists assume the political beliefs of unionist Protestants are grounded in sectarianism and/or ignorance.

Nationalists often portray Northern Protestants as erring natives or alien 'planters' (O'Halloran 1987).[22] If Protestants are really Irishmen (albeit engaged in disavowal), to refuse them access to the Irish language is to symbolically deny them membership of the Irish nation. Many Irish speakers are naturally glad to meet others, whatever their religious or political beliefs, and friendliness and tolerance are part of the Catholic communal tradition in Northern Ireland (Ruane and Todd 1996: 76). But if Protestants are conceptualized as British 'planters', then nationalist Irish speakers might resist perceived attempts to 'steal' their language, spy on them for loyalists or the British security forces, or attempts to undermine the association between nationalist ideology and language revivalism.

22 In recent years nationalists have become more willing to accept the British identities of unionists, although what this entails in a practical sense is unclear (Ruane and Todd 1996: 101).

Catholic Irish speakers occasionally disparage attempts to encourage Protestant interest in the language.[23] Gearóid Ó Cairealláin, a leading Irish language activist, satirized the 'galar' ('disease') of 'An tSlí leis an Ghaeilge a Dhéanamh Tarraingteach don Phobal Phrotastúnach i dTuaisceart Éireann' ('How to Make Irish Attractive to the Protestant Community in Northern Ireland') (*Lá*, 27 November 1997). According to one *Andersonstown News* article:

> Ní gá do Ghaeil Protastúnaigh na Sé Chontae a thabhairt leo chun an Ghaeilge a chur i réim in Éirinn arís. Gan fiacail a chur ann, tá 5 milliún duine sa tír seo agus más féidir linn leathchuid acu sin a thabhairt isteach ar an athbheochan ba chuma faoi Phrotastúnaigh na Sé Chontae. (*Andersonstown News*, 17 February 1990)
>
> [It is not necessary for Irish speakers to bring the Protestants of the Six Counties with them in restoring the Irish language in Ireland again. Without mincing words, there are 5 million people in this country and if we can bring half of them into the revival the Six County Protestants would not matter.]

Some Protestant learners of Irish have met Catholics who objected to their learning the language. This is usually communicated though hostile looks or avoidance, rather than open hostility. Ignoring Protestant learners can be a polite form of sectarianism which is ambiguous, as it can represent a genuine oversight or a malicious intent to overlook the feelings of others (see Liechty and Clegg 2001: 133). However, some Protestant learners seem to be left in little doubt. One Protestant describes his visit to the Gaelic League's *ard-fheis*, when it was held in Belfast in 1995:

> I was coming down the stairs and there was a group of them there [Belfast Irish speakers]. They were all talking but when they saw me they stopped. It was so obvious – I was the only one coming down the stairs. And I thought 'Oh, God! They know me. Do I need all this?'

This learner was shunned on further occasions and decided to stop learning Irish. His Protestant friends asked him why he bothered with Irish speakers

---

23 There are many examples of minority language groups which restrict access to their languages. Young black Creole speakers in London often resent white people learning their language, although some make allowances for friends (Hewitt 1986). In Ireland, travellers who speak Cant and Gammon are afraid that police officers and public sector workers will learn their language in order to eavesdrop on their conversations (Power 2002: 159).

when they caused him so much stress. Eventually he decided not to bother and abandoned learning Irish. Republican claims of the non-sectarianism of the IRA are met with Protestant incredulity. Many Protestants are fearful of republican Irish speakers, given their history of physical violence. One Protestant learner said to me, 'It's all right arguing with them, but at what point do your kneecaps come off?' Fears of republican intelligence gathering are so strong that some Protestants are reluctant to give their addresses or telephone numbers to their teachers. Furthermore, Protestant learners have been afraid they will be perceived to be spies for loyalists or for the British security services. Another problem concerning Protestant learners of Irish is that they often wish to fade into the 'Catholic' background, undercommunicating their Protestant identities, so Catholic Irish speakers are unaware if they have particular concerns.

The reaction by Protestant learners to hostility and other chill factors varies, but those who persist overcome their difficulties. They learn to attribute the hostility of Catholic Irish speakers to certain individuals, as they meet others who are more friendly. Sympathetic Irish speakers try to explain those who are hostile to Protestant learners as 'cúng' ('narrow-minded') or 'bitter', sometimes owing to bad experiences during the troubles, leading to sectarian attitudes. Sectarian Irish speakers are thus conceptually minoritized in terms of personal pathology, rather than as expressing Catholic communal or political values. In a similiar manner, Catholic Irish speakers who reject accounts of Protestant fears or Catholic hostility may pathologize concerned Protestant learners as 'paranoid'. However, it is not necessary to attribute the fears of Protestants to mental imbalance, especially at the initial toe-in-the-water stages of learning. One unionist learner from the majority Protestant town of Newtownards explained why he would not go to language classes in west Belfast – 'I'd be a stranger in a strange land.' Given his background and beliefs, this seems to have been a reasonable assumption.

Other challenges facing Protestant learners concern the culture of the Irish language – the phenomenon of 'languaculture' (Agar 2002). Phrases which reflect nationalist thought, nationalist songs (often in English), and discussions of republican politics and GAA matches[24] at Irish language events are examples of occasions when Protestant learners encounter intra-group interaction which exclude them, whether intentionally or otherwise. This can cause the Protestants to feel they are in a median state, encountering another culture as well as their own. They feel like 'temporary tourists' in the Irish language scene. Protestant learners may experience feelings of detachment and disengagement, adopting a strategic approach to involvement with Irish speak-

---

24 Most people in Northern Ireland appear to develop their interest in sports during their school years, and few Protestants ever encounter GAA games during their education.

ers. For example, I spoke to one nationalist Protestant learner who decided not to send his child to an Irish-medium school. He felt his children would be out of place in a working-class Catholic environment.[25]

On the other hand, Protestant learners can find the distinctiveness of the Irish language scene enlightening. Some Protestant motivations to learn Irish arise from their interest in Irish as an exotic language of a different community.[26] Discovering a new culture and ways of interpreting their surroundings often makes the experience worthwhile. One Protestant learner explains how he came to see Belfast in a new light:

> I remember in Methody [Methodist College] in my last year, I found these books in Methody library about Deirdre of the Sorrows and Cú Chulainn and things. They really captivated me 'cos I'd never heard of these people and I suddenly found that they actually lived here, and it gave the whole place this wonderful resonance of romance, which I of course hadn't seen before, because for me Belfast was big warehouses and the City Hall [laughs]. So I suddenly found that there was this 'waters of the wild' and Avalony-type things very central to the past here. I found that very intriguing. In Methody all the stories I read about castles, pools and dingly dells were all in England and England was such a wonderful place and I would have to go to England to see them. I didn't realize that they were here as well.

A learner from the Shankill Women's Centre was inspired for many reasons by a visit to an Irish-medium primary school, Gaelscoil na bhFál. She admired the standard of education, the high level of the school's organization, and the important role of women as teachers:

> I suppose I didn't expect it to be quite so well run as it is, and although I know they're in the process of getting the place refurbished and things like that, the women who run it are very very strong, and have a great sense of direction where they're going and what they want, and have a great rapport with the children. I mean we went to a P1 class and a P2 class and a P3 class, and in the P2 class I was lost because I couldn't understand what they were saying! The children all *love* it, and it's a very happy environment.

---

25 One Protestant who lives outside Belfast related how his daughter felt strange and excluded in an Irish-medium school as all her classmates were prepared for confirmation during school hours. 26 As Sam McAughtry wrote rather pithily, 'Catholics are not so curious to know about Protestants, but Protestants are always curious about Catholics' (1985: 37).

Most Protestants have positive experiences of learning Irish. There are many examples of Catholic attitudes of sensitivity and inclusivity towards Protestant learners. Some Protestant learners told me how Catholic Irish speakers recounted the traditional hostility of the Catholic Church to the Irish language in an attempt to make Protestant learners more welcome. Teachers are also known to try to put Protestant learners at their ease by saying they are interested in Scottish Gaelic – a 'Protestant' language, with a large number of Presbyterian speakers. Teachers of classes in the centre and south of the city often assume they have some Protestants in their classes, and will carefully monitor their own statements in order not to give offence.

In Northern Irish life, despite political and religious differences, individuals can develop bridging relationships in interest groups or work environments. In these situations, the identity as 'fellow worker' or 'fellow Irish speaker' are highlighted, and other differences are subsumed. Friendship can cross all divisions in Northern Irish society, as many find that life is much more complicated than nationalist or unionist ideologies will allow:

> There didn't seem to be any bother, because you were aware you were a Protestant and they would be aware that you were a Protestant too. You were welcomed because, the impression I got, because you took an interest in the culture of the country – you were made very welcome, in fact, maybe patronising a wee bit, even, at times by some people, not by them all, but by some people, you know. You'd have a bit of crack and a slagging about it, all right – but you know, it was all fun.

When Protestant and Catholic speakers of Irish meet for the first time, they often follow the social etiquette which entails the avoidance of religious and political topics of conversation. However, Protestant learners often notice that some Catholic Irish speakers depart from this etiquette, as they feel the need to demonstrate they are not republican. Thus Protestant learners often become the unintentional confidantes of Catholic Irish speakers who bitterly resent the republican image of the Irish language. This process is often two-way as many Protestant learners feel they have to distance themselves from the loyalist extremists of their own community. As one explained to me, 'We need to prove that we're not Orange bigots and they have to prove they're not Provos'.

In the absence of such 'proof', Protestant and Catholic Irish speakers often fantasize about each other's political beliefs, leading to incidents which reveal mutual misunderstandings. For example, I know of one Protestant unionist learner who is rather bemused by an Irish speaker who perceives him to be a latter-day United Irishman, leading his people from the folly of unionism to an enlightened republican perspective. This reflects the nationalist belief that unionism is a contemporary aberration from the Protestant principles of the United Irishmen (O'Halloran 1987: 24). Protestant learners can be mistaken for Catholics, especially as they often conceal or undercommunicate their backgrounds in Irish language environments. One recounted the surprise from his fellow learners when he revealed his religious background, resulting in them 'rewinding what they'd said in their heads' for a moment, in case they had said anything which could be construed as sectarian. Protestant learners find their stereotypes of Irish speakers are often challenged; one was taken aback in a west Belfast class when the teacher told him that the republican slogan 'Tiocfaidh ár lá' was 'bad Irish'. Some Protestants are surprised by the friendliness of certain republican Irish speakers, and learn to perceive them more sympathetically as individuals and not as malevolent agents of a political movement.

Ultach, a small Irish language promotion and funding organization, has a cross-community remit and its offices are situated in the 'neutral' centre of Belfast to provide ease of access to people from a Protestant background. For example, one working-class Protestant used to come into Ultach offices to enquire about Irish language learning materials. He was too afraid to go to the Cultúrlann to buy them, so Ultach staff would purchase them and he would repay them when he came to the 'safe' Ultach space. Ultach also helps interested Protestants to find suitable classes and Gaeltacht courses.

While Ultach established a fine cross-community ethos after its inception in 1989, having a cross-community board and publishing relevant materials, such as a reprint of the Revd William Neilson's *An Introduction to the Irish Language,* the organization was able to undertake more outreach work when I was employed as a cross-community officer in 1997. This included giving presentations to Protestant groups on the Irish language classes, providing classes and information on the language, and publishing information on the experiences of Protestant learners to raise awareness of Catholics (e.g. McCoy and Ní Bhaoill 2004). This work can be difficult at times, as many Protestants are hostile or indifferent towards the Irish language.[27] However, as the peace

---

27 Occasionally I have been the object of republican suspicion and Protestant hostility because of my job. Shortly after I begun work, I received a letter from the One Ireland – Two Nations group, together with an Orange song 'Here we are and here we stay' and some photocopied Sinn Féin propaganda. The letter stated, 'Those Protestants who call themselves Irish and take part in Irish culture, including Irish dancing and Irish language are traitors and collaborators and do more damage to our cause than Sinn Féin/IRA can ever do.' The solution was to create 'FREE ULSTER AREAS' where such activities would be banned, together with 'goods that promote Irish Republicanism (Caffreys etc) and those that are advertised by Irish actors (Surf, etc.)'; this is a reference to the increasing Irishness of advertisements broadcast by Ulster Television on account of its higher audience in the Irish Republic, although loyalists attribute the increasing Irishness to preparations for a united Ireland.

process gathers strength I have been given more opportunities. For example, I have taken classes for civil servants in the Departments of Health and Office of First Minister and the Deputy First Minister. I have noted that as Irish increases in status in Northern Ireland, more Protestants are enquiring about 'official' Irish – how to address the President of Ireland, for example. As more Protestants become fluent in Irish, their enquiries have become more detailed, including complex grammatical questions.

However, there remain many difficulties. A heated debate on the Irish language in Sandy Row, a staunch unionist district, was interrupted by a woman who had learned some Irish in a class in the city centre, but complained that all Irish language activities seemed to be in 'republican areas', and there would be nowhere in the city where she could explore the Irish language in a 'safe' environment. This is a legitimate concern. While Protestants who would venture into west Belfast have less fear of being seen as spies, fears of hostility or appearing conspicuous remain; as one put it, 'I'm afraid of sticking out like a sore thumb'. Some other concerns have little to do with the Irish language movement; drivers are often afraid that their cars will be stolen, given the joyriding problem in west Belfast. One ameliorating factor is the larger number of Irish language events held in the city centre since the ceasefires, reflecting a more tolerant approach by the municipal authorities and entertainment centres; nonetheless these events are still few and far between.

CONCLUSION: PROTESTANTS AND IRISH IN THE NEW BELFAST

Belfast is in a state of political and cultural flux; Irish is simultaneously the language of the Catholic ghetto and the government application form. It is regrettable, however, given the rapid physical transformation of peace-time Belfast, that cultural and community divisions remain entrenched. The image of the Irish language as a Sinn Féin shibboleth has changed little. Most working-class Protestants detest Irish, while some middle-class Protestants are developing more sympathetic views, and a minority from both classes even learn the language. The post-ceasefire period has opened up many opportunities for Protestants to learn Irish, but as we have seen, many have to tip-toe through a minefield of sectarian sensitivities, a familiar enough activity of the people of Belfast.

It is very difficult to foretell the future of Protestants and the Irish language in the city. A depressing scenario would be that the current widespread hostility to Irish would continue, given Protestant fears of the electoral rise of Sinn Féin, the persistence of communal divisions, and the replacement of the military conflict by a cultural one. A more positive scenario would be 'back to the future'; the situation may in some ways come to resemble that of the relaxed 1960s rather than the tense 1980s. Protestant learners of Irish may not find themselves caught between warring factions and tensions may ease between the two communities. The conflict would be mere history for young Catholic Irish speakers and young inquisitive Protestants. Therefore, Protestants and Catholics may be ready to discuss their differences and explore the Irish language together.

Irish-medium education in Belfast

SEÁN MAC CORRAIDH

'Irish-medium education' is a fairly recently coined title for the sector, probably influenced by the name given to French language immersion programmes in Canada which is referred to in the literature as 'French-medium education'. In the 1970s it was referred to in Irish with terms like *oideachas Gaeilge* or *scolaíocht Ghaeilge* (Irish language schooling/education in English). This form of educating children has been with us in Belfast since the 1960s when a small nursery was set up in Cumann Chluain Ard in Hawthorn Street, Belfast for children of Irish speaking parents. Strangely enough, it was also in the 1960s in Canada that the same type of educational experiment was being carried out for English speaking, mostly middle-class children whose parents wanted them, for various reasons, to become bilingual and bicultural (Baker and Prys Jones, 1998). However, while the French-medium system had the professional advice of psychologists and educationalists, Irish-medium education in Belfast was driven by the passion, faith, belief, courage and radical resolve of the original parents. These qualities were passed to other parents and the school that was opened stayed open unsupported officially for thirteen years. The Irish-medium sector in Belfast has been financially supported by the state since the 1984, thirteen years after the establishment of the first Irish language primary school in Belfast in 1971, known as Scoil Ghaeilge Bhéal Feirste (Belfast Irish Language School) at the time and Bunscoil Phobal Feirste (Belfast Community Primary School). Teacher education for those who chose the pathway of Irish-medium education in their academic career has only been available since 1996 and is offered for primary phase teachers through both the Bachelor of Education (BEd) and Post-Graduate Certificate in Education (PGCE) courses in Saint Mary's University College, Belfast. Only recently have the specific needs of Irish-medium teachers been seriously considered in the professional development courses for teachers organized by the education and library boards, who are charged with advising and supporting teachers.

THE 1950S AND A NEW PHILOSOPHY AMONG BELFAST IRISH SPEAKERS

In the 1950s, Belfast's Irish language movement was losing hope in the 'official' language movement based in Dublin and in the intentions of the Irish gov-

ernment to address the decline of Irish in Irish speaking areas and its development beyond those areas. These were the opinions of a revivalist organization by the name of Fál who presented this new philosophy in their paper
Dearcadh (Ó Fiaich, 1990). Their philosophy to a large extent was modelled on
the published writings of the Donegal Gaeltacht writer Seosamh Mac Grianna,
a major figure nationally in twentieth-century prose writing in Irish (Ó Muirí,
1999; de Brún, 2002). The 1950s were also a golden era for Irish language clubs
and societies in Belfast for a diverse range of intellectual and sporting activities including cycling, hiking, swimming, reading and drama (Maguire, 1991).
This era of clubs and societies helped prepare a theoretical foundation for the
practical approach and resultant accomplishments of the following decades, in
terms of the promotion of Irish and Irish-medium education in Belfast.

THE PRACTICAL APPROACH OF THE 1960S AND 1970S

Scéal Úr was a newspaper which featured the varied programme of events
that the Irish language community in Belfast took part in during the 1960s
(Barnes, 2001). It published news, information and material for reflection for
'our part of the Gaeltacht'. Cumann Chluain Ard, an Irish language society
with premises in west Belfast but whose Irish language classes were attended
by Belfast people from all areas and all sections of the community, was also
central to a lot of these developments. These developments included a nursery group for the children of Irish speaking families and the establishment of
the Shaw's Road urban Gaeltacht, Pobal Feirste. In 1971 a ground-breaking
initiative was launched that was to influence and shape the fate of the Irish
language and of Irish-medium education in Belfast. The Shaw's Road families opened a school in which their Irish speaking children would be educated
through the Irish language. The simple fact that when the children of Shaw's
Road Gaeltacht came of school age they needed to attend school was established by that Irish language community over one weekend in 1971. Initially,
only Irish speaking children attended and a certain homogeneity existed in
that all the pupils not only had a good understanding of Irish but could speak
it as well. This is an important point as, later on, nursery education was necessary in order to promote both Irish language receptive and production skills
in those children from English speaking families who attended the school.

AN EARLY ATTEMPT AT POST-PRIMARY PROVISION

When these original children came to the age of post-primary education in
the late 1970s, again it was decided to provide this phase of Irish-medium

education on the site of Scoil Ghaeilge Bhéal Feirste on Shaw's Road, Belfast. However, the odds were stacked against its survival. The procurement of learning, teaching and human resources proved too much. However, to their credit, a local school, St Mary's Christian Brothers' Grammar School, made strong attempts to assist the fledgling Irish language secondary school by providing instruction in Irish in some areas, especially the humanities. Nevertheless, the availability of Irish speaking teachers among staff dictated which subjects would be offered. Despite all of these efforts, therefore, the project of a new secondary school had to be put in abeyance.

RECOGNITION IN THE 1980S

Bunscoil Bhaile Stíle (Steelestown Primary School) in Derry City had been established originally as a unit within an English-medium school and it gained recognition in 1983. The following year after a long struggle with the education authorities Bunscoil Phobal Feirste (formerly known as Scoil Ghaeilge Bhéal Feirste) on Shaw's Road, Belfast gained recognition. Nevertheless, the accommodation (including the school hall, offices and staff room) was entirely made up of prefabricated huts. This situation remained until the school got a new building just a few years ago. Although the accommodation was not great, the staff's spirit, morale and sense of collegiality were very high. Bunscoil Phobal Feirste had started taking in children from English speaking families who had no previous experience of Irish whatsoever. When these children came to study the primary curriculum the collegiality among teachers mentioned above was needed in order to meet the challenges of ensuring quality learning opportunities for children in the Irish language and in all the other areas of learning. The driving force was always that the children were at the centre of all learning activities. The perceived high quality of the education that pupils were getting and indeed the success levels in the transfer process (eleven plus test) resulted in huge demand for this type of education from neighbouring communities in west Belfast and further afield in areas such as Short Strand and Ardoyne. Nurseries were also set up in these areas, carefully established with clear indications to the communities of the social and economic benefits of such ventures. Children came and still come to school in Bunscoil Phobal Feirste from these areas on buses. The second Irish-medium school in Belfast originally known as An Dara Gaelscoil (literally, the second Irish-medium school) opened in 1987 in a small room beside a bingo hall on the Springfield Road with the present author as teacher in charge. Even at this stage the vision the organizers showed is to be praised, for part of my contract was to visit on a weekly basis an experienced immersion teacher to work on my plans and schemes of work. The emphasis was firmly on the quality of provision from the outset. That school is now known as Gaelscoil Na bhFál (the Falls Irish-medium school) and is a flourishing institution today. Those associated with the nursery in the Twinbrook area negotiated with the authorities in Bunscoil Phobal Feirste and a satellite of the school was opened under the name of Scoil na Fuiseoige (The school of the lark) which is now a successful Irish-medium primary school serving the greater Twinbrook and Poleglass areas.

It is important to mention that many of the teachers who were the pioneers of Irish-medium education have now moved into vitally strategic positions in the promotion and development of the sector. These positions include the management of the Irish-medium resource centre (An tÁisaonad Lán-Ghaeilge) located in St Mary's University College, senior management of schools, language teachers in post-primary schools, principals of schools both urban and rural, teacher educators, academics, advisers and advisory teachers in education and library boards, developing curriculum and assessment materials at the Council for Curriculum Examinations and Assessment. This has an upside and a downside in that a lot of wisdom and dearly-bought experience left the sector and young inexperienced teachers came in place who may not have the same insight or pioneering spirit of those who preceded them.

POST-PRIMARY IRISH-MEDIUM EDUCATION

Early in the 1990s the provision of post-primary Irish-medium education in Belfast became a reality with a small number of pupils based in Cultúrlann Mac Adam/Ó Fiaich in west Belfast. The growth in demand for Irish-medium education at this phase closely resembled the growth in the primary phase schools and soon the premises were too small. The school proved its academic credentials and scored highly in examination results against similar types of schools with the same profile in their student intake. Its viability was obvious to parents and a strong campaign ended in recognition for the school and new premises which, at the time of writing, are being extended with a 4.3 million build and an increase of pupil population to six hundred.

THE QUALITY OF THE LEARNING AND TEACHING

I was among the first cohort of teachers who were inspected by Department of Education inspectors. It was clear to them that there was a lot of effective teaching going on, that teachers brought many professional skills to the school which created a healthy learning climate in classrooms. However, the place of English was not clearly defined. This I feel is still a dilemma in Irish-medium education today. I remember that a Welsh language adviser came to visit the school and said that we should keep English in a vacuum and not allow it to infiltrate the school. English is taught as a core curricular subject through English but, on a personal note, I believe that through a controlled, creative innovative approach, English could be exploited on a grander scale to promote the quality of teaching and learning in the sector through a greater use of bilingual glosses, for example, and other learning aids. This, and the most effective ways to develop pupils' production skills of speaking and writing Irish are areas which can be effectively promoted in an integrated way.

IRISH-MEDIUM EDUCATION COMES IN FROM THE PERIPHERY

The early years of the new millennium witnessed the establishment of Comhairle na Gaelscolaíochta (The Council for Irish-medium Education) to develop the sector, and Iontaobhas na Gaelscolaíochta (The Irish-medium Education Trust) to raise funds to aid the sector. A curriculum adviser and two advisory teachers for the areas of literacy and numeracy have been appointed to the Education and Library Boards to provide the Irish-medium perspective to the professional development and support offered to teachers.

Today in the North of Ireland there are around 65 educational sites across the three phases: nursery, primary and secondary, with around 3300 children; 165 teachers and 35 nursery directors (Comhairle na Gaelscolaíochta, 2004). In the greater Belfast area today, there are ten playgroups which children attend in order to acquire a passive knowledge of Irish which will enable them to study the primary curriculum through that language. There are also ten Irish-medium primary schools stretching from Twinbrook in west Belfast, to Cliftonville in north Belfast, and to Ormeau in south Belfast. There are three sites in the region of the education and library boards (ELBs) where Irish-medium education is presently available at the secondary level. These are in west Belfast, Derry city and Armagh city. In the Derry and Armagh cases, these are units within 'mother schools'. Belfast's Irish language secondary school Meánscoil Feirste (Belfast Secondary School), which opened in 1991, operates independently and is now being extended with new ICT facilities and lecture hall and as mentioned above recently gained permission from the Department of Education to take in up to six hundred pupils. In the region of the five ELBs, around 32 percent of all the nurseries are in Belfast with 46 percent of the pupils, 35 percent of the primary schools are in Belfast, 56 percent of the pupils and 48 percent of the teachers. There is one post-primary school in Belfast with 84 percent of pupils and 72 percent of all teachers of post-primary ImE. Irish-medium education was initiated in Belfast and it is clear that ImE remains strongest in Belfast across the five ELBs area.

ACHIEVEMENTS

The achievements of Irish-medium education in Belfast, which are the focus of this article, are significant and include the following:

- An alternative quality grassroots educational provision, which parents voluntarily buy into, has been created in Belfast by dedicated hardworking parents, teachers, and governors for their children and for the children of parents who choose it.
- The overwhelming majority of practitioners in the sector are young and vibrant teachers.
- The schools have enjoyed the support of the communities.
- The sector has given a lot of children an awareness of their Irish language heritage while being presented with the local curriculum which children locally in English-medium education also study.
- Pupils gain a competence in Irish which entails advanced skills in comprehension and fluency of production.
- Pupils retain a pioneering spirit, a strong attachment and regard for the Irish language after leaving post-primary Irish-medium education.

CHALLENGES

The challenges facing the sector are just as significant and include the following:

- A lack of resources especially in Irish literacy, resourcing learning and teaching in Irish-medium schools has been and remains a major challenge to effective teaching in the sector. Funding was secured for a resource unit back in the early 1990s in Bunscoil Phobal Feirste and this resource unit (An tÁisaonad Lán-Ghaeilge) is now located in St Mary's University College. Funded by Foras na Gaeilge, the Áisaonad has created high quality history, science, numeracy and literacy resources mainly for primary schools. So, in some ways, the days of the teacher-produced resources, in the form of black and white worksheets has gone.
- Teacher workload in translating, attending to two languages, integrating language and content.
- Shortage of teachers and substitute due to supply not meeting demand.
- Inexperienced teachers in classrooms and in management positions without experienced teachers to fall back on for advice within the schools.
- Teachers' Irish language proficiency as second language users of Irish.
- Fit-for-purpose professional development of teachers.

- Small percentages of native speakers among Irish language teachers and assistants in sector. An increased number of native speakers would add vibrancy to the Irish language environment in schools.
- School development and effectiveness.
- Attracting and recruiting teachers who are both specialists in subject areas and highly proficient in Irish is a difficulty in post-primary education.
- Developing accuracy and form in pupils' production of the Irish language.

CONCLUSION

Perhaps in the past the Irish-medium sector has not marketed itself or celebrated its many successes and the excellent education it provides loudly or often enough. The approach has always been open, reflective and, at times, self-critical with the aim of improving. In this healthy, reflective atmosphere, challenges can be addressed and overcome within a learning sector such as this one. In the urban context of a changing Belfast, it should be recognized that Irish-medium education at all levels in the last three decades has added an exciting, dynamic, challenging, innovative, bilingual aspect to the educational choices parents can make for their children. The ever-increasing numbers of pupils in the schools show that parents view Irish-medium education as a viable alternative to the mainstream educational provision. Increasingly, teachers in the sector report a growth in their sense of worth and professionalism, in that development bodies such as Comhairle na Gaelscolaíochta (The Council for Irish-medium Education) and Iontaobhas na Gaelscolaíochta (The Irish-medium Trust), and a fit-for-purpose advisory service within the education and library boards are now fully operational and available to them. These developments working in partnership can potentially enhance the practice and professional knowledge of ImE practitioners which the pioneering teachers of the final three decades of the last millennium established on the strong foundations of commitment, industry and zeal.

The Gaeltacht Quarter: promoting cultural promiscuity and wealth

SEÁN MISTÉIL

From its origins as the 'the mouth of the sandbank', the present city of Belfast is defining new meanings and fresh frontiers of industrial, economic, social and environmental achievement. Yet, significant parts of the city remain negative economic beneficiaries and their assets, such as language and culture, continue to be ignored when it comes to city-wide or regional economic planning. The Irish language community is one such location and exists as a relatively untapped mine of potential. In an age of fascination with cultural roots and riches, the Irish language is a raw material of a significant cultural capital. It is time that the city began to transform these materials into products, for competitive advantage and strategic attractiveness. The Gaeltacht Quarter is a model for achieving that. It is structured to maximize the economic opportunities provided by a growing cluster of Irish language and culture-based enterprises. Envisaged is a new physical and organizational context into which local creativity can be packaged and channelled into products and services which generate wealth. Over time this will produce a virtuous circle: people attracting people, businesses creating further businesses, a living, organic village, giving extra colour and dignity to the idea of Belfast as a vibrant, open and pluralistic city.

The potential for progress is already evident. At government level the Joint West Belfast/Greater Shankill Task Force Report recommended that the Gaeltacht Quarter be developed and a development board established to oversee delivery. Arising from this ministerial recommendation, Clive Dutton, a distinguished regeneration specialist, was commissioned by the Department of Culture, Arts and Leisure (DCAL) to assess operational issues for the development board and advise on its structure and governance. His proposed delivery model and observation that the Gaeltacht Quarter requires 'open minds and an inventive, and indeed, courageous and ambitious approach' is encouraging. Dutton goes on to state that 'The Gaeltacht Quarter is a project that relates to the heartbeat of the city of Belfast. To the history and culture of the people and the potential to achieve positive effect across Northern Ireland, the island of Ireland, and internationally – as a beacon initiative, by building on and implementing the recommendations of the joint West Belfast and Greater Shankill Task Forces Report'. At a community level, Forbairt Feirste (Belfast Development), Belfast's Irish language economic agency, continues to play a mainstream role in co-ordinating and maintaining momentum from all the partners in the process. Its mission of 'Using the richness of the Irish language to release the city's economic power' provides a benchmark to measure progress and to ensure the Gaeltacht Quarter benefits people within and outside its immediate locale.

At this formative stage the Gaeltacht Quarter has a city-wide and inclusive message to communicate as well as a set of core values and economic objectives to be explained. Those objectives can be compared to stars, which are fixed points, but which are perceived differently from one person to another according to the physical, cultural, social and historical placement of that person. We must be flexible and sensitive in responding to this diversity but also challenging to those parts which seek to advance the Irish language as a location for cultural segregation or as a zone of discomfort in terms of city-wide economic planning. It seems that suspicion of each others' cultures has a long heritage. In overcoming this negative legacy it is important that we allow others to see how the cultural structures of the Gaeltacht Quarter have grown. The Gaeltacht Quarter consolidates what is already a long story built on steady development. Two landmark events are useful in this respect—the stories of Cumann Chluain Ard and Gaeltacht Bhóthar Seoigh (Shaw's Road Gaeltacht). Each provides insights into the language's organic growth and explains that the Gaeltacht Quarter is ideologically consistent with generations of thinking stretching back to the 1930s.

West Belfast in 1936 was a place of poverty, hunger and mass unemployment. People whose every thought was how and where to obtain work and food, were in no mood to listen to what they thought was the empty idealism of Gaelic speaking. Seamus Maxwell and Liam Rooney, two unemployed young men had the courage and foresight to think differently. They formed what later developed into Cumann Chluain Ard, an Irish language club dedicated to learning and social advancement. The club was based in the back streets of the Falls Road. In a programme for the Thomas Davis Centenary Week produced in 1945, they were described as being 'alive to the facts that Gaelic speaking was not something mystical or abstract, but a definite cultural and economic objective'. Even today this is an innovative statement to make but during the urban distress of the thirties and forties it demonstrated remarkable insight. Try to imagine yourself living during that time. You are married, three young children, out of work and no prospect of gaining work. In a conversation with your wife you state that economic progress (bread on the table) is linked to learning and encouraging others to learn Irish. This is what Maxwell and Rooney believed and this is what the Gaeltacht Quarter seeks to prove.

Today, investing in culture is paraded as a proven tool of urban and social regeneration. As the new knowledge-based economy develops, it is becoming increasingly clear that cultural distinctiveness will play a critical role. Yet the Irish language still remains on the fringes in terms of area-based, city-wide and regional economic planning. The Gaeltacht Quarter seeks to reverse this trend.

In a recent paper entitled 'Bilingualism and economic development in west European minority language regions', Ab van Langevelde concludes by stating that 'bilingualism can serve as a stimulus to regional authorities to foster an economic development more in harmony with the regional culture, in which the minority language plays so salient a role. Then bilingualism would form a point of profit in the economic development of west European minority language regions'.[1] The founders of Cumann Chluain Ard and Ab van Langevelde may be separated by time but they are connected by their shared understanding that language can be a powerful economic driver.

During the 1940s, 1950s and 1960s Cumann Chluain Ard developed into the epicentre for Irish language activity in Belfast attracting young people from all over the city. It was here that the next big step in the development of the language took place – the formation of the Shaw's Road Gaeltacht in 1969. Globally, the sixties were a time for dreamers but few would have such a deep and long-lasting impact as those first families who joined together to establish the city's first urban Gaeltacht. They were taste makers, social investors, seeding social impact and theirs was a bold undertaking. They believed that the residents of a city are responsible for what they can bring out of their city. They were not interested in incremental change but preferred to operate at the other end of the change spectrum. The place where transformational change occurs. In trying to reconfigure a culturally dysfunctional city, they asked questions 'What if the language could be heard? What difference would it make to our children? What will it bring to the city?' The noise they generated stirred the city and awakened a new sense of self and history within neighbourhoods and generations. Their bold undertaking triggered the development of Irish language education and the massive growth in Irish language activity. The skyline shows physical evidence – cranes building new Irish language schools but it is the horizon of what is possible which remains their most telling contribution. They pushed it high and created space for others to follow and grow.

Many programmes have been made and column inches written about the Shaw's Road Gaeltacht but few have recognized the role of its wider constituents and supports. This is important in understanding the Gaeltacht Quarter and its relationship to the wider city. It would be wrong to think that the Gaeltacht Quarter will accrue benefit to only one part of the city

---

1 Ab Van Langevelde, 'Bilingualism and economic development in west European minority language regions:a dooyeweerdian approach'. University of Groningen.

or to only one community. Shaw's Road Gaeltacht, like the Gaeltacht Quarter, is site specific, yet, it functions on a wider geographic basis relying on an interdependent set of overlapping relationships – a partnership in which strength is shared and built. This was critical in maintaining the vision. Against a backcloth of state neglect, rising violence and oppressive threat, those first pioneering families could so easily have given in. They were sustained by the strength of their community – a city-wide community – which comprised English and Irish speaking neighbours. It is important that we remind ourselves that the Shaw's Road Gaeltacht was an initiative of the Irish speaking community in Belfast as a whole and it was from this wider, deeper well that success was achieved. Economic support was vital in maintaining momentum but there were other more powerful factors. As children of that community and from a young age we acquired a strong sense of destiny and a fearless, fierce appetite for the future. I think this is in part due to our city-wide identity. The Shaw's Road Gaeltacht provided a sense of place for many. As children we gained great strength from this reality and from the visits we received from our neighbours from throughout the city and, indeed, the island. I smile, for example, when I think of the great support we received from the Ballymun community in Dublin. People who didn't have much to give but who gave a lot. For us children, the children of other Irish speaking families such as the de Brún, Ó Maoileoin, Mac Ainmhire and Napier families provided fun and the understanding that we were part of a wider community. For the adults, individuals like Alf Ó Murchú, Brendán Mac Giolla Domhnaigh, Pádraig Ó Maolchraoibhe, Pilib Mac Mathúna, Seán Mac Goill, Séimí Ó hOdhráin, and many others, dug deep and kept heads up.

The Shaw's Road Gaeltacht is still growing but the centre of innovation has moved to the place were the next big step in driving the city and its languages forward will take place. The urbanization of the Irish language gifts Belfast with the opportunity of building new strategic capital. The Gaeltacht Quarter represents the city's most authentic model for achieving this. John Montgomery, in his paper 'Cultural quarters as mechanisms for urban regeneration', prepared for the Australia National Congress, states: 'Good cultural quarters will only succeed if they offer a distinctive and varied cultural programme.'[2] In this respect the Gaeltacht Quarter finds itself in fertile ground and provides the city with a blueprint for rewriting the rule book that defines diverse cities. The Gaeltacht Quarter is authentic, not generic, and has grown organically over a number of years.

---

2 Montgomery, John, 2003: 'cultural quarters as mechanisms for urban regeneration: a review of four cultural quarters in the UK, Ireland and Australia', paper presented to the Planning Institute of Australia National Congress.

Those familiar with regeneration policy designed to address the problems of distressed urban areas will know that encouraging increased footfall is an important part of the dynamic of change. West Belfast's indices of need and deprivation are well-documented in the Taskforce report. What is not so clear is that this part of West Belfast is already attracting enormous footfall. Physically we have a Medical/Teaching Hospital, a University and, in the Cultúrlann, the focal point for Irish language development. Culturally, we have dynamic theatre companies, film-makers, artists, writers, unique political tourism assets, an Irish language daily, cafés, a varied events programme and the biggest community festival in Europe delivered annually by the Féile an Phobail team. The message is clear. The critical mass ingredients of modern urban regeneration are already coalescing. A word about some of those ingredients.

St Mary's University College has a vibrant Irish language community with a long-standing tradition of teaching Irish at degree level. It is at the forefront of providing bilingual teacher education for Irish-medium schools both at undergraduate and post-graduate levels. It has an Irish language resource centre, a well-stocked library of Irish language materials and provides a specialized ICT learning environment for the Irish language. Of equal importance is its commitment of fully supporting the vision of the Gaeltacht Quarter and, indeed, Montgomery also spotlights the importance of education to cultural quarters. What most, if not all, the cultural quarters have in common is the presence, either within the quarter, or very close to it, of a major arts education and/or training institution, whether it's the Northern Media School in Sheffield or the Visual and Performing Arts Centre in Adelaide. Temple Bar is adjacent to Trinity College, and the Manchester Institute for Popular Culture has an office in the MNQ. In the cases of Sheffield and Adelaide this outcome was quite deliberate, and both are seeking to strengthen the links between formal education and enterprise development. Through its further education training programme, Forbairt Feirste is pioneering vocational training through the medium of Irish. Through a dynamic partnership with BIFHE and with the support of the Department for Learning, a new arena of learning and earning is emerging.

In taking the Gaeltacht Quarter forward, the following points summarize its mission, objectives and practical impacts:

Mission

Using the Irish language as its centre of gravity the Gaeltacht Quarter will help its diverse satellites of economic and cultural action to operate together as a stable and organic economic system which sustains its people and is sensitive to their needs and ambitions.

Stewardship
The responsibility for the development of the Gaeltacht Quarter is also the challenge: how to provide a solid foundation for the prosperity of local people while creating a platform for public and private sector development. The solution, which combines civic responsibility and inclusive custodianship with the performance of high-level economic planning, is contained within the Taskforce recommendation to establish 'A representative Gaeltacht Quarter Development Board.'

Role and function of the Gaeltacht Development Board
We see its role primarily as the main engine of cultural renewal and regeneration, whose function it is to turbo-boost the momentum of growth and to supervise its acceleration and promotion within a city-wide, regional and European context.

Definition
The core of the Gaeltacht Quarter is embodied by a mix of physical, cultural, economic and social infrastructural requirements. These include:

- Development of creative industry incubator units.
- Skills enhancement and training conducted in Irish.
- Development of a brand space.

The Cultúrlann already embodies this idea of a brand space. A place where language can be spoken and heard. We now need to take this a step further. The Gaeltacht Quarter and the British Government's ratification of the European Charter for Regional and Minority Languages, Part III for the Irish language, provides us with the opportunity of taking this step. For its part Pobal has already in place plans to develop an innovative and interactive learning and visitor centre. This will play an important role not only in promoting our sense of history and progress but also in facilitating intergenerational activity. There are over 3000 children attending Irish language schools but there a few places where these children and their families can meet and mix. A social disconnect has emerged and the brand space proposal represents an opportunity of bridging that gap.

Development of an evening economy, including café culture
The role of Cumann Chluain Ard is critical in this respect. Once at the cutting edge of language activity in this city, its role needs to be reconsidered. This is important because it represents an enormous historical and economic asset. This needs to be either regenerated or relocated.

Trails that connect and illuminate the area's cultural touchstones
Cultural icons are an important part of this. This part of Belfast is populated
by and attracts figures of international reknown. Yet there is little or no recognition of their connection to the area. As a way of promoting this and as a
means of connecting some of the area's physical assets we propose the development of a 'marks of time' trail.

*The creation of a beacon landmark and the development of street furniture and
frontages*
To help identify the distinctiveness of the area and spotlight its Irish language characteristics.

Signage
We need to dress the area in a way which is consistent with and is supportive of our commitment to promoting engagement with other cultural communities whilst also promoting access for tourists.

The development of merchandizing opportunities and points of sale
As consumers increasingly exercise personal choice in the services they use
and the products they purchase, culture is rapidly evolving as a dynamic economic driver. Even our television viewing is becoming interactive with increasing collaboration between viewer and programme maker shaping individually
relevant content. Twenty-first century buying and selling is now about competing in the 'experience' economy. The success levers are trust, authenticity and individual fulfillment. The Gaeltacht Quarter can provide the inti-
macy which the market craves. To begin we need to create more spaces for
the language to be heard and then we must become crusaders – encouraging
people into actions consistent with commercial opportunity. This means challenging inertia and provoking people into recognizing that much of what they
take for granted in their language and culture offers enormous economic
potential. Let me be clear, this is not about embracing a right-wing economic
agenda but it is about championing economic rights. It is about saying that
our children should prosper equally and that our business model will succeed
because it will inspire innovation and better service the requirement for indi-
vidualization. In the late nineteenth century William Morris and the pre-
Raphaelite movement set out to implement a new kind of society that would
act as an alternative to industrialization and armed rebellion. This movement
and its craft ideals spread quickly to the US, Europe and Japan. Morris like
many of his colleagues made commercial successes of their ventures. We need
to show people how to create commercial value from cultural wealth. We need
to harness the self help ethos that sustained the development of Irish-medium
education and channel it towards business and entrepreneurial activity. For

its part Forbairt Feirste is pushing forward its 'Brabach an Phobail' initiative which aims to cultivate businesses in the social economy sector. But it is also our intention to turn Brabach an Phobail into a trading company which proactively drives and markets product and service innovation within the Gaeltacht Quarter community. This approach offers exciting opportunities for partnership, participation and progress. We have a lot to offer and its time to start selling. Let's feed the appetite for anti-standardization and create a really sexy set of brands that excite the world.

Physical development of the Beechmount site

The recent agreement of Belfast City Council to transfer ownership of the Beechmount Leisure centre through a heads of agreement between Forbairt Feirste, Meánscoil Feirste and St Mary's University College provides a unique opportunity of creatively exploring the public realm. This provides the Gaeltacht Quarter with space to physically explore new possibility, to construct a theatre perhaps, creative incubator units and develop a physical brand, a touchstone that resonates with residents and visitors.

The development of cultural venues and events

The development of cultural venues and events that release opportunities for citizens or visitors to deepen their understanding of the Irish language and culture. Music, language, dance and all art-forms being manifest in public accessible places.

Accommodation

The location of St Mary's University College has led to an increase in the provision of accommodation for students. This is seasonal and tends to lie vacant at critical times when visitors want to stay in West Belfast. The Gaeltacht Quarter presents an opportunity to reconfigure the nature of accommodation provision in this part of the city. We should begin by commissioning an audit of potential sites and then find ways of developing and better communicating its availability.

Sustainability

A structured programme that supports Irish language learning courses for adults needs to be put in place. It is also important that the momentum created by the establishment of the Gaeltacht Quarter is used to build links with other cultural and language communities in the city and that a co-operative marketing approach is implemented to actively promote Belfast as a multi-cultural destination offering a unique experience of cultural diversity and inclusion.

Conclusion

The message is simple: identify resources, and put them to use. It is not that there are too many voices in Belfast – but that there are not nearly enough. Making them heard is one step in the process of making Belfast itself heard – and listened to – all over the world.

Bibliography

Adams, G.B. (1964), 'The last language census in Northern Ireland' in G.B. Adams (ed.), *Ulster dialects: an introductory symposium* (Cultra, Co. Down), 111–46.

—— (1986), *The English dialects of Ulster: an anthology of articles on Ulster speech by G.B. Adams*, ed. Michael Barry and Philip Tilling (Cultra, Co. Down).

Adams, Gerry (1995), *Free Ireland: towards a lasting peace* (Dingle, Co. Kerry).

Agar, Michael (2002), *Language shock: understanding the culture of conversation* (New York).

Agnew, J. (1996), *Belfast merchant families in the seventeenth centuries* (Dublin).

Anderson, C. (1830), *Historical sketches of the native Irish* (Edinburgh).

Anderson, J. (1888), *History of the Belfast Library and Society for Promoting Knowledge commonly known as the Linen Hall Library* (Belfast).

Andrews, J.H. (1974), *History in the Ordnance Survey map: an illustrated history* (Belfast).

Baker, Colin (1992), *Attitudes and language* (Clevedon).

Baker, C. and Prys Jones, S. (1998), *Encyclopedia of bilingualism* (Clevedon).

Bardon, J. (1982), *A history of Ulster* (Belfast).

Barnes, D. (2001), 'Scéal Úr', BEd diss. (St Mary's University College, Belfast).

Beckett, C. (1967), *Fealsúnacht Aodha Mhic Dhomhnaill* (Dublin).

—— (1987), *Aodh Mac Domhnaill: Dánta* (Dublin).

—— (1995), 'A study of Robert S. McAdam's manuscript English-Irish dictionary', PhD thesis (The Queen's University of Belfast).

Benn, G. (1877), *A history of the town of Belfast* (London).

Blaney, R. (1996), *Presbyterians and the Irish language* (Belfast).

Boyd, Andrew (1969), *Holy war in Belfast* (Tralee).

Boyne, P. (1987), *John O'Donovan: a biography* (Kilkenny).

Brady, A.M., and B. Cleeve (1985), *A biographical dictionary of Irish writers* (Dublin).

Breathnach, D., and M. Ní Mhurchú (1986) *Beathaisnéis 1882–1982 a hAon* (Dublin).

—— (1994), *Beathaisnéis 1882–1982 a Ceathair* (Dublin).

Brett, C.E.B. (1985), *Buildings of Belfast, 1700–1914* (Belfast).

Burton, Frank (1978), *The politics of legitimacy: struggles in a Belfast community* (London).

Campbell, F. (1991), *The dissenting voice: Protestant democracy from plantation to partition* (Belfast).

Carroll, D. (1995), *The man from God knows where* (Dublin).

Chart, D.A. (1931) (ed.), *The Drennan letters* (Belfast).

Chichester, Sir A.P.B (1871), *History of the family of Chichester* (London).

Chitham, E. (1986), *The Brontës Irish background* (London).

Clarkson, Leslie (1983), 'The city and the country' in Beckett et al., *Belfast: the making of the city* (Belfast), 153–65.

Cohen, Anthony P. (1994), *Self consciousness: an alternative anthropology of identity* (London).

Comhairle na Gaelscolaíochta (2004), *Bunachar Sonraí Gaelscoileanna: 2003–2004* (Belfast).

Comhluadar (2005), (Dublin).

Corkery, D. (1925), *The hidden Ireland* (Dublin).

Dawson, C. (1992), *Peadar Ó Gealacáin: Scríobhaí* (Dublin).

Day, A. (1986), 'Computer-based index to Irish Ordnance Survey Memoirs', *Donegal Annual* 38, 78–80.

——, and P. McWilliams (1990–8), *Ordnance Survey memoirs of Ireland*, 40 vols (Belfast).

de Brún, Fionntán (2002), *Seosamh Mac Grianna: an mhéin rúin* (Dublin).

de Brún, P. (1987), 'The Irish Society's bible teachers', *Éigse* 22, 54–106.

de hÓir, É. (1961), *Royal Irish Academy Centenary Exhibition: John O'Donovan (1806–61) and Eugene O'Curry (1794–1862)* (Dublin).

de Paor, P. (1990), 'Roibeard Mac Ádhaimh agus uiscí fuinniúla na hÉireann: ceannródaí Gaeilge agus teicneolaíochta', *Comhar* (Eanáir), 20–5.

Deane, A. (1924) (ed.), *Belfast Natural History and Philosophical Society centenary volume, 1821–1921* (Belfast).

Dinneen, Rev. P. (1927), *Irish-English dictionary* (Dublin and London).

Duffy, Seán (1989), *Nicholas O'Kearney: the last of the bards of Louth* (Dublin).

Dunleavy, Janet Egleson, and Gareth Dunleavy (1991), *Douglas Hyde: a maker of modern Ireland* (Berkeley).

Dunn, Seamus, V. Morgan, and H. Dawson (2001), *Establishing the demand for services and activities in the Irish language in Northern Ireland* (Belfast).

Edwards, R. Dudley (1979), *Patrick Pearse: the triumph of failure* (London).

Elliot, M. (1989), *Wolfe Tone: prophet of Irish independence* (Yale).

Evans, Estyn E. (1996), *Ireland and the Atlantic heritage: selected writings* (Dublin).

Farmer, H. (1987), *The Oxford dictionary of saints* (Oxford).

Ferguson, Lady (1896), *Sir Samuel Ferguson and the Ireland of his day* (London and Edinburgh).

Finlay, Andrew (2004), 'Me too: victimhood and the proliferation of cultural claims in Ireland' in A. Finlay (ed.) *Nationalism and multiculturalism: Irish identity, citizenship and the peace process* (Münster).

Fisher, J.R., and J.H. Robb (1913), *Book of the Royal Belfast Academical Institution: the centenary volume, 1810–1910* (Belfast).

Fishman, J. (2001), *Can threatened languages be saved?* (Clevedon).

Fitzgerald, G. (1984), 'Estimates for baronies of minimum level of Irish speaking among successive decennial cohorts 1771–1781, to 1861–1871', *Proceedings of the Royal Irish Academy*, 84, C, 117–55.

—— (2003), 'Irish speaking in the pre-Famine period: a study based on the 1911 census data for people born before 1851 and still alive in 1911' in *Proceedings of the Royal Irish Academy*, 103C, no. 5, 191–283.

Flanagan, D. (1978), 'Seventeenth-century salmon fishing in Co. Down: river-name documentation', *Bulletin of the Ulster Place-Names Society*, 2nd series, vol. 1, 22–6.

Flower, R. (1947), *The Irish tradition* (Oxford).

Fortescue, Sir F. (1858), *An account of the Rt. Hon. Sir Arthur Chichester* (London).

Froggatt, P. (1981), 'Dr James MacDonnell, MD (1763–1845)', *The Glynns* 9, 17–31.

—— (1984), 'MacDonnell, father and son: James (1763–1845); John (1796–1892), Surgeon of Dublin', *Journal of the Colleges of Physicians and Surgeons* 13, 198–206.

Gaeltacht 1965 : Treoraí na Gaeltachta (Belfast 1965).

Gaffikin, Thomas (1984), *Belfast fifty years ago: a lecture delivered in 1875* (Belfast).

Gillespie, Raymond and Stephen A. Royle (2003), *Irish historic towns atlas no. 12: Belfast Part 1, to 1840* (Dublin).

Gregory, Augusta Lady (1914), *Our Irish theatre* (London).

Gwynn, Stephen (1915), *The famous cities of Ireland* (Dublin).

Harbison, J. (1989), 'The Belfast Harpers' Meeting, 1792: the legacy', *Ulster Folklife* 35, 113–28.

Hay, Marnie (2004), 'Explaining *Uladh*: cultural nationalism in Ulster' in Taylor FitzSimon and Murphy (eds),*The Irish Revival reappraised* (Dublin), 119–31.

Hayward, R. (1952), *Belfast through the ages* (Dundalk).

Heatley, Fred (1983), 'Community relations and the religious geography 1800–86' in Beckett et al., *Belfast: the making of the city* (Belfast), 129–42.

Hempton, D., and M. Hill (1992), *Evangelical Protestantism in Ulster society, 1740–1890.* (London and New York).

Hewitt, John (1978), *John Luke: 1906–1975* (Arts Councils of Ireland).

Hewitt, Roger (1986), *White talk black talk: inter-racial friendship and communication among adolescents* (Cambridge).

Hindley, R. (1990), *The death of the Irish language: a qualified obituary* (London).

Holmer, N.M. (1965), *The dialects of Clare: Part II* (Dublin).

Hughes, A.J. (1987), 'Anecdotes relating to Peadar Ó Doirnín and Cormac na gCeann', *Seanchas Ard Mhacha* vol. 12, no. 2, 128–37.

—— and McDaniel, E. (1988), 'A nineteenth-century translation of the Deirdre story', *Emania* 5 (Autumn) 41–7; 6 (Spring 1989) 41–7.

—— and Hannan, R.J. (1992), *Place-names of Northern Ireland: Volume 2, County Down II: The Ards* (Belfast).

—— (1991), 'Irish place-names: some perspectives, pitfalls, procedures and potential', *Seanchas Ard Mhacha* vol. 14, no. 2, 116–48.

—— (1991–3), 'On the Ulster place-names: *Glynn, Glenavy, Carrickfergus* and *Forkill'*, *Ainm, Bulletin of the Ulster Place-Name Society* 5, 92–107.

—— (1992), 'Deirdre Flanagan's "Belfast and the place-names therein" in translation', *Ulster Folklife* 38, 79–97.

—— (1994), 'Gaeilge Uladh' in K. McCone et al. (eds) *Stair na Gaeilge* (Maynooth), 610–60.

—— (1994b), 'A phonetic glossary of Tyrone Irish', *Zeitschrift für Celtische Philologie* 46, 119–63.

—— (1999), 'The Virgin St Duinseach and her three Ulster churches near Strangford Lough', *Celtica: James Carney memorial volume* 23, 113–24.

—(2001), 'Gaelic poets and scribes of the South Armagh hinterland in the eighteenth and nineteenth centuries' in A.J. Hughes and William Nolan (eds) *Armagh: history and society* (Dublin), 505–58.

Hunt, Tristam (2004), *Building Jerusalem: the rise and fall of the Victorian city* (London).

Hyman, Louis (1972), *The Jews of Ireland: from the earliest times to the year 1910* (Shannon, Co. Clare).

Jamieson, J. (1959), *History of the Royal Belfast Academical Institution, 1810–1960* (Belfast).

Kachuk, Patricia (1994), 'A resistance to British cultural hegemony: Irish-language activism in West Belfast', *Anthropologica* 36, 135–54.

Kennedy, David (1967), 'The early eighteenth century' in Beckett and Glasscock (eds) *Belfast: the origin and growth of an industrial city* (London), 39–54.

Killen, J. (1990), *A history of the Linenhall Library, 1788–1988* (Belfast).

Kramsch, Claire (2000), *Language and culture* (Oxford).

Kudos, *Our common heritage: a study into attitudes and perceptions of the unionist community related to the Irish language* (Derry, n.d.).

Lennon, Brian (2004), *Peace comes dropping slow: dialogue and conflict management in Northern Ireland* (Belfast).

Liechty, Joseph, and Cecelia Clegg (2001), *Moving beyond sectarianism: religion, conflict and reconciliation in Northern Ireland* (Dublin).

Mac Carráin, Liam (1982), *Is Cuimhin liom an tAm ... Cuimhní Cinn Sean-Ghaeil.* (Belfast).

Mac Giolla Domhnaigh, Gearóid (1995), *Conradh Gaeilge Chúige Uladh ag Tús an 20ú Chéid* (Monaghan).

Mac Giolla Domhnaigh, G., and G. Stockman (1991), *Athchló Uladh* (Belfast).

Mac Grianna, Seosamh (1936), *Pádraig Ó Conaire agus Aistí Eile* (Dublin, 1969).

Mac Lochlainn, A. (1995), 'The Famine in the Gaelic tradition', *Irish Review* 17/18, 90–108.

Mac Maoláin, Seán (1940), 'Uaigneach sin!' in *An tUltach* 17:11.

— (1942), *I mBéal Feirsde Domh* (Dublin).

— (1969), *Gleann Airbh go Glas Naíon* (Dublin).

Mac Póilin, Aodán (2003), 'The Irish language in Belfast until 1900' and 'Irish language writing in Belfast after 1900' in Nicholas Allen and Aaron Kelly (eds) *The cities of Belfast* (Dublin), 41–61; 127–151.

Mac Suibhne, Breandán, and David Dickson (2000) (eds), *The outer edge of Ulster: a memoir of social life in nineteenth-century Donegal* (by Hugh Dorian) (Dublin).

MacLysaght, E. (1972), *The surnames of Ireland* (Dublin).

Madden, R.R. (1843), *The United Irishmen: their lives and times*, vols 1–3, 3rd series (Dublin).

Magee, J. (1988), 'The Neilsons of Rademon and Down: educators and Gaelic scholars', *Familia – Ulster Genealogical Review* vol. 2, no. 4 , 64ff.

Maguire, Gabrielle (1991), *Our own language* (Clevedon).

Maguire, W.A. (1993), *Belfast* (Keele).

Martin, F.X. and F.J. Byrne (1973) (eds) *The scholar revolutionary: Eoin Mac Néill and the making of modern Ireland* (Dublin).

Mawhinney G. (1992) (ed.), *O.S.L. Derry John O'Donovan's letters from County Londonderry, 1834* (Ballinascreen Historical Society).

May, Stephen (2001), *Language and minority rights: ethnicity, nationalism and the politics of language* (London).

McCall, H. (1881) *The house of Downshire* (Belfast).

McCaughtry, Sam (1985), 'Being Protestant in Northern Ireland' in J. McLoone (ed.) *Being Protestant in Ireland* (Naas).

McCavitt, J. (1998), *Sir Arthur Chichester: lord deputy of Ireland, 1605–16* (Belfast).

McCoy, Gordon (1997), 'Protestant learners of Irish in Northern Ireland' in A. Mac Póilin (ed.), *The Irish language in Northern Ireland* (Belfast). (article available at http://cain.ulst.ac.uk/issues/language/mccoy97.htm)

—— and Róise Ní Bhaoill (2004), *Protastúnaigh an Lae Inniu agus an Ghaeilge: contemporary Protestant learners of Irish* (Belfast).

McGimpsey, C.D. (1994), a paper in P. Mistéil (ed.), *The Irish language and the unionist tradition* (Belfast), 7–16.

McManus, D. (1991), *A guide to ogham* (Maynooth).

McNeill, M. (1960), *The life and times of Mary Ann McCracken* (Dublin).

Merrick, Tony (1979), 'Glimpses of old Belfast, *XIX*' in *Irish Weekly & Ulster Examiner* 02 June 1979.

—— (1984), *Gravestone inscriptions: Belfast. Volume 2: Friar's Bush and Milltown graveyards* (Belfast).

Moody, T.W. and J.C. Beckett (1959), *Queen's University Belfast, 1845–1949: the history of a university* 2 vols (London).

Morris, H. (1921), 'Two Belfast Gaels [Samuel Bryson and Robert MacAdam]', *Irish Book Lover* 13 (Aug–Sept), 1–6.

Murphy, Michael J. (1941), *At Slieve Gullion's foot* (Dundalk).

Neilson, Revd William (1808), *An introduction to the Irish language* (Belfast, 1990).

Nelson, Sarah (1984), *Ulster's uncertain defenders: loyalists and the Northern Ireland conflict* (Belfast).

Newmann, K. (1993), *Dictionary of Ulster biography* (Belfast).

Ní Chinnéide, M. (2001), *Speaking Irish at home* (Dublin).

Ní Uallacháin, Pádraigín (2003), *A hidden Ulster: people, songs and traditions of Oriel* (Dublin).

Ó Buachalla, B. (1962), *Clár na Láimhscríbhinní Gaeilge i Leabharlann Phoiblí Bhéal Feirste* (Dublin).

—— (1963), 'An Bíobla i gContae Aontroma', *Feasta* (Deireadh Fómhair, Samhain, Nollaig).

—— (1968), *I mBéal Feirste Cois Cuain* (Dublin).

—— (1975), *Cathal Buí: Amhráin* (Dublin)

Ó Casaide, S. (1930), *The Irish language in Belfast and County Down A.D. 1601–1850* (Dublin).

Ó Conluain, P. (1989), 'The last native Irish speakers of Tyrone', *Dúiche Néill* 4, 101–18.

Ó Dónaill, N. (ed.) (1977). *FGB Foclóir Gaeilge-Béarla: Irish-English dictionary* (Dublin).

Ó Dubhda, Peadar (1936), *Tríd an Fhuinneog* (Dublin).

Ó Duibhín, C. (1991), *The Irish language in Co. Down since 1750* (Cumann Gaelach Leath Cathail).

—— forthcoming: booklet plus cassette of the Irish texts recorded by Dögen.

Ó Fiaich, B. (1990), 'Fál agus Dearcadh' MA diss. (University of Ulster, Coleraine).

Ó Fiaich, T. and Ó Caithnia, L. (1979), *Art Mac Bionaid: Dánta* (Dublin).

Ó hAilín, T. (1969), 'Irish revival movements' in B. Ó Cuív (ed.), *A view of the Irish language* (Dublin), 81–100.

Ó Laighin, Seán (1990) (ed.), *Ó Cadhain i bhFeasta* (Clódhanna Teoranta).

Ó Mainnín, M. (1992), *The place-names of Northern Ireland, volume 3, County Down III: The Mournes* (Belfast).

Ó Maolfabhail, A. (1989), 'An tSuirbhéireacht Ordanáis agus Logainmneacha na hÉireann 1824–34' *Proceedings of the Royal Irish Academy* 89, C, 3–66.

Ó Muilleoir, Máirtín (1999), *Belfast's dome of delight: City Hall politics, 1981–2000* (Belfast).

Ó Muireadhaigh, Lorcán (1927), *Amhráin Chúige Uladh* (Dublin, 1984).

Ó Muireasa, Énrí (1915), *Céad de Cheolta Uladh* (Newry, 1983).

Ó Muirí, Pól (1999), *A flight from shadow: the life and work of Seosamh Mac Grianna* (Belfast).

Ó Muirí, R. (1994), *Láimhscríbhinn Staire an Bhionadaigh: Comhrac na nGael agus na nGall le Chéile* (Monaghan).

Ó Murchú, M. (1989), *East Perthshire Gaelic* (Dublin).

Ó Néill, S. (1966), 'The hidden Ulster: Gaelic pioneers in the North', *Studies* 55, 60–6.

Ó Snodaigh, P. (1995), *Hidden Ulster: Protestants and the Irish language* (Belfast).

Ó Tuama, S. (1972), *The Gaelic League idea* (Cork).

Ó Tuathail, É. (1933), *Sgéalta Mhuintir Luinigh: Munterloney folk-tales* (Dublin).

O'Byrne, Cathal (1946), *As I roved out* (Belfast).

O'Halloran, Claire (1987), *Partition and the limits of Irish nationalism: an ideology under stress* (Dublin).

O'Hanlon, William. M. (1853), *Walks amongst the poor of Belfast* (1971).

O'Laverty, Revd J. (1878–95), *An historical account of the diocese of Down and Connor ancient and modern*, 5 vols (Dublin).

O'Rahilly, T.F. (1932), *Irish dialects past and present* (Dublin).

—— (1946), *Early Irish history and mythology* (Dublin).

O'Reilly, C.C. (1993), 'The development of the Irish language in Belfast: a brief historical background', *Ulster Local Studies*, vol. 15, no. 1 (Summer) 72–9.

O'Reilly, Camille (1995), 'Fíor-Ghaeil agus Fíor-Ghaelach: tradition, heritage and authenticity in the Irish language revival', unpublished paper given at the Association of Anthropology in Ireland Conference.

—— (1999), *The Irish language in Northern Ireland: the politics of culture and identity* (Basingstoke).

OSL Down, 'Letters containing information relative to the antiquities of the County of Down collected during the progress of the Ordnance Survey in 1834'. Supplement to *Leabharlann*, 3 (1909).

Patton, Marcus (1993), *Central Belfast: an historical gazetteer* (Belfast).

Pender, S. (1939) (ed.), *A census of Ireland, circa 1659* (Dublin).

Power, Jimmy (2002), 'Cant: an Irish Traveller's perspective', in John M. Kirk and Dónall P. Ó Baoill (eds) *Travellers and their language* (Belfast).

Robb, J. (1946), 'A famous Irish grammar', *Irish News* 9 January 1946.

Roberts, Celia et al. (2001) (eds), *Language learners as ethnographers* (Cleveden).

Robinson, P. (1986), *Carrickfergus: Irish historical towns atlas no. 2* (Dublin).

Ruane, Joseph, and Jennifer Todd (1996), *The dynamics of conflict in Northern Ireland: power, conflict and emancipation* (Cambridge).

Shearman, H. (1935), *Belfast Royal Academy, 1785–1935* (Belfast).

Sinn Féin (1984), *Learning Irish: a discussion and information booklet* (Belfast).

Smith, Anthony D. (1986), *The ethnic origins of nations* (Oxford).

Smith, G. (1902), *Belfast Literary Society, 1801–1901: historical sketch* (Belfast).

Smyth, J. (1993), 'Freemasonry and the United Irishmen', in D. Dickson et al. (eds),

The United Irishmen: republicanism, radicalism and rebellion (Dublin), 167–75.

Stokes, W. (1905) (ed.), *Félire Óengusso Céli Dé: The Martyrology of Óengus the Culdee* (London).

The Agreement: Agreement reached in the multi-party negotiations (London, 1998).

Thompson, G.B., and G.B. Adams (1964), *Ulster dialects: an introductory symposium* (Cultra, Co. Down).

Todd, Jennifer (1988), 'The limits of Britishness' in *Irish Review*, 5 (Autumn), 11–16.

Toner, G. and Ó Mainnín, M. (1992), *The place-names of Northern Ireland, volume 1, County Down 1: Newry and South-West Down* (Belfast).

Uí Laighléis, Gearóidín (2003), *Seán Mac Maolain agus Ceart na Gaeilge* (Dublin).

Wagner, H. (1958), *Linguistic atlas and survey of Irish dialects*, vol. 1, maps (Dublin).

—— and Ó Baoill, C. (1969), *Linguistic atlas and survey of Irish dialects*, vol. 4, Ulster, with appendices for the Isle of Man and Scotland (Dublin).

—— and Mac Congáil, N. (1983), *Oral literature from Dunquin* (Belfast).

Walker, B.M. and A. McCreary (1994), *Degrees of excellence: the story of Queen's, Belfast, 1845–1995* (Belfast).

Walsh, Revd L. (1844), *The Home Mission unmasked* ...(Belfast).

Watson, S. (1984), 'Séamus Ó Duilearga's Antrim notebooks – I Texts', *Zeitschrift für Celtische Philologie* 40, 74–117.

—— (1987), 'Séamus Ó Duilearga's Antrim notebooks – II Language', *Zeitschrift für Celtische Philologie* 42, 138–218.

Welch, R. (1996) (ed.), *The Oxford companion to Irish literature* (Oxford).

Whitaker, T.K. (1982), 'James Hamilton Delargy', *The Glynns* 10, 20–5.

Williams, F. (1995), 'Six hundred Gaelic proverbs collected in Ulster by Robert MacAdam', *Proverbium* 12, 343–55.

Williams, Glyn (1992), *Sociolinguistics: a sociological critique* (London).

Young, R. (1894–5), 'The Irish harpers in Belfast in 1792', *Ulster Journal of Archaeology*, 2nd series, vol. 1, 120–7.

Zimmermann, George D. (2001), *The Irish storyteller* (Dublin).

Zwickl, Simone (2002), *Language attitudes, ethnic identity and dialect use across the Northern Irish border: Armagh and Monaghan* (Belfast).

Acknowledgments

The editor gratefully acknowledges the help and support of the following groups and individuals in the production of this book:

The editors and staff of Four Courts Press; Geraldine Begley who compiled the index; Foras na Gaeilge; UK Data Archive; Eneclann; the staff of various libraries, including St Mary's University College Library, Belfast Central Library, the Linenhall Library and Queen's University Library. Stephen Gallagher of the Faculty of Liberal Arts, St Mary's University College for his technical expertise.

Jacaí de Brún; Séamus agus Máire de Brún; Anna Beckett; Cormac Ó hAdhmaill; Meábha Uí Chriagáin; Séamus Mac Seáin; Séamus Mac Diarmada; Kieran McConville; Cardinal Ó Fiaich Library, Armagh; Aoife Ní Riain, Belfast Central Library; Proinsias Ó Broin; Ciarán Ó Duibhín; Seán Mac Labhraí; Nan O'Hara; Leo D'Agostino; Pól Mac Fheidhlimidh; Joe Ó Labhraí; Colm Mac Aindreasa; Mícheál Mac Goilla Ghunna; Ruairí Mac Leanacháin; Marcas Ó Murchú.

An earlier version of the two essays by A.J. Hughes, 'Robert MacAdam and the nineteenth-century Irish language revival' and 'The Ulster Gaelic Society and the work of MacAdam's Irish scribes' appeared as the introduction to *Robert Shipboy MacAdam: his life and Gaelic proverb collection* (Belfast, 1988); an earlier version of Aodán Mac Póilin's essay, 'The Irish language in Belfast until the eighteenth century' appeared in Nicholas Allen and Aaron Kelly (eds), *The cities of Belfast* (Dublin, 2003).

Illustrations

appear between pages 128 and 129

1 Title page of *Bolg an tSolair or Gaelic Magazine* (1795); courtesy Belfast Central Library.
2 Dr William Neilson.
3 Dr James MacDonnell.
4 The Ulster Unionist Convention of 1892 with its Erin-go-Bragh slogan.
5 Crooked Lane, later Chapel Lane, Belfast; courtesy PRONI.
6 Fishdealer, Belfast, *c.*1905; courtesy PRONI.
7 Coláiste Chomhghaill's certificate in teaching Irish awarded to Seán Beckett, signed by Seaghán Ó Catháin, 1909; courtesy Anna Beckett.
8 An Ardscoil Ultach, headquarters of the Belfast Gaelic League in Queen's Street, 1913; courtesy Cormac Ó hAdhmaill.
9 Modh Díreach charts used in Ardscoil classes; courtesy Anna Beckett.
10 Advertisement in *Craobh Ruadh*, a Gaelic League publication, 1913.
11 Advertisement in *Craobh Ruadh* for Eudhmonn Mac Aonghusa, tobacconist, the first Belfast shopkeeper to display his name in Irish above his shop (1901).
12 Irish volunteers marching in Smithfield, *c.*1914; courtesy PRONI.
13 Belfast Gaelic League group at Coláiste Bhríde, Omeath, in 1916 with Fr Dónall Ó Tuathail (seated, right); courtesy Anna Beckett.
14 P.T. McGinley (Peadar Toner Mac Fhionnlaoich).
15 Seán Mac Maoláin.
16 Opening night of Cumann Chluain Ard's new premises in Hawthorn Street, 1944 with Séamus Mac Fearáin as 'fear an tí' and Alf Ó Muireadhaigh (Lurgan) as guest speaker (both men were later to become presidents of the GAA); courtesy Méabha Uí Chriagáin.
17 Thomas Davis centenary march Oakman Street, Falls Road, Belfast, 1945; courtesy Marcas Ó Murchú.
18 *Scoraíocht* (social evening) for young people attending the Ardoyne branch of Gaelic League in 1950.
19 Aisteoirí Naomh Bríd actors rehearsing in 1950 (*left to right*) Eibhlín Vaughan, Méabha Uí Chriagáin, Seosamh Mistéil, Bob Crombie (director).
20 Committee of Cumann Chluain Ard, 1962 (*left to right*) Liam Ó Duibhir, Seán Mac Aindreasa, Alf Ó Murchú (chair), Bríd Nic an tSionnaigh, Tomás Ó Monacháin (secretary), Séamus de Brún (treasurer); courtesy *An tUltach*.
21 Bríd Nic Gaoithín of An Ceann Garbh, Co. Donegal, teaching in Cumann Chluain Ard 1962; courtesy *An tUltach*.
22 Staff and pupils of the first Meánscoil in 1978 (*left to right*) Máire Mhic Sheáin, Áine Mhic Aindreasa, Bríd Mhic Sheáin, Colm Mac Aindreasa, Conall Ó Coisneacháin, Adam Mac Giolla Chatháin, Eilis Ní Bhruadair, Nuala Nic Sheáin; courtesy Séamus Mac Seáin.
23 Orange Order banner of the 1303 lodge, Ireland's Heritage.

Contributors

FIONNTÁN DE BRÚN is a senior lecturer in Irish, St Mary's University College, Belfast; his published work includes a critical study of the writings of Seosamh Mac Grianna, *Seosamh Mac Grianna: an Mhéin Rúin* (2002) and a collection of short stories, *Litir ó mo Mháthair Altrama agus Scéalta Eile* (2005).

PATRICK McKAY has been a research fellow with the Northern Ireland Place-Name Project since 1992. He is honorary secretary of the Ulster Place-Name Society and the author of *Place-Names of Northern Ireland, vol. 4: the baronies of Toome* (1995); *A dictionary of Ulster place-names* (1999) and *Place-Names of Northern Ireland, vol. 8: Lisnaskea and district* (2004).

A.J. HUGHES is a senior lecturer in Irish at the University of Ulster in Belfast. He is the author of many books and articles on Irish language and literature, including *Robert Shipboy MacAdam: his life and Gaelic proverb collection* and has also translated modern Irish prose and poetry into English, French and Breton.

AODÁN MAC PÓILIN is Director of Ultach Trust, a cross-community Irish language funding body. He has written and lectured on cultural and linguistic politics, language planning, education, broadcasting, literature and the arts, and has published translations of poetry and prose from Irish. He edited *The Irish Language in Northern Ireland* (1997) and was Irish language editor of the literary magazine *Krino*.

GORDON McCOY grew up in Saintfield, Co. Down and now resides in Belfast. In 1992 he graduated with a degree in Celtic and Sociology from Queen's University Belfast, and afterwards remained at the university to examine Protestant learners of Irish for a doctoral thesis in the Department of Social Anthropology. He is currently employed as a cross-community officer with the Ultach Trust.

GABRIELLE NiGUIDHIR is a principal lecturer in Irish-medium Initial Teacher Education at St Mary's University College, Belfast. She is the author of *Our own language* (1991), a study of the Shaw's Road urban Gaeltacht.

SEÁN MAC CORRAIDH is the adviser for Irish-medium education for the five education and library boards in Northern Ireland. He has recently completed a doctoral thesis at Queen's University Belfast on teachers' practices and beliefs on teaching through the medium of Irish as an immersion language.

SEÁN MISTÉIL was born in Belfast in 1964 and raised in Gaeltacht Bhóthar Seoighe. He established a communications partnership in 1990 delivering a broad range of creative services throughout Ireland. He is a director of the West Belfast Partnership Board and Chair of Forbairt Feirste, the Belfast Irish Language economic development agency.

Index